The Don Giovanni Moment

COLUMBIA THEMES IN PHILOSOPHY, SOCIAL CRITICISM, AND THE ARTS

[Detail] Engraving by J. H. Ramberg, 1831. See figure 6.2.

The Don Giovanni Moment

ESSAYS ON THE LEGACY OF AN OPERA

Edited by

Lydia Goehr Daniel Herwitz

COLUMBIA UNIVERSITY PRESS   NEW YORK

Columbia University Press
Publishers Since 1893
New York Chichester, West Sussex

Library of Congress Cataloging-in-Publication Data

The Don Giovanni moment : essays on the legacy of an opera /
editors, Lydia Goehr and Daniel Herwitz.
    p. cm. — (Columbia themes in philosophy, social criticism, and the arts)
Includes bibliographical references.
ISBN 0-231-13754-0 (alk. paper) — ISBN 0-231-51064-0 (ebook)
1. Mozart, Wolfgang Amadeus, 1756–1791. Don Giovanni.
2. Don Juan (Legendary character) in literature.
3. Music and literature. 4. Opera. I. Goehr, Lydia.
II. Herwitz, Daniel Alan, 1955– III. Series.
ML410.M9D63 2006
782.1—dc22   2005033481

Casebound editions of Columbia University Press books are printed
    on permanent and durable acid-free paper.

Printed in the United States of America

c 10 9 8 7 6 5 4 3 2 1

Columbia Themes in Philosophy, Social Criticism, and the Arts presents monographs, essay collections, and short books on philosophy and aesthetic theory. It aims to publish books that show the ability of the arts to stimulate critical reflection on modern and contemporary social, political, and cultural life. Art is not now, if it ever was, a realm of human activity independent of the complex realities of social organization and change, political authority and antagonism, cultural domination and resistance. The possibilities of critical thought embedded in the arts are most fruitfully expressed when addressed to readers across the various fields of social and humanistic inquiry. The idea of philosophy in the series' title ought to be understood, therefore, to embrace forms of discussion that begin where mere academic expertise exhausts itself, where the rules of social, political, and cultural practice are both affirmed and challenged, and where new thinking takes place. The series does not privilege any particular art, nor does it ask for the arts to be mutually isolated; we encourage writing from the many fields of thoughtful and critical inquiry.

Dedicated to Bernard Williams

Contents

Contributors

NIKOLAUS BACHT received his education in music and philosophy and his doctorate from King's College, London, in 2002 with a dissertation entitled "Music and Time in Theodor W. Adorno." He has held doctoral research positions at Harvard and Cambridge Universities and is currently a postdoctoral Research Fellow at King's College, Cambridge. He is continuing to work and write on aesthetics, music, and the history of ideas.

RICHARD ELDRIDGE is professor of philosophy at Swarthmore College. He is the author of *On Moral Personhood* (1989), *Leading a Human Life: Wittgenstein, Intentionality, and Romanticism* (1997), *The Persistence of Romanticism* (2001), and, most recently, *An Introduction to the Philosophy of Art* (2003).

BORIS GASPAROV is professor of Slavic languages and literatures at Columbia University. He is the author and coeditor of (among others): *Cultural Mythologies of Russian Modernism* (1988), *Christianity and the Eastern Slavs*, 3 vols (1989), *Pushkin's Poetic Language* (1992, 2000), *Language and Memory* (1996), *Five Operas and a Symphony: Words and Music in Russian Culture* (2005).

LYDIA GOEHR is professor of philosophy at Columbia University. She is the author of *The Imaginary Museum of Musical Works* (1992) and *The Quest for Voice: Music, Politics, and the Limits of Philosophy* (1998). In 1997 she was the Ernest Bloch Professor in the Music Department at the University of California,

Berkeley, where she gave a series of lectures on Richard Wagner. In 2002–2003 she was the Aby Warburg Professor in Hamburg and a fellow at the Wissenschaftskolleg zu Berlin. She is currently completing a book on the relationship between philosophy and music in the work of Theodor W. Adorno entitled *Notes to Adorno*.

THOMAS S. GREY received M.A. and Ph.D. degrees in music from the University of California, Berkeley, and has taught at UCLA and Stanford Universities. Since 1997 he has been associate professor of music at Stanford University. He is the author of *Wagner's Musical Prose: Texts and Contexts* (1995) and editor and coauthor of the Cambridge Opera handbook on Wagner's *Flying Dutchman* (2000), and a forthcoming *Cambridge Companion to Wagner*. His current projects include a book on music and visual culture in the nineteenth century and editing a two-volume history of opera for Cambridge University Press. He served as editor of the *Journal of the American Musicological Society* from 1999 through 2001.

AGNES HELLER was a friend and student of Georg Lukacs. She rose to fame in postwar Europe for her work in Marxian theory and moral and political philosophy. After active involvement in the Hungarian Revolution, she was dismissed from her academic position. In 1977 she emigrated to Australia. She taught in Germany and America, after which she accepted a position, which she still holds, in the Graduate Faculty Department of Philosophy at the New School for Social Research in New York. After 1989 she was elected to the Hungarian Academy of Sciences. Since then she has split her teaching between Budapest and New York. The recipient of numerous academic prizes, she has been the subject of several documentaries and is the author of more than twenty books.

DANIEL HERWITZ is director of the Institute for the Humanities and Mary Fair Croushore Professor of Humanities at the University of Michigan. A six-year residence in South Africa led to his most recent publication, a book on the South African transition, *Race and Reconciliation* (2003). He has written on many subjects in philosophical aesthetics and avant-garde art.

BERTHOLD HOECKNER is associate professor of music and the humanities at the University of Chicago. He was educated in Germany, England, and at Cornell University. In 1997 he won the Albert Einstein Award of the American Musicological Society for the best article published by a younger scholar. His book *Programming the Absolute: Nineteenth-Century Music and the Hermeneutics of the Moment* was published in 2002.

PHILIP KITCHER is professor of philosophy at Columbia University. He is the author of many articles and seven books, the most recent of which are *Science,*

Truth, and Democracy (2001) and *In Mendel's Mirror: Philosophical Reflections on Biology* (2003).

ERNST OSTERKAMP is professor of German literature at the Humboldt-Universität zu Berlin. His books include *Lucifer: Stationen eines Motivs* (1979), *Im Buchstabenbilde: Studien zum Verfahren Goethescher Bildbeschreibungen* (1991), and *Rudolf Borchardt und seine Zeitgenossen* (1997). He is currently completing a book on the poetry of Stefan George.

INGRID ROWLAND is Andrew W. Mellon Professor in the Humanities at the American Academy in Rome. Her books include *The Culture of the High Renaissance: Ancients and Moderns in Sixteenth-Century Rome* (1998), *The Ecstatic Journey: Athanasius Kircher in Baroque Rome* (2000), and *The Scarith of Scornello: An Etruscan Fraud* (2004). She is completing a biography of Giordano Bruno.

RICHARD SCHACHT is professor of philosophy and Jubilee Professor of Liberal Arts and Sciences at the University of Illinois, Urbana-Champaign. He teaches and writes on developments in post-Kantian European philosophy and on questions relating to human reality, value, and normativity. His books include *Hegel and After* (1975), *Nietzsche* (1985), *The Future of Alienation* (1994), and *Making Sense of Nietzsche* (1995).

BRIAN SOUCEK received his Ph.D. in philosophy at Columbia University in 2005 with a dissertation on the analogy between artworks and persons. He is currently a Collegiate Assistant Professor and Harper Fellow in the Society of Fellows at the University of Chicago.

HANS RUDOLF VAGET is the Helen and Laura Shedd Professor of German Studies and Comparative Literature at Smith College. He was educated at the Universities of Munich and Tübingen, the University of Wales at Cardiff, and at Columbia University. He has published widely in the field of German Studies from the eighteenth century to the present, focusing primarily on Goethe, Wagner, and Thomas Mann as well as music history and film. A recipient in 1994 of the Thomas-Mann-Medaille for his edition of the correspondence of Thomas Mann and Agnes E. Meyer (1992), he is also one of the chief editors of the new edition of the works, letters, and diaries of Thomas Mann. In 2001 he was awarded a Forschungspreis by the Alexander von Humboldt Foundation.

BERNARD WILLIAMS was one of the best-known moral philosophers of the twentieth century. His influence was far-ranging and profound. He wrote extensively on philosophy and music.

Introduction

LYDIA GOEHR AND DANIEL HERWITZ

*I*n the history of opera there is perhaps no moment of greater consequence than that of the opening of Mozart's *Don Giovanni*. Though written almost entirely in the buoyant joviality of the major mode, the opera's first D-minor chord strikes terror as it moves hauntingly toward an irrevocable cadence. Almost immediately revoked by the major mode, the minor opening is destined to return, and so it does. Having watched the Don's erotic romping and destructive rampage, the Commendatore finally appears to deliver his judgment. Entering as a statue of the eternally dead, he heralds the death of the Don. But the Don is not ready to die and invites the statue to dinner. The bravado of his invitation only confirms his lack of remorse. The statue arrives. Acting as if his power and success in life will not fail him even when threatened with the supernatural, the Don again refuses to repent and is accordingly engulfed by flames. Yet what follows seems to negate the intensity of the punishment. No character formerly wounded by the Don treads sadly upon his ashes. Each rather joins hands with the other to sing with what some think is merely a dripping falsetto cheerfulness of a world that has once more been made pleasant. During the nineteenth century this final scene struck some in the musical world as so obviously false that they omitted it entirely, believing the opera ended better perishing in D minor.

Others read the ending differently. Overall, that performers and directors felt (as they still do) they had the power to decide how the opera should end, that the ending posed a genuine question for the work as a whole, guaranteed for this work a fascinating reception and legacy.

On one reading the D-minor motif, or the so-called Don Giovanni chord, opens the opera to tell us that it is there also to close it, or at least to shut the pages of the book of life on a figure whose actions have been measurable in the size and scope requiring, in Nietzsche's words, "the seriousness of the 'Stone Guest' [to] leap out of the wall and shake the listener to his very intestines." Of course, the listeners only come to know this at the end. Still, what they learn on the way is that everything that happens—all the singing, seduction, and slaying—subsists on little more than voice and air. For while the opera unfolds or, one might say, for nearly as long as it takes Leporello to list his master's conquests, both the music and plot are propelled by an inexhaustible energy: the unrelenting drive of (musical) seduction. The Don is a figure too big to be curtailed, too significant merely to grow old and die in a mediocre and ordinary world. He is rather the absolute drive and scope of music itself. When the moralizing D-minor motif thus returns to interrupt his musical course, the audience now knows for whom the bell tolls and with what inexorable consequence. But to what ultimate end? Does this moralizing chord, this consignment of the Don to the flames, necessitate the reintroduction of morality in the form, as some have read it, of a banal conventionality? Or does it rather signal a settling of scores long overdue—even the raw return of something like oedipal justice? Or is the point yet different, that it symbolizes the fact that this opera must end, that even music's immortal voice cannot last forever, where to become immortal and then to die is, in the theatrical words of Eugene Ionesco, the very point of life? If this last thought captures something right, then the Don's death signifies less a moralizing restitution of the bourgeois green fields of happiness than a return to the condition of a much deeper conception of life and living.

Of life and living in *Don Giovanni*: this is the theme most perfectly discussed by Bernard Williams in his classic essay "Don Juan as an Idea." As a tribute, we as the editors decided early on to include this essay in the present volume as it has appropriately been included in others. Sadly, Bernard Williams's untimely death required us also to dedicate our volume to him in memoriam. We would have preferred, as we had originally intended, to dedicate this book as a tribute to a great thinker still in the throes of life.

Don Giovanni lives only so long as it is performed: it is known, as all opera is known, through the history of its interpretation and performance. Performances of *Don Giovanni* have been extraordinarily variegated, risky, and audacious. Some present the Don's life as ahistorical; others situate him historically to try perhaps to counter the seeming universal significance of his acts. Some adulate the Don as a cosmic principle: irrepressible, magnificent, living out the true art of life. Think of the Don that Cesare Siepi created in the opera houses of Europe (especially the 1952 Salzburg, Furtwängler performance), with all his grand gestures, topped by a dazzling hat in the style of a Toulouse Lautrec. Others have presented the Don as a hopelessly craven neurotic, a man who cannot stop. Or, differently again, recall Joseph Losey's 1979 film with its strangely pallid and repressed Don, played by Ruggiero Raimondi, whose good looks are rendered sinister through excessive makeup and unexpected camera angles. At one moment Raimondi's lips are seen pressed tightly together to signify a kind of tension, perhaps a repressed homosexuality, a narcissism, or an impotence. Here the Don appears as physically vicious: his speech is violent, his demeanor and actions are exaggerated. But still there is a decaying and decadent luxury in which his fantasies are played out. Losey thus portrays him as an artifact of his morbid time. Or at least Losey seems to believe this about the time, given the Gramscian epigram, seen in his opening shot, scribbled on a wall as if it were graffiti.

The present volume focuses less on the debate about how best to produce the work than on the complexity of its reception. Sometimes with a brush of adulation, sometimes with that of lambaste, the contributing authors investigate how far this opera as a work of embodied myth redefines the relationship between art and morality. Power, seduction, judgment: these are the main themes. Many of the essays show that the work assumes a kind of limit or condition for art that cannot coherently be surpassed: that one can only go so far in the art of seduction before being interrupted by the moral voice. Such a view, not incidentally, is confirmed also by Losey in his film, where he shows that the propensity of this work to define for itself an absolutely sui generis field of glory is among its chief illusions. The play between the aesthetic and the moral, or the dynamics of the work's erotic power, is intended, furthermore, to challenge the (professed) allegiances of an established Viennese bourgeoisie.

This volume is not so much about the work that is *Don Giovanni* itself; it is about the works written in the opera's shadow. The contributing authors thus concentrate on the many appropriations, rewritings, and retellings of *Don Giovanni* in the form of other, and sometimes at first sight unrelated, works. They attend to works that stand to *Don Giovanni* in a special and interesting relationship, perhaps of influence, analogy, or competition. That the source work itself is about paternity (in the figure of the Commendatore) and about the refusal of paternity (in the figure of the Don) justifies the interest in its progeny, in works written in tribute to it, in works that have wanted to acknowledge or even to move beyond this parental master(piece).

Not wanting to step on the pages of the enormous body of musicological literature on this opera, or repeat the findings, the contributing authors were chosen to write predominantly from the perspectives of philosophy and literature. Their explorations range from the dramatic contributions of Byron, Grabbe, Hoffmann, Kierkegaard, Mörike, and Shaw to the operas or music dramas of Wagner and Strauss. Some essays place Don Giovanni or Don Juan in comparative context, as a competitor to other figures of heroic status in German Romanticism and Modernism. No better and no closer competitor, so at least one author argues, can be found than the disobedient figure of Faust.

We are of the impression that "the Don Giovanni moment"—the D-minor chord—returns so often in the subsequent history of opera as to have virtually defined its own minilegacy: hence the title of the present volume. It may not even be unwarranted to claim that this moment becomes for modern opera overall the way to symbolize fate, judgment, and learning, recalling perhaps Aristotle's key moment of recognition and reversal in his theory of tragedy (and comedy). Furthermore, the mellifluous insinuations of a Giovanni aria are found so often in subsequent poetry and literature as to serve as a kind of inspiration from which the sensuous-seductive voice of a writer wishes to draw breath. This genuflection before the opera is utterly commanded by its themes: it is exactly what the Don requires of every woman who comes close. They will love him, so demands the music. They must submit, as we apparently are to submit, to its seductive power—or not. For perhaps this opera teaches us about our ability to resist and transcend its power to seduce in the move toward moral consciousness. As Kierkegaard writes, and as many of our authors discuss, it is not merely the man that demands submission but the Idea, and we may not want to be taken in by it. The power of the music is intended, according to a developing nineteenth-century aesthetic, to allow Don Giovanni as seducer to be transfigured by his own music into the very idea of seduction. But that this transfiguration is not allowed fully to succeed leaves us with a deep conflict between the work's aesthetic power and its implied judgment or morality, with what Bernard Williams often liked to describe as a state of uncertainty or indeterminacy. The conflict in this opera is, for many of the contributors to this volume, about the confrontation that the aesthetic poses to the moral and the moral to the aesthetic. The Don Giovanni moment cannot be only a moral moment; a moral moment must rather coexist with the albeit conflicting aesthetic drive. The moment thus lasts much longer than the time it takes for the Commendatore to issue his judgment; it lasts for the entire run that is Giovanni's aesthetic, seductive, and erotic life. As with Aristotle, the moment of recognition demands the entire form and unfolding of the action as a whole.

In the interrelated essays by Lydia Goehr and Daniel Herwitz, the conflict between the aesthetic and moral is made to work self-reflectively, to bear on the very nature and medium of opera, music, and art. Drawing on Kierkegaard's claim that *Don Giovanni* is "the only classic example of its kind," Goehr argues for a contender in Wagner's *Tristan und Isolde*. She explores two concepts, first that of the absolutely musical, in contradistinction to that of absolute music, and second that of an *Erlebnis*, to sustain a relationship between the absolutely musical experience that is the work and the absolute demand the work makes upon the listener. As Kierkegaard places himself as a lover of the opera that is *Don Giovanni*, so Wagner's *Tristan* makes a seductive claim upon its audience, to deceive, to seduce, to draw them away from a world that is real toward one defined by the "purely aesthetic." Goehr pursues the political and moral dangers of the erotic drive of the "absolutely musical" in terms of a promise that is also a curse. Herwitz draws on Kierkegaard's work to ask how philosophy itself becomes not only seductive but also operatic. He sets his Kierkegaardian-inspired reading against a consideration of the opera's sexism—loving as a woman, acting as a man. He concludes that the dialectical preoccupation with gender in the work stands in an inextricable relation to the aesthetic and moral tensions evident in Kierkegaard's own operatic style of writing philosophy.

Ernst Osterkamp's essay begins the chronological unfolding of *Don Giovanni*'s legacy. He explores Goethe's relationship to *Don Giovanni* as it affected the creation of *Faust* and thus the deep interaction between these two great literary myths. His discussion focuses on how both figures came comparably to engage in a constant border crossing between knowledge and learning, on the one hand, and pleasure and desire, on the other. Each was driven by music, the force of which, so Osterkamp maintains, was deeply rooted in Goethe's development of modern individualism. Many of Goethe's followers—Lord Byron, Nikolaus Lenau, Christian Dietrich Grabbe—then tried to produce works in Goethe's shadow. The attempts were not always successful, but together they demonstrated that the attempt to merge the drama of Faust with that of Don Giovanni was at once impossible although somehow, after Goethe, unavoidable.

Richard Eldridge's essay interprets E. T. A. Hoffmann's classic short story on Don Juan. It explores the musical, dramatic, philosophic, and sexual preoccupations of its protagonist to establish a central trope of German Romanticism, namely, as Eldridge argues, that we are drawn toward a kind of surrender to uncontrollable passion as the fullest realization of earthly action, but therein also pulled toward death in the refusal of all reciprocity and acknowledgment.

Thomas S. Grey traces the Byronic and Gothic elements of the Don Juan figure as an archetype in German Romantic opera, drama, and poetry. He focuses on Wagner's *Flying Dutchman* and Liszt's *Réminiscences de Don Juan* to show an emerging paradox, to wit, that at the same time that the figure of the Don becomes Gothicized and vampirized it became also domesticated, which is to say, adapted to a postrevolutionary and specifically German *Vormärz* bourgeois sensibility. Grey views Wagner's *Dutchman* as a completion of this adaptive process.

Boris Gasparov explores a particular trope of European Romanticism through the work of Pushkin. Whereas some Romantics such as Byron and Hoffmann showed a fascination with Don Juan as a figure belonging to a pre-Romantic past, unburdened by reflection and self-doubt, Pushkin pulled his hero, from which he was personally unable to distance himself, fully into the Romantic or self-reflective domain. In his early work, Pushkin gave his Don Juan figure a double identity, reflected in his paradoxical attempt to cross over from Mozart's *Don Giovanni* to Benjamin Constant's *Adolphe*. In his later work, however, the figure came increasingly to be identified with the authoritative figure of the Commendatore and by extension with the authority of the Russian autocracy. The Commendatore's seeming immobility and eventual triumph was exemplified in the late Pushkin's fatalistic view, as Gasparov describes it, of Tzar Nicholas's Russia.

That the subsequent appropriation by other operas may improve or render more explicit the thematic character of *Don Giovanni* is a claim made by Philip Kitcher and Richard Schacht in their shared investigation of Wagner's *Ring*. Placed in comparison with *Don Giovanni*, they argue that Wagner's work revolves around questions of authority and judgment: who makes what kinds of judgment and with what authority? Considering how these questions arose first in *Don Giovanni* and then in the larger canvas of the *Ring*, the authors read the latter as having taken up one of the challenges of *Don Giovanni* with more variation and complexity, the challenge specifically of confronting how and whether a human life achieves or holds onto meaning in a world that constantly turns.

In, as it were, the final gasp of Romanticism at its most self-conscious phase, Brian Soucek argues that although Richard Strauss and Hugo von Hofmannsthal made explicit the fact that two of their collaborations stood in analogy to two of Mozart's operas, they did not mention arguably the best analogy of all, namely, *Ariadne auf Naxos*'s relation to *Don Giovanni*.

Both operas stem from many of the same sources, include a parallel mix of comedy and tragedy, exist in two significantly different versions, and, since their beginnings, have been subject to similarly divergent interpretations. But if, as Soucek further argues, *Ariadne* is an analogue to *Giovanni* then it is a self-conscious one. Not only does it inherit the interpretative problems of Mozart's work; it also assumes a reflective stance on those very problems.

And then enters that wag of a wit, George Bernard Shaw, whose *Man and Superman: A Comedy and a Philosophy* (1903) does not, so argues Agnes Heller, actually rewrite Don Juan; it rather rather deconstructs the very myth. Heller explores the sense of the comic by comparing Shaw to earlier versions of the Don Juan figure, as seen, say, in Tirso de Molina's *El burlador de Sevilla* (1630) and Moliere's *Don Juan ou Le Festin de pierre* (1665). Mozart's music contrarily endows the figure with a kind of grandeur incompatible with the comedic. Heller shows the complexity of Shaw's transition, how he returns the legend to the comic genre by employing the language of prose drama and reversing almost all the traditional roles. Through the extended lens of Wagner and Nietzsche, Shaw was able to produce in the form of art something approximating a reflective "essay" of contemporary social relevance, one that bore significantly on the then prevalent forms of nihilism, socialism, and feminism.

In his essay Hans Rudolf Vaget aims to recover Mörike's interpretation of Mozart's creative process as described in his famous novella of 1855, *Mozart's Journey to Prague* (en route to attending the premiere of *Don Giovanni*). Against the blanket condemnations of many nineteenth-century interpretations of the opera by critics such as Edward Dent and Albert Einstein, Vaget argues for the value of Mörike's interpretation, in particular, by drawing on the identification of Mörike's own creative process with that of Mozart. In Vaget's essay the identification of authorial process is sustained by a comparison not of biography or intention as such but on the basis of the works.

The philosopher and musician Theodor W. Adorno also sought to recover Mozart's opera, not only by paying tribute to Kierkegaard but also by producing a small vignette on and explicitly in homage to Zerlina. The final two essays of this volume explore this homage. Berthold Hoeckner offers both a translation of Adorno's piece as well as a philosophical commentary upon it, illustrating a dialectical turn away from the figure of Don Juan toward a more neglected character. The small vignette and the small character fit Hoeckner's reading of Adorno's dialectic between the absolute, explosive, and intensive moment and the work as an extended whole. Nikolaus Bacht's essay situates Adorno's homage in a broader context of Adorno's lifelong engagement with the opera, in particular with his response to an early Klemperer performance.

In this response Bacht finds a typically Adornian play of dialectics between freedom and pleasure, on the one hand, and reconciliation and fate, on the other.

One thing this volume wants to show is that it is a clearly a sign of the power of *Don Giovanni* that it has prompted such diverse reimaginings and interpretations. Our ordering of the essays follows a roughly chronological pattern, although it begins in an unexpected place. It starts at a moment in fact before the start, with a deeply culinary essay by Ingrid Rowland on the origins of the Don Juan figure in an ancient Mediterranean cult of magical statues and necromancy. Although, as Rowland argues, it was Tirso de Molina's *El burlador de Sevilla* that marks the first appearance of Don Juan as a full-blown figure, a more significant development of the cultish aspects of the figure was found in the sixteenth-century Italian philosopher Giordano Bruno, whose dialogue *La Cena de le Ceneri, The Ash Wednesday Supper,* presented parallels to the portentous supper that led Don Juan to Hell—and us, as listeners, to possible intestinal damage.

We wanted the D-minor chord to ring with as much brawn as Zerlina's aria rings with its own *certo balsamo*. The arguments of this volume's essays envisage an opera whose terms of reference are as forceful and overwhelming today as they were two centuries ago, when Mozart journeyed to Prague to the opening of his work that would survive a Europe increasingly overrun with statues and cemeteries the more it pulled itself into hell. The legacy of *Don Giovanni* is that of a world in which we would be lonely without its main character, thus the arguable tediousness of the final reconciliation scene after his death. But the legacy is also of a world that forces us to live, when we must live within the ambit of its authority, in some sort of constant state of rebellion. Studying some part of the immense range of this opera's influence, as these essays do, is a way to reassess the opera and to appreciate its scope. We venture to say that the legacy of *Don Giovanni* is the road back to the opera itself, the very road in reverse that Mozart's carriage traversed to bring him to the beginning of its afterlife. We think it therefore notable that, for all the extensive writing on this opera, there has never been, as far as we can tell, a collection of essays specifically about its legacy as shown in works other than itself. We hope this collection will inaugurate others to be produced so that, over time, another list may be unfolded in a different key.

New York and Ann Arbor, 2004

The Don Giovanni Moment

One

Don Giovanni: "And what communion hath light
with darkness?"

INGRID ROWLAND

*I*t is generally acknowledged that the character we know as Don
Juan first emerged about 1630 in Counter-Reformation Spain,
the protagonist of a play, *El burlador de Sevilla o el convidado de piedra* (*The
Trickster of Seville; or, the Stone Guest*), written by a Spanish friar, Gabriel de
Tellez, who took the pseudonym Tirso de Molina.[1] The Burlador, named Don
Juan Tenorio, has three good qualities in the eyes of his peers: noble birth,
great courage, and adamant fidelity to his word. Otherwise, he is evidently
good for nothing: a shameless bully, a seducer, a grandee too quick with his
sword who recklessly skewers the father of one of his conquests, the powerful
Don Gonzalo. One evening, heaping insult on mortal injury, Tirso's trickster
happens by Don Gonzalo's tomb, an extravagant marble structure boasting a
family chapel with a full-sized portrait statue of Don Juan's outraged victim.

Tweaking the statue's stony beard, Don Juan invites the image to dinner on
the eve of what is to be the rake's own wedding night. To Don Juan's surprise
and the delight of Tirso's audience, the stone guest arrives for dinner and
politely, in turn, invites Don Juan to come back to his place for a reciprocal
treat. This repast, served in the tomb chapel amid shifting sarcophagi, proves
to be a meal of vipers and scorpions, wine replaced by vinegar water. Don
Juan's good breeding emerges in the courtly alacrity with which he downs the

repulsive food, but at a certain point a flaming sensation in his inward parts leads him to realize that he has repeated the ancient error of Persephone in Hades: by partaking of this infernal meal he has consecrated himself to the realms of Hell. This first Don Juan is damned, in other words, not because he has been a cad, a rapist, or a murderer, but specifically and exclusively because he has first insulted and then dined with a citizen of the world beyond.[2] This is why the Stone Guest shares the play's title; he is as integral to the story as the Don himself.

In devising the Trickster of Seville, Tirso de Molina created a full-blown myth, with a myth's profound exploration of the relationship between mortal humanity and the supernatural.[3] And like every good myth, that of Don Juan was destined for its own glorious afterlife, perhaps never more glorious than during those frenzied weeks of 1787 when Wolfgang Amadeus Mozart teamed with the Venetian librettist Lorenzo Da Ponte to create their *Don Giovanni* in the proverbially magic city of Prague.

Myths, however, seldom spring full-blown from the head of a single creator. Don Juan's myth had been abuilding for centuries, if not, as his connection with the Persephone story suggests, for far longer than that. Like Persephone, he had certainly been baked in the sun of southern Europe, where ancient Greek statues had often been rumored to talk and occasionally to come to life.[4] Medieval Madonnas and crucifixes, in Italy especially, followed in the same pattern, and in the fifteenth century a rediscovered Greek manuscript bearing the name of Thrice Great Hermes, Hermes Trismegistos, asserted to scholars of the dawning Italian Renaissance that the ancient Egyptians had employed statues to call down and localize the powers of heaven.[5] By some fifty years before the writing of Tirso de Molina's *Trickster of Seville,* the Don, or someone very much like him, seems to have been on the mind of an Italian expatriate in the England of Elizabeth I. This volatile soul, in fact, would perish, like the Spanish grandee of story and song, enveloped in flames, although those flames came not from Hell itself but from a stake erected by the secular arm of the Roman Inquisition.

The Italian expatriate was Giordano Bruno, the defrocked Dominican friar who met his end at dawn on February 17, 1600, in Rome for espousing an abundant set of heretical principles.[6] These heresies included the contention that the sun was the center of but one planetary system in an infinite universe, belief in an immortal world soul, pronounced skepticism about the virgin birth of Jesus Christ, and utter certainty that his own philosophy, a mixture of Kabbalah, Neoplatonism, Hermetism, new science, and ancient mnemonic arts, would offer its practitioners a more secure path to enlightenment than any of his century's prevailing religions. Bruno came from Nola, a small town in the hinterland of Naples, and throughout his life referred to himself in the third person as "il Nolano" and to his credo as the "Nolan philosophy." But Nola held il Nolano for only a short time; after entering the Dominican convent of San Domenico Maggiore in Naples at seventeen (one of the places, in fact, where a crucifix once spoke to St. Thomas Aquinas), he began to exhibit both his genius and his ungovernable temperament. After a brush with the Inquisition sent him running from Naples in 1576, he spent the rest of his life on the move and in trouble; like Don Juan Tenorio, he chafed under the bonds of conventional morality but could never abandon it altogether.

Giordano Bruno's connection to Don Juan and to statues will require some elaboration; it stems from a remark near the beginning of what may be his most brilliant creation, the vernacular dialogue *La Cena de le Ceneri* (*The Ash Wednesday Supper*), written and printed in London early in 1584.[7] Italian books had a lively market in England, the country under Elizabeth I was filled with Italians and Italophiles, beginning with the queen herself, who conversed wittily in just the kind of courtly vernacular that prevailed in Florence and Rome. Her language was not quite the same language as Bruno's Neapolitan, heavily laced as it was with Spanish expressions, but in those days preceding the attack of the Spanish Armada there were many learned Londoners who knew Spanish as well. *La Cena de le Ceneri* was printed by a London printer, John Charlewood, who added to the book's international flavor by claiming to have printed it in Paris.

Bruno set his *Cena de le Ceneri* in London in the Lenten season of 1584, not long after an invitation to lecture at Oxford had met with dismal failure.[8] The university, firmly committed to Aristotle's philosophy and the world system of Ptolemy, had invited Bruno to debate the validity of Copernican astronomy with a local don, but after his first appearance he was accused of having simply plagiarized the Neoplatonic philosopher Marsilio Ficino. This accusation threw Bruno into one of his proverbial rages; as he saw it, his adversary, Dr. Underhill, was an arid pedant who failed to see the radical originality with which Nolan philosophy departed from Ficino's Neoplatonism—and although Bruno's philosophy does in fact bear a notable debt to Ficino, it does depart as radically as he claimed. It is unlikely, however, that the Oxford audience could have heard this originality through Bruno's thick accent and effusive gestures, especially as the dons were not particularly sympathetic to Ficino or Copernicus, let alone to Bruno himself.[9] Nor would they have much of a chance to clarify their thinking: the tiny Italian stormed back to London and his rooms in the French Embassy.

In the French ambassador's residence, among embassy staff and the courtiers of the Virgin Queen, Bruno found more congenial company. He made friends with the dashing poet Sir Philip Sidney and with two men who also appear in the Ash Wednesday supper: Fulke Greville and the Anglo-Italian writer John Florio, who lived, like Bruno, in the French Embassy between Fleet Street and the River Thames. *La Cena de le Ceneri* could count, therefore, on a substantial reading public in London. Though he claimed to know only a few words of English, Bruno got by in Italian, French, and Latin; indeed, his command of these languages had already allowed him to dwell among Dominican friars in Naples and Rome, Swiss Calvinists in Geneva, freethinking French courtiers in Paris, and the disparate denizens of several places in between. Yet if his facility with language afforded him the means to live among a varied assortment of his fellow creatures, Bruno's ill-concealed impatience with stupidity, his arrogance, and his incandescent temper fits always urged him to move on under a cloud of opprobrium. His escape from Naples had earned him defrocking from the priesthood, expulsion from the Dominican order, and excommunication from the Catholic Mass.[10] A tartly critical pamphlet he published after little over a month in Geneva brought him to trial for libel and excommunication from the Calvinist communion.[11] By the time Bruno reached London, he was probably Christian only in the most tenuous sense; by the end of his life, in most respects, he was no longer Christian at all.[12]

He arrived in an England still searching for a resolution of its own religious situation. As for academic matters, Bruno would show in *La Cena de le Ceneri* that the English were if anything more dogmatic than their peers on the Continent. The dialogue begins by reporting an encounter between Fulke Greville and himself near Fleet Street:[13]

> Prithee, Signor Nolano, let me know the reasons why you believe that the earth moves. To which [the Nolan] replied: he could furnish him no reason whatsoever without knowing his capabilities, and not knowing the extent to which he would be understood *he feared doing as those people do who say their piece to statues and go off to converse with the dead*. Would [Greville] then please first make himself better known by proposing the reasons that persuaded him to the contrary, because according to the brightness and power of mind he might demonstrate in adducing these [reasons, the Nolan] could give him appropriate answers.

Better still, Bruno said that he would like to debate qualified proponents of Ptolemaic cosmology, an idea to which Greville eagerly assented.

> Next Wednesday, eight days from now, which will be Ash Wednesday, you will be invited to a banquet with many gentlemen and learned persons, so that after eating we may hold a discussion of many fine things.[14]

The Nolan assented, "But, I pray you, do not bring ignoble persons before me, ill educated and ill versed in similar speculations."[15]

The dialogue continues by detailing how Bruno's high expectations were systematically dashed, beginning with the schedule. Banqueting in Italy meant an invitation for midday, but by lunchtime on Ash Wednesday Bruno, having heard nothing, went off with some Italian friends. He returned at dusk to find his housemate John Florio and their friend Matthew Gwynne at the embassy door, nervously waiting to collect him for supper. The Nolan urged them to calm themselves:

> "Up to now only one thing has gone wrong for me; that I had hoped to conduct this business in the light of day, and I see that the debate will happen by candlelight. . . . But now," said the Nolan, "let us set out, and pray that God will guide us in this dark evening, on so long a journey, down such hazardous streets."[16]

Ash Wednesday, the penitential holy day that marks the beginning of Lent, is not normally marked off by feasting but by abstinence, the stark climax of Shrove Tuesday's gluttonous revels. Catholic tradition counted penitence among the seven sacraments; English Protestants reduced this number to the two ceremonies explicitly attested in the Gospel: Baptism and Communion (or, as they termed it, the Lord's Supper). By inviting guests to dinner on a day that Catholics normally devoted to fasting, Bruno's Protestant hosts made public their own position in the religious debates that had divided England, often violently, for much of the sixteenth century. In addition, however, by deciding to spend the evening in learned discussion among scholars they actively redefined penitence as thoughtfulness and introspection rather than merely participation in ritual. Their Ash Wednesday supper, when it begins, is therefore fraught with glimmers of enlightenment as well as symbolism.

For Bruno, however, a walk through muddy London streets and the Englishmen's attempts at learned discussion soon proved as trying as forty days of Lenten privation:

> The Nolan says that in all ten months he has stayed in England he never drew as much profit as he did on this single evening from doing penance and earning pardons. This evening was for him a sufficient beginning, middle, and end of Lent. "This evening," he said, "I expect to have earned more by my penance than by forty damn days of fasting, and forty nights besides. This evening I was in the desert, where, not for one, or three, but for forty temptations I garnered forty thousand years of plenary indulgence."[17]

The climax of *La Cena de le Ceneri*, like that of the Don Juan story, occurs, then, over a nocturnal dinner. It is an age-old setting for profound encounters, as in Homer's *Iliad*, where the Trojan king Priam makes a phantasmagoric twilight passage across enemy lines to the tent of the Greek hero Achilles, who has killed Priam's son Hector and kept the body with him as a gruesome memento of his own rage.[18] Priam resolves to ransom back Hector's body for proper burial, an act that will bring an end both to the cycle of Hector's life and to Achilles' extravagantly brutal wrath. The old man makes his way down from the citadel of Troy accompanied by Hermes, the divine escort who shepherds the souls of the dead to the underworld, and this god's presence in the bleak nocturnal landscape makes Priam's journey across the battle lines a literal passage through the "valley of the shadow of death." Priam appeals to Achilles with the terrible words: "I dare what no other mortal on earth has dared: to reach out my hands to the mouth of the man who has killed my children." As Achilles looks up from his obsessive watch over Hector's corpse, old Priam suddenly reminds him of his own father, and he agrees to give the body up. Abruptly returned to the world of the living, he has his Myrmidons wash Hector and prepare him for burial and then invites the aged king to sit down for a meal, noting that the mythic heroine Niobe had remembered to eat even after losing all twelve of her children, six sons and six daughters.[19] So, in the midst of devastation, in the presence of Hector's corpse, the two warriors come to recognize one another's humanity and signal that recognition by dining together. In this strange intimacy Achilles at last puts away the consuming wrath that has been the subject of the *Iliad*, and within a few more lines Homer brings his epic to a close.[20]

By a similar narrative logic the premonitory atmosphere of the Last Supper, another nighttime meal, gives way to Jesus's terrible vigil in the Garden of Gethsemane, when he prays to be spared his imminent suffering and death and walks instead into the ambush set by Judas Iscariot.[21]

By casting his dialogue as an Ash Wednesday supper, Bruno, with a daring that borders on recklessness, invites comparisons with the Last Supper, and hence with the Last Supper's ritual commemoration in the liturgy of the Eucharist. The Eucharist, in turn, had been a subject of fervent and sometimes violent debate between Catholics and Protestants. Bruno's experience with the Calvinists in Geneva had left him with a sharp distaste for radical Protestants, and his late arrival at the Ash Wednesday meal spares him the passing of the "loving-cup" in an English ritual that pointedly evokes the Protestant communion in two kinds, both bread and wine, in the most negative possible light. Fastidiously neat, Bruno was clearly revolted by sharing the Elizabethan loving-cup so closely with his less hygienically minded dinner companions who collected scraps of food in their beards and neglected to wipe their mouths before drinking.[22]

Against this tenebrous background of courtiers and academics gathered in a dark, wood-paneled dining room at Whitehall in the last dank vestiges of English winter to exchange their barbarous ceremonies, the Nolan philosophy and its proponent are intended to blaze like the sun, and they do, but the unworthiness of Greville's two donnish guests forces Bruno into a contradiction: the Nolan must, after all, talk to statues and converse with the living dead. The dialogue begins with a scathing portrait of them, in a conversation between the intelligent Smitho and Teofilo, the character who represents Bruno:

SMITHO: Did they speak good Latin?
TEOFILO: Yes.
S: Gentlemen?
T: Yes.
S: Of good reputation?
T: Yes.
S: Learned?
T: Most competently.
S: Well bred, courteous, civil?
T: Not enough.
S: Doctors?
T: Yes Sir, yes, Father, yes Ma'am, yes indeed; from Oxford, I believe.
S: Qualified?
T: Of course. Leading men, of flowing robes, dressed in velvet; one of whom had two shiny gold chains around his neck, the other, by God! with that precious hand (that contained twelve rings on two fingers) he looked like a rich jeweler; your eyes and heart popped out just looking at it.
S: Were they steeped in Greek?
T: And in beer, too, forsooth.[23]

Like the eucharistic aura he lends to the tableau of the loving-cup, Bruno's brief remark about his unwillingness to talk to statues emphasizes another sore point among the later sixteenth century's raging religious controversies. Statues, particularly religious statues, were a touchy subject in Elizabeth's England. The Protestant reform throughout Europe, but particularly in its Calvinist version, contained a powerful iconoclastic element. In Nuremberg iconoclasts would break the talented hands of the sculptor Tilman Riemenschneider in 1525 to prevent him from carving, as they claimed, more idols.[24]

In England the iconoclasts would ravage churches, smashing stained glass windows, pulverizing statues, and gouging paintings. What was only a gathering storm under Elizabeth reached gale force in the next century with the murder of King Charles I and the ascendancy of Oliver Cromwell: Charing Cross, the thirteenth-century stone cross that serves as a signpost to Giordano Bruno en route to his Ash Wednesday supper, was destroyed by Puritan vandals in 1647.[25]

In fact, Bruno's own distaste for traditional Catholic veneration of the saints was almost Protestant in its vehemence; his companions in prison would tell the inquisitors that

> he said that one should not adore the relics of the saints, nor honor them, because in this way one could end up adoring the bone of a dog—saying, "How do you know that these things are really the bones of saints?"
>
> He criticized the images of saints, saying that it was idolatry to venerate them, and he made fun of them with some ugly and profane gestures. . . . In Naples he was tried twice [by the Inquisition], first for having given away certain figures and images of saints, and having kept a single crucifix, and for this reason he was accused of disparaging the images of saints.[26]

The twenty-second article of the thirty-nine that were adopted by Elizabeth's Anglican Church as the fundamental tenets of their faith was fully in line with Bruno's expressed opinion on these matters:

> The Romish Doctrine concerning Purgatory, Pardons, Worshipping, and Adorations, as well of Images as of Reliques, and also invocation of Saints, is a fond thing vainly invented, and grounded upon no warranty of Scripture, but rather repugnant to the Word of God.[27]

Thus by insisting that he would not speak to statues and converse with the dead, the Nolan was not only warning Greville that he refused to debate with dullards. He was suggesting more broadly that he wanted to be able to discern reality from its image, in human nature, in religion, and in the infinite reaches that the Nolan philosophy, uniquely in its time, ascribed to outer space.[28] The Nolan philosophy promised to guide its adepts surely through a world of oscillating appearances. Shortly after publishing *La Cena de le Ceneri,* Bruno would make this claim to certain guidance explicit in the introduction to the last and most ambitious of all his vernacular dialogues, *De Gli Heroici Furori, On the Heroic Frenzies,)* of 1585:

But here contemplate the harmony and consonance of all the spheres, intelligences, muses, and instruments together, where heaven, the movement of the worlds, the works of nature, the discourses of intellect, the mind's contemplation, the decrees of divine providence, all celebrate with one accord the lofty and magnificent vicissitude that equals the lower waters with the higher, exchanges night for day, and day with night, so that divinity is in all things, so that everything is capable of everything, and the infinite goodness communicates itself without end according to the full capacity of all things.[29]

It was the need to communicate "according to the full capacity of all things" that brought Bruno to question the capacity of Fulke Greville in their opening exchange in *La Cena de le Ceneri*. (The same art, of course, is practiced on a less ambitious scale, and usually only with intent to deceive, by Lorenzo Da Ponte's Don Giovanni, who boasts that "there is no talent more fertile than mine.")[30]

If talking to statues raised the specter of idolatry in *La Cena de le Ceneri*, conversing with the dead brings up another dubious practice, this time one with which Bruno was definitely associated, at least by hearsay: necromancy. One of the figures in Elizabeth's court with whom the Nolan is likely to have come into contact was the bibliophile and mathematician John Dee.[31] Whether or not Dee and Bruno were actually acquainted, their arcane, complicated activities struck some contemporaries as similar. And Dee, with the help of his shady assistant Edmund Kelley, most certainly made experiments at calling up the dead and talking to angels. The English public's conflation of the work of Dee and Bruno, and their amusement at it, drives the action in Robert Greene's comedy, *Friar Bacon and Friar Bungay*, whose two eccentric philosopher-friars combine Bruno's hyperactive rhetorical style with out-and-out necromancy.[32] The results are comical, but like Aristophanes' satire of Socrates in *The Clouds*, Greene plays to popular perception of a misfit who will eventually pay for that eccentricity with his life.[33]

With remarkable economy, therefore, Giordano Bruno's short aside at the beginning of *La Cena de le Ceneri* to Fulke Greville, a man he is just getting to know, insists that the Nolan philosophy is an art guided by the pure light of reason rather than shadowy occult powers. This is why Bruno says in addition that he would rather defend his philosophy in daylight rather than under cover of night. Indeed, the shadowy elements of the Nolan philosophy seem to have resulted chiefly from Bruno's own inability to explain it all without losing patience with his listeners. In his own view his philosophy was the most plainly enlightened and the most reasonable in history:

The point on which we should fix our mind's eye is this: whether we abide in the daytime with the light of truth above our horizon, or whether we are in the regions of our adversaries, our antipodes? Whether we stand in the shadows, or rather they? Whether, in conclusion, we, who begin to renew the ancient philosophy, stand in the morning to put an end to the night, or in the evening to put an end to the day?[34]

After this bracing preamble *La Cena de le Ceneri* insists that the wisest ancients of all are in fact those who inhabit the present:

I mean to say that we are older, and have greater antiquity, than our predecessors. That is, at least so far as this applies to certain opinions like the one under discussion [sc. the Copernican cosmology] . . . the argument that our contemporaries are not more aware of things than those who came before them, or than the majority of those alive in our own time, has no point anymore: this happens because people, both living and dead, have never participated in other people's lives, and, what is worse, they live their own lives as if they were dead![35]

The inquisitors who examined, perhaps tortured, and finally killed Giordano Bruno were, in his own words, asses, pedants, fools, discordant lutes, ugly dog cuckolds, and more.[36] When they read out his condemnation, he replied: "Perhaps you are more afraid to read me that sentence than I am to receive it."[37] His death did not go unremembered. The moral difficulties involved in killing Giordano Bruno simply for holding his ideas proved enough to induce that same Inquisition, and one inquisitorial examiner, Robert Cardinal Bellarmine, to spare the lives of two younger contemporaries for whom the light of reason also served as a powerful image: Tommaso Campanella and Galileo Galilei. It was the Counter-Reformation that bred the beginnings of Mozart and Da Ponte's Enlightenment hero, the libertine whose freedom of action stood above all for freedom of thought.

Which returns us, at last, to Don Juan Tenorio, the Trickster of Seville, and ultimately to Don Giovanni. Don Juan Tenorio earns his fate by doing what Giordano Bruno explicitly hopes not to do, and finally does, in *La Cena de le Ceneri*; he talks to a statue and reckons with the dead. He is crushed, like Giordano Bruno, by the engines of the Counter-Reformation, whose ancient fears and prohibitions, as Tirso warns, are rooted in an unchanging supernatural reality. Indeed Bruno himself, like Don Juan Tenorio, goes to a figurative Hell for the same transgressions. A tortuous nighttime journey from the French Embassy to the Ash Wednesday supper in Fulke Greville's rooms at Whitehall embarks the Nolan philosopher and his companions on a ferry boat that ostensibly plies the river Thames, but the leaky vessel with its two sinister ferrymen soon reveals itself to be the barge of Charon, the mythological ferryman who took the souls of the deceased across the River Styx.[38] The journey en route to the Ash Wednesday supper is, therefore, presented as a journey through Hell, although Bruno transforms that mythic Hell into a figurative inferno of darkness, ignorance, and bad manners. The Nolan philosophy promises to liberate humanity from this damnation, and indeed Hell has no place in Bruno's infinite cosmos; as a prisoner of the Inquisition in Venice he told his cellmates that eventually God would pardon even the demons.[39] His parting gift to the readers of *La Cena de le Ceneri* is a reference to another book of his that is now lost. Its title was *Purgatorio dell' Inferno*: Hell's Purgatory, or, perhaps better, The Purification of Hell. "And there," he promises, "you shall see the fruits of redemption."[40]

As for Don Juan Tenorio, who sins against both Christian creed and the Nolan philosophy, there is still something in him of Giordano Bruno. Tirso de Molina's protagonist retains his own version of heroic integrity by keeping his word with death, facing his fate with his trust as a gentleman inviolate and his courage unwavering, his human qualities pitted against the machinery of organized religion successfully enough to create a character of mythic vitality. Still, Tirso's play is a melodrama, and his libertine grandee is probably not, on the whole, much imbued with the Nolan philosophy. His story nonetheless expresses a defiantly libertarian spirit that the Nolan philosophy also tapped. Molière would be the first writer to lend an overtly intellectual dimension to the instructive tale of the Spanish Don, but it was once again an Italian, Lorenzo Da Ponte, who would supply the witty words to go with a Mozart score in which music incontrovertibly pitted Don Giovanni's all too human brilliance against the numinous darkness. Bruno's self-description from *La Cena de le Ceneri* gives humanity a transcendent power that is not so unlike what Søren Kierkegaard ascribes to Don Giovanni in his description of the overture to Mozart's opera:

> Now, what shall I say about the Nolan? . . . If in ancient times Tiphys was praised for having discovered the first boat, and crossed the seas with the Argonauts . . . if in our time Columbus is praised . . . what should one make of the man who has found the way to ascend to heaven, run the circumference of the stars, and leave at our backs the convex surface of the firmament? . . . Look who has traversed the air, penetrated the heavens, raced the stars, passed beyond the margins of the world, and with the key of subtle inquiry opened all the cloisters of the truth that can open to us, exposed veiled nature, given eyes to the blind, loosened the tongue of the mute, straightened the lame . . . [41]

The point of Don Giovanni, as Kierkegaard sees him, lies not in his sordid ways but in the combination of his primal energy and his defiance, the super-human force of his humanity:[42]

Hear the beginning of his life, as the lightning flashes forth from the murk of the thunderclouds, so he bursts forth from the depths of earnestness, swifter than the lightning's flash, more inconstant and yet as constant; hear how he rushes down into the manifold of life, how he dashes himself against its solid dam; hear those light dancing tones of the violin, hear the signal of gladness, hear the exultation of lust, hear the festive happiness of enjoyment; hear his wild flight, he is transported beyond himself, ever swifter, ever more impetu-ously; hear the unbridled demands of passion, hear the sighing of love, hear the whisper of temptation, hear the whirlpool of seduction, hear the stillness of the moment, hear, hear, hear Mozart's Don Juan!

NOTES

The subtitle is taken from 2 Corinthians 6:14.

1. See Laura Dolfi, ed., *Tirso de Molina. Immagine e rappresentazione. Segundo Coloquio Internacional, con un' appendice sul tema del Don Giovanni. Atti del convegno di studi, Salerno, 8–9 maggio 1989* (Naples, 1991); Josep M. Sola-Solé and George E. Gingras, eds., *Tirso's Don Juan: The Metamorphosis of a Theme* (Washington, D.C., 1988).

2. See Friedrich Dieckmann, *Die Geschichte Don Giovannis: Werdegang eines erotischen Anarchisten* (Frankfurt, 1991); Han S. Meyer, *Doktor Faust und Don Juan* (Frankfurt, 1979); Giovanni Macchia, *Vita, avventure e morte di Don Giovanni* (Turin, 1978): Helmut Kreuzer, ed., *Don Juan und Femme Fatale* (Munich, 1994).

3. See José Bergamin, "Moralidad y misterio de Don Juan (Lo que va del hombre al nombre)," in Dolfi, *Tirso de Molina*, 253–291.

4. Erwin Rohde, *Psyche. Seelencult und Unsterblichkeitsglaube der Griechen,* 3d. ed. (Tübingen and Leipzig, 1903), 190, 193–194 (Greece); Franklin Brunell Krauss, "An Interpretation of the Omens, Portents, and Prodigies Recorded by Livy, Suetonius, and Tacitus" (Ph.D. diss., University of Pennsylvania, 1930), 176–179 (ancient Rome; see especially the statue of Zeus Olympios in Athens that laughed at the Emperor Caligula when he tried to haul it off to Rome, 178–179); for the fundamentally dif-ferent phenomenon of "talking statues" in Renaissance Rome, see Valerio Marcucci, *Pasquinate romane del Cinquecento* (Rome, 1983).

5. The most explicit ancient source on animated statues is the Hermetic dialogue *Ascle-pius*, composed in Greek in the late Roman imperial age, probably in Alexandria, and known to the Middle Ages in Latin translation; see André Jean Festugière, *Le révé-lation d'Hermès Trismégiste* (Paris, 1949–1954); D. P. Walker, *Spiritual and Demonic Magic from Ficino to Campanella* (London, 1958); Frances Yates, *Giordano Bruno and the Hermetic Tradition* (London, 1964); Garth Fowden, *The Egyptian Hermes:*

A Historical Approach to the Late Pagan Mind (Princeton, 1986); Sebastiano Gentile, ed., *Marsilio Ficino e il ritorno di Ermete Trismegisto* (Florence, 1999); Carlos Gilly and Cees van Heertum, eds., *Magia, Alchimia, Scienza dal '400 al '700. L'influsso di Ermete Trismegisto/Magic, Alchemy, and Science from the Fifteenth to the Eighteenth Centuries: The Influence of Hermes Trismegistus* (Florence, 2002).

6. Saverio Ricci, *Giordano Bruno nell' Europa del Cinquecento* (Rome, 2000); Michele Ciliberto, *Giordano Bruno* (Rome and Bari, 1997); Hilary Gatti, *Giordano Bruno and Renaissance Science* (Ithaca, 1999); Hilary Gatti, ed., *Giordano Bruno, Philosopher of the Renaissance* (Aldershot, 2002); Eugenio Canone, ed., *Giordano Bruno 1548–1600, Mostra storico documentaria, Roma, Biblioteca Casanatense 7 giugno—30 settembre 2000* (Florence, 2000); Nuccio Ordine, *La soglia dell'ombra: Letteratura, filosofiea e pittura in Giordano Bruno* (Venice, 2003); Vincenzo Spampanato, *Vita di Giordano Bruno* (Rome, 1988; repr. Messina, 1921).

7. A critical edition of this dialogue has been produced by Giovanni Aquilecchia, Giordano Bruno, *La Cena de le Ceneri, Giordano Bruno Oeuvres Complètes,* vol. 2, *Le Souper des Cendres* (Paris, 1994).

8. Giovanni Aquilecchia, "Bruno at Oxford Between Aristotle and Copernicus," in Michele Ciliberto and Nicholas Mann, eds., *Giordano Bruno, 1583–1585: The English Experience/L'esperienza inglese* (Florence, 1997), 117–124; Miguel A. Granada, "Thomas Digges, Giordano Bruno e il copernicanesimo in Inghilterra," ibid., 125–155; Ricci, *Giordano Bruno,* 214–216; Hilary Gatti, "Tra magia e magnetismo: La cosmologia di Giordano Bruno a Oxford," *Paradigmi* 18.53, n.s. (May-August 2000), 237–260.

9. Giovanni Aquilecchia, "Giordano Bruno in Inghilterra, 1583–1585: Documenti e testimonianze," *Bruniana e Campanelliana* 1 (1995), 33–36.

10. Ricci, *Giordano Bruno,* 100–111.

11. Ibid., 125–137.

12. Bruno's doubts about Christ were one of the chief reasons for his eventual sentence by the Inquisition; see Luigi Firpo, *Il processo di Giordano Bruno* (Rome, 1993), 109–113.

13. Bruno, *Cena,* 75: "All'ora gli disse il Signor Folco Grivello: 'Di grazia, signor Nolano, fatemi intendere le raggioni per le quali stimate la terra muoversi.' A cui rispose, che lui non gli arebbe possuto donar raggione alcuna, non conoscendo la sua capacità: e non sapendo come potesse da lui essere inteso, temerebbe far come quei che dicono le sue raggioni a le statue et andano a parlare co gli morti. Per tanto gli piaccia prima farsi conoscere con proponere quelle raggioni, che gli persuadeno il contrario: per che secondo il lume e forza dell' ingegno che lui dimostrerà apportando quelle, gli potranno esser date risoluzioni."

14. Bruno, *Cena,* 77: "Mercoldì ad otto giorni che sarà de le ceneri, sarete convitato con molti gentil'omini e dotti personaggi, a fin che dopo mangiare si faccia discussione di belle e varie cose."

15. Bruno, *Cena,* 77: "Ma vi priego che non mi fate venir innanzi persone ignobili, mal create e poco intendenti in simile speculazioni."

16. Bruno, *Cena,* 79: "Orsù," disse il Nolano, "andiamo e preghiamo Dio che ne faccio accompagnare in questa sera oscura, a sì lungo camino, per sì poco sicure strade."

17. Cited in Giordano Bruno, *Dialoghi italiani: dialoghi metafisici e dialoghi morali,* ed. Giovanni Aquilecchia, with notes by Giovanni Gentile (Florence, 1985), 78: "Dice il Nolano che in diece mesi ch' ha soggiornato in Inghilterra: non ha profittato quanto

questa sera in far penitenze, et guadagnar perdoni. Questa sera gli fu bene accomodata ad esser principio, mezzo, et fine de la quarantina. Questa sera (disse) voglio che vaglia per la penitenza ch'arrei fatta diggiunando quaranta giorni benedetti, et quaranta notte ancora. Questa sera son stato nel deserto; dove non per una, o tre, ma per quaranta tentazioni ho guadagnato quarantamilia anni d' indulgenzia plenaria." *Benedetti* has been translated in its colloquial sense; literally the phrase says "forty holy days of fasting."

18. Homer, *Iliad*, book 24, lines 141–469.

19. Ibid., 24.505–506: "the man who has killed my children" is the more concise *andros paidophonoio*.

20. The Niobe passage is ibid., 24.601–620.

21. Mark 14:32–36: "And they came to a place which was named Gethsemane: and he saith to his disciples, Sit ye here, while I shall pray. And he taketh with him Peter and James and John, and began to be sore amazed, and to be very heavy; And saith unto them, My soul is exceeding sorrowful unto death: tarry ye here, and watch. And he went forward a little, and fell on the ground, and prayed that, if it were possible, the hour might pass from him. And he said, Abba, Father, all things are possible unto thee; take away this cup from me: nevertheless not what I will, but what thou wilt."

Matthew 26:36–39: "Then cometh Jesus with them unto a place called Gethsemane, and saith unto the disciples, Sit ye here, while I go and pray yonder. And he took with him Peter and the two sons of Zebedee, and began to be sorrowful and very heavy. Then saith he unto them, My soul is exceeding sorrowful, even unto death: tarry ye here, and watch with me. And he went a little farther, and fell on his face, and prayed, saying, O my Father, if it be possible, let this cup pass from me: nevertheless not as I will, but as thou wilt."

22. Bruno, *Cena*, 325–327.

23. Ibid., 27–29.

> SMITHO: Parlavan ben latino?
> TEOFILO: Si.
> SMITHO: Galant'uomini?
> TEOFILO: Si.
> SMITHO: Di buona riputazione?
> TEOFILO: Si.
> SMITHO: Dotti?
> TEOFILO: Assai competentemente.
> SMITHO: Ben creati, cortesi, civili?
> TEOFILO: Troppo mediocremente.
> SMITHO: Dottori?
> TEOFILO: Messer si, padre si, madonnasi; madesi; credo da Oxonia.
> SMITHO: Qualificati?
> TEOFILO: Come non? Uomini da scelta, di robba lunga, vestiti di velluto: un de' quali avea due catene d'oro lucente al collo; e l'altro (per Dio) con qualla preziosa mano (che contenea dodeci anella in due dita) sembrava uno ricchissimo gioielliero, che to cavava gli occhii et il core, quando la vagheggiava.
> SMITHO: Mostravano saper di greco?
> TEOFILO: E di birra eziamdio."

24. Julien Chapuis, ed., *Tilman Riemenschneider: Master Sculptor of the Late Middle Ages* (Washington, 1999). Even this atrocity could not stop the artist, however.

25. David Piper, *The Companion Guide to London* (Woodbridge, 2000), 95; Gillian Tindall, *The Man Who Drew London: Wenceslaus Hollar in Reality and Imagination* (London, 2002), 77–78, 99–100.

26. Firpo, *Il processo di Giordano Bruno*, 278–279: "Diceva che non si dovevano adorare le reliquie dei santi, né honorare, perché si poteva cosí adorare un' osso di un cane, dicendo 'Che sapete voi che sia di questo santi?'" 279: "Biasimava l'imagini e diceva ch'era un'idolatria, e se ne burlava con certi gesti brutti e profani . . . a Napoli era stato processato due volte, prima per haver dato via certe figure et imagini de' santi e ritenuto un crocefisso solo, essendo per questo imputato di sprezzare l'imagini de' santi."

27. The thirty-nine articles are appended to most English editions of the Anglican *Book of Common Prayer.*

28. See Gatti, *Giordano Bruno and Renaissance Science.*

29. Giordano Bruno, *De Gli Heroici Furori*, in Bruno, *Dialoghi italiani* (Florence, 1985), 947: "Appresso si contempla l'armonia e consonanza de tutte le sfere, intelligenze, muse ed instrumenti insieme; dove il cielo, il moto de' mondi, l'opre della natura, il discorso de gl'intelletti, la contemplazion della mente, il decreto della divina provvidenza, tutti d'accordo celebrano l'alta e magnifica vicissitudine che agguaglia l' acqui inferiori alle superiori, cangia la notte col giorno, ed il giorno con la notte, a fin che la divinità sia in tutto, e l' infinita bontà infinitamente si communiche secondo tutta la capacità delle cose."

30. "Più fertile talento del mio non si ha."

31. Peter J. French, *John Dee: The World of an Elizabethan Magus* (London and New York, 1987); Yates, *Giordano Bruno and the Hermetic Tradition*; Deborah E. Harkness, *John Dee's Conversations with Angels: Cabala, Alchemy, and the End of Nature* (Cambridge, 1998).

32. Robert Greene, *Friar Bacon and Friar Bungay* (London, 1926).

33. For the relationship between Socrates and Aristophanes see W. K. C. Guthrie, *A History of Greek Philosophy*, vol. 3 (Cambridge, 1968), 359–377; K. J. Dover, *Aristophanic Comedy* (Berkeley, 1972), 101–120; *Aristophanes' Clouds*, ed. K. J. Dover (Oxford, 1968), xxxii–lvii. Dover omits, deliberately, the immortal Benjamin Bickley Rogers, *The Clouds of Aristophanes* (London, 1916), xxi–xxxvii. A. M. Bowie, *Aristophanes* (Cambridge, 1993), 112–124, emphasizes Socrates' characterization as a magician in *The Clouds.*

34. Bruno, *Cena*, 63: "Quello dumque al che doviamo fissar l'occhio de la considerazione, è si noi siamo nel giorno, e la luce de la verità è sopra il nostro orizzonte, overo in quello de gli aversarii nostri antipodi; si siamo noi in tenebre, o ver essi; et in conclusione si noi che damo principio a rinovar l'antica filosofia, siamo ne la mattina per dar fine a la notte, o pur ne la sera per donar fine al giorno."

35. Bruno, *Cena*, 57–59 : "Si voi intendeste bene quel che dite, vedreste, che dal vostro fondamento d' inferische il contrario di quel che pensate: voglio dire, che noi siamo più vecchi ed abbiamo più lunga età, che i nostri predecessori: intendo, per quel che appartiene in certi giudizii, come in proposito. Non ha possuto essere sì maturo il giudizio d' Eudosso, che visse poco dopo la rinascente astronomia, se pur in esso non rinacque, come quello di Callippo, che visse trent' anni dopo la morte d' Alessandro magno; il quale come giunse anni ad anni, possea giongere ancora osservanze

ad osservanze. . . . Più ne dovea vedere Macometto Aracense milleducento e dui anni dopo quella. Più n' ha veduto il Copernico quasi a nostri tempi. . . . Ma che di questi alcuni, che son stati appresso, e che la moltitudine di que' che sono a nostri tempi, non ha però più sale, questo accade per ciò che quelli non vissero, e questi non vivono gli anni altrui, e, quell che è peggio, vissero morti quelli e questi ne gli anni proprii."

36. Firpo, *Il processo di Giordano Bruno*, 281: "When the prisoners who were friars said the breviary, he said that these whispering friars had no idea what they were saying, and when he had the breviary in hand it made his head ache, because it was badly put together, like a lute out of tune . . . and the person who compiled it was a great fucked cuckold"; "Franciscus Gratianus concarceratus Venetiis dicit . . . con occasione dei frati prigioni, che dicevano il breviario, diceva che questi frati susurroni non sapevano quello si dicessero, e che quando haveva il breviario in mano, li faceva doler la testa, perché era mal fatto e come un leuto scordato . . . e che quello che l'haveva fatto era un gran becco fottuto."

37. Gaspar Schoppe to Conrad Rittershausen, February 17, 1600, cited in Firpo, *Il processo di Giordano Bruno*, 351–352: "Then they degraded him, as we say, excommunicated him, and handed him over to the secular magistrate for punishment. When these things had been done, he made no other reply than, in a menacing tone, 'You may be more afraid to bring that sentence against me than I am to accept it.' And so he was led to prison . . . and so he perished miserably by burning, to proclaim, I believe, to all those other worlds he made up, how blasphemers and impious men are treated in Rome."

38. Bruno, *Cena*, 81: "un che pareva il nocchier antico del tartareo regno, porse la mano al Nolano; et un altro che penso ch'era il figlio di quello, benché fusse uomo di sessantacinque anni in circo." Adi Ophir, in the preface to *Cena*, xliv–l, sees the journey as a political allegory; Eugenio Canone regards it as a prefiguration of the dinner itself, "Una cinericia cena," in Eugenio Canone, *Il dorso e il grembo dell' eterno: Percorsi dell a filosofia di Giordano Bruno* (Pisa/Rome, 2003), 25–52, especially 49.

39. Firpo, *Il processo*, 266: "Franciscus Gratianus concarceratus Venetiis: Dicea che non vi era Inferno né Purgatorio, ma se pur vi era una di queste due cose, vi era il Purgatorio, ch' era più ragionevole che l' Inferno, perché se bene il fuoco era eterno, non era peró la pena eterna, perché finalmente tutti sariano salvi, e che l' ira di Dio non era eterna, allegando 'Nunquid in aeternum Deus irascetur?' dicendo ancora che nel fin del mondo si sariano salvati fino li demonii, perché 'Homines et iumenta salvabis Domine.' E se bene io li replicavo di ció, nondimeno lui mi diceva ch' ero una bestia e capraro, e che non sapevo niente"; "Francesco Graziano, fellow prisoner in Venice: 'He said that neither Hell nor Purgatory existed, but if one of them had to exist, it would be Purgatory, which was more reasonable than Hell, for even if the fire were eternal, it did not follow that the punishment would be eternal, because in the end everyone would be saved, and that God's wrath was not eternal. He cited [Jeremiah 3:5] Will he reserve his anger forever? and also said that at the end of the world even the demons would be saved, because [Psalms 36:6] O LORD, thou preservest man and beast. And if I argued with him, he said that I was beast and a goatherd, and that I knew nothing.'"

40. Bruno, *Cena*, 281,283: "Teofilo. A voi, Smitho, mandarò quel dialogo del Nolano, che si chiama *Purgatorio de l' inferno*; e ivi vedrai il frutto della redenzione"; "Teofilo. To

you, Smitho, I will send the Nolan's dialogue called *Hell's Purgatory*, and there you will see the fruit of redemption."

41. Bruno, *Cena*, 43–49: "Or che dirò io del Nolano? . . . se vien lodato lo antico Tifi per avere ritrovata la prima nave e co gli Argonauti trapassato il mare . . . se a' nostri tempi vien magnificato il Colombo . . . che de' farsi di questo che ha ritrovato il modo di montare al cielo, discorrere la circonferenza de le stelle, lasciarsi a le spalli la convessa superficie del firmamento? . . . Or ecco quello ch' ha varcato l'aria, penetrato il cielo, discorse le stelle, trapassati gli margini del mondo . . . Cossì al cospetto d'ogni senso e ragione, co la chiave di solertissima inquisizione aperti que' chiostri de a verità che da noi aprir si posseano, nudata la ricoperta e velata natura; ha donati occhi a le talpe, illuminati i ciechi . . . sciolta la lingua a muti . . . risaldati i zoppi."

42. Søren Kierkegaard, *Either/Or*, trans. Howard V. Hong and Edna H. Hong, *Kierkegaard's Writings*, vol. 4, part 2 (Princeton, 1988).

Don Juan and Faust: On the Interaction Between Two Literary Myths

ERNST OSTERKAMP

On December 29, 1797, Friedrich Schiller wrote to Goethe from Jena, "I always had a certain confidence in the opera, that from it the tragic drama would unfold in a nobler form, as from the choruses of the old Bacchanalia." Schiller hoped that the opera would stimulate a new conception of tragic drama. At the time he was working on his great drama *Wallenstein* after a long hiatus in his poetic production. Schiller's new conception of tragic drama was intended to satisfy the requirements of an aesthetics of autonomy, because, so he wrote, opera's artificiality frees the poet from all "servile imitation" and allows him a "freer play" of art.[1] Goethe was sympathetic to Schiller's aim not least because, just two days earlier, he had had another chance to see in Weimar a performance of his favorite opera, Mozart's *Don Giovanni*. On December 30 he replied to Schiller, "You would have seen your hope for opera fulfilled in high degree in *Don Giovanni*; but at the same time this piece is also utterly isolated, and since Mozart's death all prospects for something similar have been dashed.[2]

But was Mozart's *Don Giovanni* really so isolated in Goethe's eyes? In December 1797 Goethe had resumed work on his tragedy *Faust* of which, up to this point, only a fragment had been published. Wasn't it inevitable that, fresh from the impact of seeing a performance of *Don Giovanni*, Goethe would have felt compelled to apply Schiller's idea of renewing tragic drama out of the spirit of opera to his *Faust* project? In *Faust: A Fragment* (1790), Goethe had advanced the plot of his planned drama to the point where Faust is threatening to turn himself into a Don Juan. Given his thirst for knowledge, Faust works his way through all the departments of the university and, after the rapid failure of his experiments in the "alternative" sciences, succumbs to an incurable disgust with academic knowledge. Putting himself in the hands of the metaphysical entertainer Mephistopheles, he accomplishes exactly one thing, the destruction of a passionately loving and desirous young girl of just fourteen years of age. Faust catches sight of Margarethe on the street, approaches her, and is just as rapidly rejected by her. He reacts by issuing an order to Mephistopheles: "Listen, you must get me the wench!" When the clever devil, well seasoned in matters of seduction, replies that for this he will need "at least two weeks," Faust is quick to respond. Understandably impatient after decades of celibacy, he points with a certain pride to his own powers of erotic attraction:

> Had I but seven hours time
> I wouldn't need a devil's help
> To seduce a creature of that kind.

"You're almost starting to sound like a Frenchman!"[3] Mephistopheles replies with amazement. For the readers of the *Faust* fragment, which first appeared in print in April 1790, a variant of Mephistopheles' answer may already have suggested itself: "You're almost starting to sound like a Don Juan!"

The premiere of Mozart's *Don Giovanni* in Prague—with Casanova in the audience—had been given only three years before, launching the opera's triumphant tour of Europe's theaters. The thematic direction in which Goethe had taken his Faust fragment responded in an almost demonic way to the contemporary Don Juan euphoria: Faust seduced his Gretchen, quickly tired of her, and went off in search of new adventures, while the object of his seduction, plagued by bad conscience, collapsed during mass in a swoon. This was just the point at which Goethe had left his *Faust* fragment. Would it not therefore have been perfectly natural for him, now in 1797, under the influence of Schiller's reflections on the relation between opera and tragedy, to end his drama in the same spirit, with a scientist mutated into a Don Juan?

The thought is perhaps made yet more compelling when we realize that Goethe had already acquired an intimate knowledge of *Don Giovanni*. On January 1, 1792, having assumed the directorship of the Weimar theater a year earlier, he had personally arranged for the Weimar premiere of the opera, performed with the sung recitative and not therefore in the *Singspiel* version that was then in general use. By 1817, when Goethe retired as the theater director, there had been no less than sixty-eight performances. And yet, it may have been precisely his obviously intimate acquaintance with the work that prevented Goethe from continuing to create his tragic drama out of the spirit of *Don Giovanni*. For, to have allowed his tragedy of cognition to be transformed into a tragedy of erotic repetition compulsion would have meant trivializing both myths, Faust no less than Don Juan. For Goethe's dramatic purposes it would have been enough to have replaced only once the theme of transgressing scientific boundaries with that of erotic transgression. This is because Faust—in contrast to Don Juan—never repeats himself; for him it is enough to know that he could become Don Juan, a possibility revealed to him through the tragedy of Gretchen. There would be nothing more boring for him than to reproduce the repetitive scheme of Leporello's list, to transform the idea of the eternal return into the constant repetition of the "ever the same" (*ewigen Wiederkehr des Gleichen*). Faust is not interested in the sport of record setting: he is a libertine of the spirit not, as Goethe knew, of the body.

Hence, for Faust, who avoids repetition as Mephistopheles avoids the Pentagram, there can be only one more erotic relationship: the one with Helena (in part 2, act 3), the symbolic embodiment of ideal feminine beauty. Whereas Gretchen represents the bourgeois reality of femininity, Helena embodies femininity as an ideal. It is to this ideal that Faust attaches his erotic desire. The moment the ideal is shattered by the horrors of reality and is revealed to be no more than an illusion, Faust's erotic desire is extinguished forever.

In other words, Goethe knew exactly that he would have hollowed out the substance of the Faust material had he brought it any closer to the Don Juan myth than he had already done in the Gretchen tragedy. Thus, it was in the realm not of material (content) but of form—the form in fact of musicality—that Goethe sought now to realize Schiller's concept of the renewal of tragic drama out of the spirit of opera. Goethe's *Faust* was a musical drama through and through.[4] Its dramaturgy in part 1, with the Gretchen songs, spirit choruses, and melodramatic passages, had already crossed the threshold into the musical sphere. In the much more complex part 2 (1832) Goethe intensified its musicalization. In this multimedia world theater the heightened verbal art repeatedly makes recourse to musical means: from battle music to choruses, from cantata and oratorio forms to the grandiose "word-opera" of the Helena act. The "opera of all operas" was how, in 1913, Hugo von Hofmannsthal would eventually characterize *Faust*.[5]

That Goethe saw *Faust's* "very serious jokes"[6] as closely related to Mozart's *dramma giocoso*, precisely on the basis of its musicality, is demonstrated in his conversations with Johann Peter Eckermann. When Eckermann, on February 12, 1829, expressed his hope that a suitable music might be found for *Faust*, Goethe reacted skeptically: " 'It is quite impossible,' Goethe said. 'The revolting, the disgusting, the terrible that it would have to contain in some places would go against the times. The music would have to be in the character of Don Juan; *Mozart* would have had to compose Faust.' "[7] While he thus avoided the blending of his Faust with Don Juan in the realm of the material, Goethe, with his inner ear, allowed Faust to assume the character of Don Juan musically. And yet, with his inner eye, this would not have been possible had the two myths not borne deep affinities to each other. Faust and Don Juan were both figures of transgression. This allowed the plot of Goethe's drama to push ahead into the sphere of "the revolting, the disgusting, the terrible." In fact, for the music of the "very serious jokes" of his *Faust* Goethe could have imagined no music other than that of Mozart's *Don Giovanni*, whose dual character of lightness and profound seriousness he never ceased to admire.[8]

So Goethe began to bring these two great myths of modern individualism together,[9] despite his keeping the seriousness of his Faust separate from the jokes of Don Juan. The two myths had been formed around 1600 within an interval, in fact, of only twenty-five years between them. In 1587, the original text of the Faust myth appeared in Frankfurt with the *Historia von D. Johann Fausten* and, in 1613, the drama that introduced the figure of Don Juan to literature, *El burlador de Sevilla* by Tirso de Molina, appeared for the first time in Spain. Following upon the major changes in worldview during the Renaissance, two myths were created that introduced plot traditions circling around figures of radical transgression. From the beginning both myths were inscribed with a warning structure. In Faust's case, in the spirit of Protestantism, a warning is issued against godless science, which, driven by the cardinal sin of curiosity, wants to break through traditional limits and seek new paths for knowledge. In Don Juan's case, in the spirit of the Counter-Reformation, the warning is against a loss of restraint, which strains the narrow limits of the early modern moral code. Both sins, *curiositas* and *voluptas*, are punishable by eternal damnation: the devil comes for both Faust and Don Juan. But in the process of Enlightenment the warning inherent in each myth begins to weaken, both when tribute is paid to the joys of knowledge under the sign of reason and when human sensuality is itself emancipated. In his own *Faust* fragment Lessing had already reevaluated the human drive for knowledge to render it the noblest of all drives. Given this rendering, Goethe could no longer let his Faust simply vanish into hell just because he aspires to what is now valued. At the same time, the myth of Don Juan became intermingled with the reality of the great libertines. For his innumerable adventures of love, the greatest of them of all, Casanova, received just one punishment, namely, to be forced to write about everything he once had been allowed to experience, thereby replacing his once lived pleasure with a now merely imaginary pleasure. To the ancien régime this must have seemed the most up-to-date form of damnation.

For the bourgeoisie of the nineteenth century there could no longer be limits to knowledge the transgression of which would be punished. On the contrary, the bourgeoisie hoped to gain its political and economic emancipation precisely by advancing knowledge. With a worried, sidelong glance at this bourgeois optimism, Goethe, in the second part of his *Faust*, transferred the warning structure of the Faust myth from knowledge itself to its potentially dangerous consequences. In the last act Faust rules over a world in which all human relations have been destroyed by economic and technical rationality. Driven by progressive optimism, Faust has established hell on earth: no wonder, then, that he experiences death as if it were an ascent into heaven.

At this time, too, the warning structure of the Don Juan myth was transformed so that the drama of erotic transgression became a drama of both repetition and ennui. The other side of the bourgeois work ethic was *eudaemonism,* which happened also to be its very motivation. If technical progress and economic prosperity had endless wish fulfillment as their goal, then this goal was no longer punishable; however, there undoubtedly arose a fear (à la Schopenhauer) that when every desire is satisfied and every wish fulfilled there follows the boredom of eternal return. Thus, in the nineteenth century, Don Juan became the pale brother of the even paler Tannhäuser who wants to live anywhere—just not in Venusberg.

For Goethe's young admirers, followers, and competitors in European Romanticism, given the breaking of the limits of intellectual cognition and the breaking of the limits of desire, and given the asceticism of spiritual knowledge and the hedonism of corporeal pleasures, Faust and Don Juan remained equally attractive and, more important, intertwined figures. Why should the one exclude the other, especially if, as the progress-oriented bourgeoisie hoped, the intensification of knowledge would bring with it the intensification of worldly pleasure? Thus the two great myths of modern individualism, which in Goethe came close enough to be heard if not seen, drew still closer together in the early nineteenth century. It was symptomatic of this development that Lord Byron, whom Goethe, in the Helena act, elevated to Faust's son Euphorion, produced his own version of *Faust* in *Manfred, a Dramatic Poem* (1817). And then, at the end of own dramatic life, he wrote his own *Don Juan*, a great satirical epic that, however, remained a fragment. Yet he never let there be any doubt that both figures were nothing but two masks behind which the same individual appears, i.e., the Romantic poet, for whom, at least in imagination, there are no more limits either to knowledge or to morality. The Romantic poet is autonomous and bound by no law other than that of art. For Byron, therefore, Don Juan melted into Faust as Faust into Don Juan through the figure of the Romantic poet. Understanding this, Goethe made Lord Byron into the son of Faust and of Helena who is, after all, the feminine-passive counterpart of Don Juan. Goethe knew, however, that in modernity such figures could not survive: Byron/Euphorion paid for his flights of imagination with a fatal plunge.

In the politically conflicted Biedermeier era, when the deathly stillness of Restoration fell over the social, scientific, and cultural dynamics of industrialization, the relationship between Faust and Don Juan assumed its most compelling power. Nikolaus Lenau, the poet par excellence of Biedermeier Weltschmerz, wrote a *Faust* in 1835 and a *Don Juan* nine years later. Both were written as dramatic poems in verse. But it was the politically narrow confines of the Metternich era that created insurmountable barriers for the titanic subjectivism of both heroes. Lenau transformed them into embodiments of Weltschmerz and inner disintegration: the ideal representatives of the dynamic of bourgeois individualism who by breaking all bounds meet with the same death—in suicide. They were too big for their times. Faust's individualism turns the corner into nihilism and he stabs himself; Don Juan's lust for life turns into disgust with life and he lets his mortal enemy stab him. Don Juan says:

> My mortal enemy is now at my mercy,
> This too is boring, as is all of life.[10]

In Lenau the mythic figures of Faust and Don Juan closely approximated each other, even if the poet maintained a distinction between the two stories. Both figures, as in Byron, were mirror images of the poet's sense of life. In contrast to Byron, however, whose Manfred/Faust and Don Juan figures expressed two clearly differentiated possibilities of his ego, Lenau allowed his figures to express the same emotional tenor. Their destruction is not brought about by a higher power but by an existential disgust, a weariness with life, an emptiness and boredom that simply seizes them. In their deaths, as in their lives, these figures are brought together typologically. Given the restrictions of the age, which impose narrow political constraints on the bourgeois individual's will to act, the individual seeks fulfillment not on the public stage but rather in private love affairs. Lenau's Faust loves and seduces all the women whom he encounters; in fact he becomes what Goethe's Faust only suggests as a possibility: a Don Juan who replaces his metaphysical motives with physical ones. In comparison with Lenau's *Faust*, Goethe's shows its radicalism, for, in the last act, at the end of his life, Faust envisions grand, world-changing plans. In Lenau's *Faust*, only three years after Goethe's death, nothing of this radicalism remains. Filled only with the sense of his godliness, Lenau's Faust tries to satisfy his drive for knowledge. Yet he allows himself to seek in practice the satisfaction of quite different desires. He is a Biedermeier and hence a melancholic Don Juan. It is possible that Lenau's decision not to complete and publish his *Don Juan* (it appeared posthumously in 1851) was a consequence of his having already seen in his *Faust* a figure long since consigned to hell.

In the year Lenau's *Don Juan* appeared, Heinrich Heine made note, in his comments on his "dance poem," also of "the odd coincidence of the Faust legend with the legend of Don Juan."[11] He did not elaborate. Perhaps he did not need to, because the thought had long since become a commonplace for a generation that had grown up with Hegel's dialectics and was used to finding the relationship of opposites in the spirit of system building.[12] Those who wanted to synthesize the representatives of intellect and physical desire would have been able to draw on any number of structural and thematic affinities between the two myths, from the spirit of rebellion against social and religious norms to the ruthlessness and erotic attraction of the two characters, from the seduction of innocent young women and the removal of competitors in duels to final descents into hell.[13] If this were not already enough, then they might simply have noticed that Faust and Don Juan bear the same name: Johannes, Juan, Giovanni.

In 1809 the writer Niklas Vogt produced a libretto that, though never set to music, aimed to show "how Doctor Faust and Don Juan could be joined together in a great opera."[14] In the background lay the Romantic intention to create "a new mythology," in the spirit of Friedrich Schlegel, as "the most supremely artistic of all artworks," because it would "incorporate all others [i.e., artworks]."[15] By unifying the two important myths of modernity, those of Goethe's *Faust* and Mozart's *Don Giovanni*, the "new mythology" would reach its highest aim and produce the most supremely artistic of artworks. Certainly Vogt, with his limited talent, was not up to the task of producing a work of this sort. He was, furthermore, limited by the then prevalent spirit of Catholic restoration. Hence his particular attempt to amalgamate the two myths fell into the darkness of forgotten literature.

It was not Friedrich Schlegel's programmatic demand for a new mythology that inspired the most artistically ambitious blending of the two myths of modern individualism. Instead, it was the sense the young authors of the 1820s and 1830s had, as epigones of the classical period, that they needed a gesture grand enough to surpass their great predecessors. Christian Diedrich Grabbe (1801–1836), whom Heinrich Heine called "one of the greatest German poets" and (with equal justification) "a drunken Shakespeare,"[16] nursed a resentment against Goethe that was typical of the era and that, to some extent, was politically motivated, as we can see, say, in the left-wing Junges Deutschland movement. In a letter written in 1885 Grabbe called Goethe a "merchant's brat turned nobleman";[17] yet, at the same time, he was never able to shake off his fascination with Goethe. By 1823, at the age of twenty-two, Grabbe had already conceived his tragedy *Don Juan und Faust*, although he did not complete it until six years later, an indication of the difficulties that even his creative audacity encountered when it came to bringing together the two extremes of the European conception of humanity, "'*Don Juan und Faust*' is [turning out to be] *theatrical*; but it also has a trace of opera, something that, if I am not a pathetic philistine, will only prove useful to it" (3:116). Thus, Schiller's prognosis of a renewal of the tragic drama out of the spirit of opera found its realization, oddly enough, in the tragedy by Grabbe, who, at the time of its writing, was not yet aware of the epistolary exchange between Goethe and Schiller, but who, when he finally read that correspondence, subjected it to a scathing review. The music for the play's premiere—in fact the only performance during Grabbe's lifetime—was written by Albert Lortzing, soon to become the most famous composer of German opera. Lortzing also played the role of Don Juan.

Grabbe freely described his intention, in an anonymous review he wrote of his own play, to bring together "two tragic legends . . . of which one represents the downfall of the too sensual, the other the downfall of the too spiritual nature in human beings" and in this way to enter into direct competition with two of modernity's greatest dramas: "Mozart's *Don Juan* and Goethe's *Faust*—what works of art! And how bold, after these Masters, to take the stage again with these two plot materials!" (3:118). The review clearly was not sparing in self-praise. Thus, the poet, with a triumphant gesture, first identifies the agonistic constellation to which his play owes its inspiration and then goes on to give assurances of its immense success: "The composition, the blending of the two legends, shows great genius—in the two characters we have before us the extremes of the human condition, and outwardly, too, in the dramatic action, the poet has understood how to bring them together in an outstanding fashion" (3:119).

But the confrontation of the "extremes of the human condition"—supreme sensuality and supreme spirituality—could only be elevated to tragic conflict if Faust and Don Juan were contrasted not as allegorical representations of alternative lives between which one could freely choose but, rather, as an internal split within the selfsame ego. The conflict could only become tragic if Faust discovered the Don Juan within himself and Don Juan discovered the Faust in himself; in other words, if the allegorical bearers of an idea were transformed into human beings tormented by their own internal contradictions. However, Grabbe allowed only one of his heroes to suffer this particular fate, namely Faust, the modern intellectual who, in his absolute will to knowledge, embarks on becoming an *Übermensch*. The life alternatives that result were clearly marked by Grabbe in the third act, when Faust, who loves Donna Anna and is holding her prisoner, confronts Don Juan on Mont Blanc. Don Juan has come to free her and return her to Rome. "Why be superhuman / If you remain a man?" asks Don Juan. Faust replies: "Why be a man / If you don't strive for the superhuman?" The Latin sensualist has a straightforward answer for his deeply philosophical Teutonic counterpart:

> A *Super*man, whether devil or angel,
> Knows as little of woman's love as any
> *Sub*human thing, whether it be
> A baboon, a frog, or an ape—and, my friend,
> *I'm* the one who lives in Donna Anna's heart!

(1:481)

The sensualist's advantage over the metaphysician is so crushing to Faust that he can only respond with violence. He thus declares the impossibility of his adhering henceforth to philosophical principles. As the *Übermensch* who craves love but does not receive it, he throws the man who so effortlessly achieves it from the icy planes of abstraction—Mont Blanc—back into the real life of temperate Rome. The sensualist of course enjoys the trip. Why this paralysis of the metaphysician, particularly when confronted by the hedonist?

Like every artistically significant adaptation of mythic material, Grabbe's tragedy transformed Faust and Don Juan into contemporaries of the author and his readers. Grabbe's art of dramatic characterization created two of the best-loved literary types of the first half of the nineteenth century: the individual suffering from Weltschmerz and the virtuoso. Measured against the virtuoso, the suffering person has no chance. During the Biedermeier period those who suffered from Weltschmerz renounced their belief in happiness, yet their melancholy thoughts dwelt on how it might have been achieved. This is why Faust makes his pact with the devil. He does not seek happiness itself ("I give up this practice"); instead he expects the devil to show him the way "by which [he] *could* have found / Peace and happiness!" (1:432). This makes matters very easy for the devil. He just has to show Faust Donna Anna, or that the path to happiness is the one followed by Don Juan. And so what happens next is what we expect: Faust quickly relinquishes all striving for knowledge and degenerates into a particularly pathetic Don Juan who gets control of Donna Anna, with much assistance from magic and demons, but gains nothing in the process. By contrast, Don Juan merely needs to look at Donna Anna for her to be as overwhelmed by him as a nineteenth-century audience would have been in the presence of a virtuoso. Grabbe's Don Juan is *the* virtuoso par excellence. The virtuoso is not interested in the subject matter—his lover of the moment; he is focused entirely on his technical abilities, the means for his success. He must continually give new proof of the perfection of his abilities and conquer his public with the same brilliance of performance that Don Juan uses to conquer his lovers. If even a single seduction fails, the virtuoso is no longer a virtuoso. In the end this is what motivates Grabbe's Don Juan; when Faust kidnaps Donna Anna and takes her to Mont Blanc, Don Juan has no choice but to follow them. He must get her back.

In act 2, as Don Juan is casting his spell over Donna Anna with words, glances, and gestures drawn from the boundless arsenal of seduction, he is suddenly interrupted by the appearance of her fiancé Octavio. This causes Don Juan immediately to fall out of his role: "Damn, I was /Doing so well. Dozens of images / Flowed from my mouth" (1:443). This is how a virtuoso reacts when a philistine deprives him of his reward. After Faust has captured Donna Anna, Don Juan despises him also as a philistine, but now specifically as a cultural philistine who seems to possess only economic and technical resources to keep a woman in his possession and who therefore understands not the slightest thing about the art of love.

This modern cultural philistine, however, has one advantage over the virtuoso: he can despair. Faust, this Titan of the intellect who has mutated into a pathetic Don Juan, has learned to love, is not loved in return, kills Donna Anna, and stands now forlorn. He has become Professor Unrat eighty years before his time, and now the Devil arrives to take him to hell. Contrarily, Don Juan cannot despair so long as the possibility of further performance is available to him. Virtuosity is his form of existence; to it he owes his success and only in his success does he exist. He is and possesses nothing but the technique to seduce: the one, the many, all. For this reason one cannot demand of him that he have a soul separate from his seductive nature. There is no soul as such that can regret, much less despair. He can despair as a virtuoso only when he fails to conquer his public. He can regret only when, in the act of seduction, he chooses the wrong sentence, the wrong gesture, the wrong tone. After Don Juan kills the governor (Donna Anna's father), and later, at the end of the drama, after the statue appears, Don Juan responds to the statue's plea for his remorse with a "Je ne regrette rien." This can only symbolize one thing, that to force him to regret his actions is to destroy his virtuosity. "What / I *am*, I *remain*! If I am *Don Juan* / Then I am nothing if I become *another*!" (1:511). The virtuoso is such that he must always take us by surprise yet never change, because his public must know what to expect. The fearlessness of the virtuoso, which permits him to function as long as there is no rupture in his character, assures that the devil will come for him and that Don Juan and Faust will forever be joined in hell: "I know, you both strive for / The *selfsame* goal, though carting on *two* wagons!" (1:512).

Grabbe's sympathy clearly lies with Don Juan, on whom he lavishes all his skill in character development; less with Faust, whose example is all too obviously designed to bring back the flights of German idealism down to earth. Nevertheless, Faust is the more modern because he is the more fractured figure. While Don Juan, despite all the effort expended on his character, remains a type with no development and is therefore unchanged throughout the entire play, Faust is split into two irreconcilable parts. It is this rupture that causes his downfall. That his will to the absolute is broken by unrequited love makes him, this intellectual, no more than a caricature of Don Juan. The unrealized striving for absolute knowledge turns into the unrealizable desire for absolute love.

But if this is so, then Faust's striving for absolute knowledge and Don Juan's striving for absolute pleasure are only variants of the same desire for limitlessness, for the removal of all barriers. Given the conditions of human existence, the desire, however, is bound necessarily to fail. Perhaps this is what the devil means when he chains Don Juan and Faust together in hell with the charge that they have striven toward the same goal. From which it follows that the final result of the tendency to combine the myths of Don Juan and Faust in the artistic production of the nineteenth century was not merely a link but a merger. For erotic and intellectual transgression had become merely names for two possibilities within the soul of a single human being. The myths of Faust and Don Juan were inseparable because the tendencies they signified were inseparable in the human being. No one recognized this more clearly than the great dramatist Friedrich Hebbel, who wrote in his journal in 1862: "Grabbe probably thought he was doing something amazing when he wrote *Don Juan und Faust*. But they are not two people at all, for every Don Juan ends as a Faust, and every Faust as a Don Juan."[18] What this meant was that the characters thus represented as types arrived thereby at the end of their usefulness. And so the story that had begun with Goethe and Schiller now came to an end with the complete merger of the myths. In modernity the myths continued to live on only through a process of psychologizing that merely served further to blur the differences between these two extremes of human existence.

The nineteenth-century tendency for Faust to transform himself into a Don Juan on every possible occasion showed just how quickly the intellectual becomes a hedonist. The further development of the Don Juan myth comparably showed that the sensualist can arrive at no better solution than to transform himself into an intellectual. No better example of the merged myths can be found than in Max Frisch's comedy *Don Juan oder die Liebe zur Geometrie* (1953), where Don Juan becomes no less than a mathematician. With him the merger reaches a Cartesian consummation. Stripped from the myths, the longing for absolute sensual pleasure and the desire for perfect knowledge remain inexhaustible themes of contemporary literature, from the novels of Vladimir Nabokov all the way to David Lodge's campus novels. Or perhaps the myths are present still, but appear only as mythic remains in Woody Allen's comedies, where the modern urban intellectual cannot help but strive to become the virtuoso of love, and the lover an intellectual, even as he realizes every moment that he must fail at both.

Translated by Susan H. Gillespie

NOTES

1. Johann Wolfgang Goethe, *Sämtliche Werke nach Epochen seines Schaffens*, Munich ed., vol. 8.1, *Briefwechsel zwischen Schiller und Goethe in den Jahren 1794 bis 1805* (Munich, 1990), 477 ff.

2. Ibid., 479.

3. Goethe, *Sämtliche Werke*, vol. 3.1, *Italien und Weimar 1786–1790* (Munich, 1990), 554 f.

4. See Hans Joachim Kreutzer, *Faust. Mythos und Musik* (Munich, 2003), 57–84.

5. Hugo von Hofmannstahl's *Einleitung zu einem Band von Goethes Werken, enthaltend die Singspiele und Opern,* in *Reden und Aufsätze I. 1891–1913,* ed. Bernd Schoeller with Rudolf Hirsch (Frankfurt am Main, 1979), 447.

6. "Sehr ernste Scherze": this is Goethe's famous expression in his last letter to Wilhelm von Humboldt on March 17, 1832; *Goethes Briefwechsel mit Wilhelm und Alexander von Humboldt,* ed. Ludwig Geiger (Berlin, 1909), 287.

7. Goethe, *Sämtliche Werke*, vol. 19, Johann Peter Eckermann, *Gespräche mit Goethe in den letzten Jahren seines Lebens* (Munich, 1986), 283 ff.

8. In conversation Goethe emphasized that in Mozart's opera it was "only amusing on the surface, but in the depths reigns seriousness, and the music expresses this very double character excellently"; *Goethes Gespräche. Eine Sammlung zeitgenössischer Berichte aus seinem Umgang auf Grund der Ausgabe und des Nachlasses von Flodoard Freiherrn von Biedermann,* ed. Wolfgang Herwig, 4 vols. (Zurich and Stuttgart, 1965–1984), 2:938.

9. See Ian Watt, *Myths of Modern Individualism: Faust, Don Quixote, Don Juan, Robinson Crusoe* (Cambridge, 1996).

10. Nikolaus Lenau, *Sämtliche Werke und Briefe. Bd. I. Gedichte und Versepen. Auf der Grundlage der historisch-kritischen Ausgabe von Eduard Castle mit einem Nachwort*, ed. Walter Dietze (Leipzig, 1970), 939.

11. Heinrich Heine, *Sämtliche Schriften*, ed. Klaus Bregleb, vol. 11, *Schriften 1851–1855* (Munich and Vienna, 1976), 375 f.

12. Cf. Petra Hartmann, *Faust und Don Juan. Ein Verschmelzungsprozess* (Stuttgart, 1998), 21.

13. See Beatrix Müller-Kampel, "Faust und Don Juan. Thematische Überblendungen in der deutschen Literatur des 19. und frühen 20. Jahrhunderts," in *Europäische Mythen der Neuzeit: Faust und Don Juan. Gesammelte Vorträge des Salzburger Symposions 1992*, ed. Peter Csobádi et al. (Anif/Salzburg, 1993), 1:137–152.

14. Niklas Vogt, *Der Färberhof oder die Buchdruckerei in Maynz*, in *Die Ruinen am Rhein* (Frankfurt, 1809), 115; quote from Hartmann: *Faust*, 8.

15 *Kritische Friedrich Schlegel Ausgabe*, vol. 2, *Charakteristiken und Kritiken I (1796–1801)*, ed. and intro. Hans Eichner (Munich/Paderborn/Vienna, 1967), 312.

16. Heine, "Memoiren," *Sämtliche Schriften*, 565.

17. Christian Dietrich Grabbe, *Werke*, ed. Roy C. Cowen (Munich and Vienna, 1975–1977), 3:332; further references will appear parenthetically in text.

18. Friedrich Hebbel, *Tagebücher, Bd. 3 1848–1863* (Munich, 1984), 322, no. 5981.

Three

"Hidden Secrets of the Self": E. T. A. Hoffmann's Reading of *Don Giovanni*

RICHARD ELDRIDGE

If one considers the libretto of *Don Juan* alone, without ascribing to it any deeper significance, but appreciating it only as a story, it is scarcely understandable how Mozart could conceive and compose such music as he did.
—E. T. A. Hoffmann, *Don Juan*

*I*t is not easy to summarize the plot of *Don Giovanni*. The libretto, as Julian Rushton has noted, has a distinctly "episodic nature."[1] One can, of course, just say which events succeed one another. But any such account soon verges on a chronicle or disconnected list of events rather than standing as a summary of a coherent action with a beginning, middle, and end. Robert Pack, in his synopsis, offers merely a succession of declarative sentences of the form "Character X does Y" (escapes, interrupts, flirts, etc.) stitched together with empty connectives such as "next" and "meanwhile."[1] Certainly, it is not clear—at least not in the libretto alone—exactly how or why one event leads to another "by necessity or by probability" as the events of a tragic drama should, at least according to Aristotle.[2]

Yet the opera is nonetheless *not* characteristically experienced by its audiences as incoherent or incomplete, nor do those audiences characteristically simply wallow in disconnected spectacles of vocalization and stagecraft. Instead, the typical audience engagement is something more like mounting horrified fascination as Don Giovanni approaches his seemingly inevitable end. Somehow this horrified fascination and feeling of inevitability overcome the fragmentariness of the plot considered in isolation from the music. Something like this inchoate fascination is likely what Kierkegaard had in mind when he noted that in opera in general, and preeminently in *Don Giovanni*,

> the situation cannot be perfectly developed or full-blown but to a certain degree is sustained by a mood. The same is true of action in an opera. Action in the strict sense of the word, action undertaken with consciousness of the goal, cannot be expressed in music, but what one could call immediate action certainly can.[3]

Just what, then, is the immediate action of *Don Giovanni*, an action embodied in a plot-wedded-to-music that is dominated by mood? How and why do we follow this action with horrified fascination? What is the peculiar nature of the action's inevitability?

E. T. A. Hoffmann's 1813 short story *Don Juan* offers us a way of taking up these questions. It is neither a piece of music criticism alone (though Hoffmann wrote a good deal of music criticism), nor a critical-explicatory essay on the opera alone (though it contains a brief essay), but a fiction, a kind of fantasia on the opera. In its freedom of response to the opera and in its own emotionalism, this fantasia both enacts and literalizes the kind of horrified fascination that *Don Giovanni* typically evokes. The musical, dramatic, philosophical, and sexual preoccupations of *its* protagonist both model and make explicit for us our own peculiar preoccupations with *Don Giovanni*. This protagonist's desires play out fantastically, more according to their own internal logic than according to any logic of realist plausibility of action, in such a way that for readers its internal logic is brought to the fore. That is to say, through his protagonist Hoffmann repeats and works through the very fact of desire in human life that dominates the opera. In so doing, he establishes a central trope of Romanticism: the ineradicability of desire, leading to a sense of outsiderliness and stiltedness in relation to the ordinary, leading often even to longing for death.

The plot of Hoffmann's story is almost as episodic and elliptical as that of *Don Giovanni*. In a provincial German city a traveler falls asleep early. He is awakened by the sound of an orchestra tuning up. He learns from an attendant that his hotel room is directly connected to the theater. A hidden door in his room leads to a small "guest loge" from which, if he wishes, he will be able to hear that night's performance of *Don Giovanni*. Amused by this possibility, he enters the loge and finds—surprisingly in this provincial backwater—both expert musicianship and a performance in Italian. He focuses principally on Donna Anna, whose "eyes flash love, anger, despair" and whose "notes, cast of ethereal metal, shine like glowing flashes of lightning," and on Don Giovanni, "a powerful, commanding figure" with "something Mephistophelean to his expression at times" that "causes involuntary dread" (64). Toward the end of the first act the traveler feels "a gentle warm breath behind me" and hears "the rustle of a silken garment" (66). Intent upon the performance, he pays no attention. But as the first act curtain falls, he turns to find that his companion is none other than Donna Anna. She speaks to him in Tuscan and reveals that she knows him to be himself a composer of operas with which she is especially intimate. "'Yes,' she breathes, "I have sung *you*, for *I* am your melodies'" (67). As the intermission bell rings, Donna Anna suddenly disappears, "saying quietly, 'Unhappy Anna, your darkest moment is upon you'" (67). The traveler returns his attention to the opera, after which he hurries "back to my room in the most exalted state of mind I had ever experienced" (68). The hotel attendant calls him to the hotel's table d'hôte, where he overhears "general praise" for the performance, but also many "little remarks" that "showed that probably no one had the slightest idea of the deeper significance of this opera of all operas" (68). Returning to his room but unable to sleep, the traveler-composer carries "a little table, two candles, and writing materials" (69) into the loge, where he composes an essay on *Don Giovanni* in the form of a letter to his friend Theodore, apparently a poet, who is the addressee of the story. As he finishes his letter,

> the clock strikes two. A warm electrifying breath glides over me. I recognize the faint fragrance of the Italian perfume that yesterday informed me of my fair neighbor's presence. I am seized by a blissful feeling that I could only express in music. The air stirs more violently through the house; the strings of the grand piano in the orchestra vibrate. . . . From a great distance, I think I hear Anna's voice.
>
> (72)

During midday conversation at the hotel table the next day, the traveler learns that the signora who had sung Donna Anna had died at exactly two o'clock in the morning.

Throughout the story's action the traveler-narrator's thoughts and feelings are foregrounded. It is not only or so much what happens—the performance of the opera, the appearance of Donna Anna, the midday meal the following day—that matters as the narrator's patterns of thought, feeling, and attention. For these patterns offer us, the audience, a model of how we too might think, feel, and attend to the work. That the traveler-narrator's thoughts and feelings are the center of the action of the story is highlighted in three ways: through the physical setting, through the intensity of his concentration on and relationship with the Donna Anna singer, and through the treatment of Don Giovanni himself as a kind of doppelgänger of the narrator and a figure for humanity in general.

Physically, the narrator is an isolated sole auditor. Loge number 23, the visitor's box, is reached "through a concealed door . . . behind the tapestry." It holds "two or at most three people," and it offers an especially intimate relation to the performance, "near the stage, all upholstered in green with a lattice to ensure privacy"(63). It is no surprise, then, that the narrator is "happy to be alone in the loge, to embrace this superb performance of the masterpiece with every nervous fibre of my being as though through tentacles, and to draw it into my innermost self" (65). The narrator's physical setting here condenses (and casts as like) the voyeuristic fantasies of both pure epistemological spectatorhood, where the world is performed and the viewer is without responsibilities or implication in it, and sexual spectatorhood, as though from the womb, on the erotic vocal transports of the singers (Donna Anna in particular). (In the grip of this same fantasy, and perhaps even remembering Hoffmann's story,[4] Kierkegaard, or his narrator A., tells us that "I have sat close to the front [at performances of *Don Giovanni*]; I have moved back more and more; I have sought a remote corner in the theater in order to be able to hide myself completely in this music.")[5] In this private space, the action is the action of the narrator's fantasy and desire.

The fantasy is further one of privately and intimately giving oneself over to or being overcome by the music, and by sexual presence, in a kind of communicative transport beyond ordinary communication—the fantasy, one might say, of operatic singing itself. "It was as if the long-promised fulfillment of the most unearthly dreams was now being granted in real life; as if the ecstatic intimations of the enchanted soul were now embodied in sounds, moulding themselves into rare disclosures." (67) The appeal and enchantment of the singing exceed ordinary communication, seeming to take the narrator (and us) into the soul itself, even ambiguously into the soul that he (and we) share with both the singer and her role. As David J. Baker has written,

> Box No. 23 is magical, the theater as dream, a heightened form of opera consumption. The metaphorical space calls to mind modern listeners' own private "stagings" of operas—in or near our bedroom—by way of recordings. When we listen to recordings, we are in a "guest loge" where no inappropriate visual details can disturb the identification we establish between a voice and a role. In this private, privileged zone, Donna Anna/the soprano seems present in our room: she is both involved to perfection in the action we hear and imagine, and also standing close beside us, singing only for us.[6]

By situating the narrator in this zone of intimacy, Hoffmann models for us the fact that opera, and especially this opera, are to be followed from within, through imaginative participation in vocal lines and gestures. This participation takes one beyond the ordinary and into the pure form of movement of ensouled desire.

The narrator's initial concentration on Donna Anna and subsequent encounter with her reinforce the intimacy of the setting and the importance of following from within the vocal movement. As she first appears in his box, the narrator emphasizes his imaginative captivation by her, her functioning for him as a kind of bridge from the ordinary to the supernatural.

> Just as in a happy dream the strangest things seem natural, and just as a pious faith understands the supernatural, fitting it in with the so-called natural events of daily life, so too I fell into a kind of somnambulism in the presence of this amazing woman. I realized, too, that there were secret bonds linking her so closely to me that she could not be parted from me even by her appearance on the stage.
>
> (66–67)

Unprompted, Donna Anna/the soprano recognizes the narrator as a composer, and indeed as the composer of her own inmost voice and passions.

> She said that music was her only reality and that she felt she could grasp through singing many otherwise hidden secrets of the self that no words could express. "Yes, it becomes clear to me when I sing," she continued with burning eyes and agitated voice, "but everything about me is dead and cold, and when I am applauded for a difficult roulade or a successful effect, it is as if icy hands clutch at my glowing heart! But you, you understand me, for I know that you too are at home in the wonderful romantic realm where tones are infused with sublime magic. . . . I know the frenzy and yearning love that were in your heart when you wrote the part of—in your most recent opera. I understand you; your soul revealed itself to me in song. Yes"—here she called me by my first name—"I have sung *you*, for *I* am your melodies."
>
> (67)

To sing, to compose, and to understand, or at the very least to feel oneself to sing, to compose, and to understand, are, this passage suggests, identical with one another, at least in this extraordinary region of Mozart's music. The activities of singing and composing are here metonyms for an intimacy of communication and an ecstasy that are not achievable within ordinary life but rather require escaping from it.

When one then follows the action of the opera and the music from the inside, as though participating in their gestures, what does one find? The principal plot suggestion that the narrator makes is that Don Giovanni's attempted seduction of Donna Anna has in fact been successful. "You will undoubtedly have noticed, my dear Theodore," he writes in his essay/letter,

> that I have spoken of Donna Anna as seduced, and I shall tell you in a few words to the best of my ability at this late hour, when thoughts and ideas come from the depth of my mind, how the music alone, quite apart from the text, seems to me to reflect the whole conflict between these opposing natures, Don Juan and Donna Anna. . . . When he fled the deed was done.
>
> (71–72)

This claim on the part of the narrator is, to be sure, explicitly denied in the text of the libretto. "Finally the dread and horror of the infamous attack increased my strength, and by twisting and struggling I tore myself away,"[7] Donna Anna tells Don Ottavio. Despite her explicit denial, however, the seduction theory has been endorsed by numbers of commentators, including Wagner, Berlioz, and Alfred Einstein.[8] Edward J. Dent, in contrast, objects that the seduction theory "is entirely [Hoffmann's] own invention, and its only value is to illustrate the German romantic mind,"[9] fallen, presumably, into misunderstanding through its own excessive enthusiasms. Is there, then, anything the seduction theory might mean, any truth toward which it points?

Invention, in some sense, the seduction theory may be. Donna Anna explicitly denies it—though she has good reason to lie to her fiancé Don Ottavio about any actual seduction. But the narrator claims that it is "the music alone, quite apart from the text" that supports this thought. It is *in* the music that "Donna Anna is in all natural endowments the counterpart to Don Juan" (71). In the narrator's hearing, both Don Giovanni and Donna Anna are vocally excessive, beyond the conventions of ordinary communicative behavior. Don Giovanni is excessive in his Promethean desire: "fired by a longing which sent the blood boiling through his veins, he was driven to the greedy, restless, pursuit of experiencing all phenomena of this earthly world, hoping in vain to find satisfaction in them" (70). Donna Anna is excessive in her fury for revenge for the death of her father, a fury that the narrator reads as itself stemming from a deep sensuality. At the moment of seduction, the narrator argues, "The fire of a superhuman sensuality, a fire from hell, surged through her being, and she was powerless to resist. Only he, only Don Juan, could arouse in her the erotic madness with which she embraced him, he who sinned with the superhuman frenzy of the hellish spirits within him" (72).

After Don Giovanni's murder of her father, this same erotic madness takes the form of a superhuman, unwavering desire for revenge, a desire that matches in both its incessancy and its death drive Don Giovanni's desire for women.

> The love that in a moment of ecstasy had flooded her being . . . now burns as annihilating hatred. . . . She feels that only Don Juan's destruction can bring peace to her mortally tortured soul; but his peace demands her own earthly destruction. Thus she incessantly spurs her indifferent bridegroom to revenge. She pursues her betrayer herself, and relents only after the powers of the underworld have dragged him down into the pit.
>
> (72)

Vocally, Donna Anna and Don Giovanni are matched at two crucial moments. As the Commendatore dies, Don Giovanni's melody in the F-minor trio is identical with the melody in which Donna Anna first demands vengeance and vows to "pursue [her attacker] forever like a desperate Fury!"[10] As Don Giovanni is engulfed by flames, "the chorus of demons"—arguably the demons who have driven Don Giovanni from within to this fate—"exactly reflects the cadences of the vengeance duet at the beginning of Act I."[11] This vocal matching reflects a thought about the human subject. Both Don Giovanni's repudiation of the Commendatore's call to repentance and Donna Anna's pursuit of vengeance are assertions of the independent energy of the self to work its particular will in human life. This energy of independent, particularized willing is, it seems, not something that is easy to give up, and it is central to what we respond to in the characters of both Don Giovanni and Donna Anna. Repentance and the abandonment of vengeance would, in contrast, be a return to a common anonymity, which presents itself here as a sacrifice of independent subjecthood.

Nowadays we are perhaps more likely to hear Donna Elvira as Don Giovanni's counterpart. Her arias "Ah taci, ingiusto core!" (Be silent foolish heart) and "Mi tradì quell'alma ingrata" (That ungrateful man has betrayed me!) show her in the grip of strong conflicting emotions, almost moved by them as contending forces within her, just as Don Giovanni appears to be unremittingly impelled from within. But Donna Elvira's vocal echoing of Don Giovanni is not inconsistent with Donna Anna's role as his proper counterpart. In a quartet with Donna Elvira, Don Ottavio, and Don Giovanni, Donna Anna sings that she feels "a torment in my soul that secretly reveals to me a hundred things about this poor unhappy girl [Donna Elvira; but also perhaps Donna Anna herself, as a half-double of Donna Elvira's in response to Don Giovanni] that I don't understand," just as Donna Elvira sings "I feel scorn, rage, spite, and fear turning within my soul, telling me a hundred things about this libertine that I don't yet understand."[12] Under the pressure of Don Giovanni, almost no one—and especially neither Donna Anna nor Donna Elvira—seems in control of thought or feeling. Feeling moves in and moves them. As Kierkegaard's equation has it, in these characters (save for Don Ottavio, who in contrast worries over proprieties) "the immediate erotic [is] identical with the musical erotic."[13] A natural erotic force within them moves them into song.

Above all, this natural erotic force within the characters, otherwise often suppressed, is called forth by the voice and presence of Don Giovanni himself. As one critic has remarked, "Giovanni adapts the style of each of his victims"[14]—or vice versa. Kierkegaard, noting the same echoing of vocal styles, suggests that

> The very secret of this opera is that its hero is also the force in the other characters. Don Giovanni's life is the life principle in them. His passion sets in motion the passion of the others. His passion resonates everywhere; it resonates in and supports the Commendatore's earnestness, Elvira's wrath, Anna's hate, Ottavio's pomposity, Zerlina's anxiety, Mazetto's indignation, Leporello's confusion. . . . The other figures in the opera are not characters, either, but essential passions, which are posited by Don Giovanni and to that extent, in turn, become musical. In other words, just as Don Giovanni entwines everybody, so all of them entwine Don Giovanni; they are the external consequences that his life continually posits.[15]

Hoffmann's narrator, in his concentration on the figure of Don Giovanni, helps us to understand how all these resonances are possible. He describes the nature and action of the passion within Don Giovanni that enables him to exercise this mysterious seductive power. The narrator emphasizes Giovanni's singular power of command, specifically his ability to be wholly *himself* in his action, achieving a purer form of passionate action as such than compromising and conventionalized individuals typically achieve. "Believe me, Theodore," he writes,

> nature fashioned Juan as the dearest of her children, with everything that raises man toward divinity, everything that elevates him above the commonplace, above the factory products which are ciphers for lack of individuality. This destined him to conquer and command: a powerful, handsome physique, a personality radiating the spark which kindles the most sublime feelings in the soul, a profound sensibility, and a quick, instinctive intellect.

(70)

Don Giovanni has a personality "raised toward divinity" and capable of kindling the experience of the sublime in us (and in the principal characters). The experience of the sublime involved is that of being challenged or threatened by excessive force or power, but then recoiling from this sense of threat to an experience of one's own dignity and power, arriving thence at a sense of felt possibility to match the original force, to answer power with power. Don Giovanni's seductions combine—the narrator argues—full personal feeling (where most of us, along with the provincial villagers, are often half-hearted) with full resoluteness of will, as though only *this*—what Don Giovanni does—were really or authentically a human action as a full flowering of both personal desire and will. No wonder, then, that both the characters and the opera's auditors should find themselves echoing its hero.

The difficulty, however—a difficulty that will come to seem the obverse of the very force and authenticity of Giovanni's desiring action—is that his desiring and acting are restless. He is so driven to command response and command it again that he cannot cathect stably to any single definite erotic object. Anyone who responds to his command cannot be as authentically forceful as he is and so cannot confer the recognition he seeks. Anyone whom he cannot command—apparently no one—must be sunk below possibilities of passionate response and action, more vegetable than human. As a result,

> just when he [was] striving for that perfection [—of passionate action—] which most expresses his divine nature . . . he was driven on by a deep contempt for the common features of life, to which he felt himself superior. He felt bitter scorn for a humanity which hoped to find in love, and the homely union it produces, some slight fulfillment of the higher aspirations which nature has treacherously placed in our hearts. He was forced to rebel against the thought of any such relationship and to wreck it whenever he found it. Thus, he was at war with that unknown Being which guides our destiny, a Being which seemed to him to be a malicious monster playing a cruel game with the wretched creatures it created. . . . He really wants more and more to leave life, but only to plunge deeper into hell. The seduction of Anna, with its attendant circumstances is the very summit of his achievement.
>
> (71)

What this passage makes clear is that the real action of the opera is *within* Don Giovanni, in his effort to live up to or to live out the possibility of fully human action for which he seems uniquely suited. He is "driven on" and "forced to rebel," in the narrator's reading, by his heightened internal capacity for action. As the narrator elsewhere remarks, Giovanni arrives at "the doom which [he] *must* bring on himself" (65; emphasis added).

This internal compulsion that drives Don Giovanni toward his doom is clearly a kind of Prometheanism. In the penultimate scene, in reply to Donna Elvira's urging him to change his way of life, Giovanni exults in his independence and his defiance of the divine. "Long live the women! Long live good wine! Forever may they exalt and sustain humanity!"[16]—without any assistance from God. Likewise Giovanni enacts independence and defiance of social life. Early on, having sworn on his honor not to be angry with Leporello and after then being reproached by Leporello for his dishonest way of life, Giovanni immediately replies, "I don't remember any promises."[17] Ordinary social reciprocities simply do not count for him, any more than reciprocity with or dependence on God does. Kierkegaard captures this Prometheanism well when he remarks that Giovanni's

> life is the sum of *repellerende* moments that have no coherence, and his life as the moment is the sum of moments and as the sum of moments is the moment. Don Giovanni lies within this universality [of self-repelling moments], in this hovering between being an individual and a force of nature.[18]

His final "No" in reply to the statue's plea or command to "Repent! Change your way of life! It's your last chance!"[19] is the simple culmination of his continuous imperviousness to both reflection and reciprocity and of his attachment to the demands of desire in the moment.

In the face of Giovanni's Promethean natural force of desire and attraction, evident and active at each moment, the other characters are typically confused: both attracted by something given, something natural-human, about the force of Giovanni's momentary desire and repelled by its imperviousness to reflection, admonition, and repentance. Donna Elvira's "scorn, rage, spite, and fear turning within my soul, telling me a hundred things about this libertine that I don't yet understand"[20] are typical of the reactions of the others (except perhaps the excessively conventional Don Ottavio), including us, who are likewise among Don Giovanni's audience.

It is no accident then that Hoffmann's narrator argues that Don Giovanni makes manifest "the essence of earthly life" in "the conflict between the divine and the demonic forces" that he plays out (70). Desire seems in part to be something given and natural. Action seems to flow from and express desire. The capacity for action is definitive of the human. Fully authentic, perfect action should, it seems, flow from desire with the most immediacy and the least openness to reflection and the demands of reciprocity. To interrupt this flow and attend to those demands, as Don Ottavio typically does, is to become a pale figure of empty conventionality. Willing that issues in action should be responsive immediately to the natural-human-given force of desire within, if the resultant action is to be fully one's own—or so, at least, we, along with the others within the opera, are moved to feel.

Yet it cannot be that action is either only or properly thus immediate and impervious to reflection. Desire should—it seems—be open to shaping by reflection and it should lead to the development rather than the repudiation of reciprocities, to (one might say) marriage rather than seduction, or so too we are moved to feel by the pains of the betrayals we witness.

What, then, is one to do in the grips of passion? "Here on earth," Hoffmann's narrator tells us, "nothing so much elevates the inner nature of man as love. It is this which, by its mysterious yet powerful agency, destroys or improves the elements of our being" (70). Destroys—if it drives us, as it has driven Don Giovanni, into the momentary, unable to cathect to others and to ordinary routine fully and with reciprocity; improves—if, mysteriously, it supports such cathexis and reciprocity.

How shall we know? How shall we achieve the cathexis and reciprocity, of which an ideal marriage is both a figure and an enactment, that are the closest we can come to earthly salvation, at least as Mozart and Hoffmann would have it? Are love and desire something given, the claims of which are to be accepted and acted on fully? Or are they—insofar as human—always in principle assessable and properly under the sway of the demands of reason? "Both": both this opera and this story tell us. We cannot and ought not repudiate the naturalness and givenness of desire in favor of submission to a pale and tottering ideal of reason. Our fascination with Don Giovanni is an acknowledgment of the proper force of natural desire in human life. But we cannot and ought not deny the availability of reflection and the demands of daily reciprocity. To do that would be to seek to live, as Hoffmann's narrator puts it, along with Giovanni, "forever above our narrow life, above Nature, above the Creator," to want "more and more to leave life . . . only to plunge deeper into hell" (71).

So how shall these opposed oughts be accepted and negotiated? This question, for Mozart and for Hoffmann (and for Kierkegaard) has no answer. In the words of Hoffmann's narrator, again, "the conflict between the divine and the demonic forces is the essence of earthly life." (70) To repudiate the existence of that conflict in oneself is to step outside the bounds of the human, either into Giovanni's hellish Prometheanism or into Ottavio's paleness. The just claims on us of both natural, given passion and reflectively supported reciprocity and dailiness ought to reconciled, and yet they cannot be, at least not in any way that we can superintend. If they *are* reconciled, that reconciliation comes mysteriously, as a gift, not an act of will.

Here, in a point that both Hoffmann and Kierkegaard emphasize and that is perhaps the central conceit of *Don Giovanni* itself, our responsiveness to music is a figure for our responsiveness to our own passions and to those who inspire them. We wish to and can *surrender to* the music, to feel with it. This kind of investment or feeling-with is essential to our musical responsiveness. As Kierkegaard puts it, "sensuousness in its elemental originality is the absolute theme of music";[21] "the immediate erotic [is] identical with the musical erotic."[22] As Hoffmann puts it in another essay,

> How wonderful is music, and how little are we able to fathom its deepest secrets. But does it not dwell in the human breast, filling the soul completely with its enchantment, so that one's whole disposition turns toward a new, transfigured life, free from this world and its depressing torments? Truly, a divine power passes through us, and by surrendering ourselves to whatever the power provokes with an innocent, childlike spirit, we are able to speak the tongue of the unknown, of the romantic realm of spirits, assimilating it unconsciously as the apprentice who has read aloud from the master's book of magic. Wonderful visions dance on the stage of life, filling all who are able to see them with an infinite yet inexpressible desire.[23]

In the final effusion of his epistolary essay, Hoffmann's narrator rhapsodizes similarly about the powers of music, embodied in the Anna soprano.

> I think I hear Anna's voice: Non mi dir bell'idol mio! Open out, oh distant, unknown realm of spirits! Open out, you land of genies! Open out, realm of glory, in which an inexpressible heavenly pain, akin to the most ineffable joy, brings fulfillment beyond all earthly promises to the enraptured soul! Let me enter the circle of your lovely apparitions! From thy dreams, which may terrify or serve as benign messengers to earthly men, choose me one which will carry my spirit to the ethereal fields as my body lies imprisoned in the leaden bonds of sleep!
>
> (72–73)

Ought we then to give way to this power of music and to the force of natural desire that can well up within us, to allow ourselves to be swept away by an unusual destiny in the blue sea of August, to follow Don Giovanni? We can and may wish to. But Don Giovanni is engulfed by the flames of hell. In the epilogue to Hoffmann's story the Donna Anna soprano who "said that music was her only reality" (67) and who assures the narrator-composer

"I have sung *you*, for *I* am your melodies" (67) "died this morning at exactly two o'clock" (73), in the report of a "clever man (taking a pinch of snuff from [his snuffbox])" (73). To surrender to this power, fully, unambiguously, and without reflection, in pursuit of the purest form of embodied action, appears to be, for us—we who follow these gestures in horrified fascination—both the way of earthly salvation and the way of death. Yet to dismiss the appeal of this surrender is to be merely clever, empty, and pale. That we *are* thus pulled involuntarily in our earthly existence (by others, by passions, by music) toward this kind of surrender, as the name of earthly action, but thence pulled inevitably toward Promethean death in the refusal of reciprocity are Hoffmann's—and Mozart's—hidden secrets of the self and a central figurative truth of Romanticism.

NOTES

E.T.A. Hoffmann, *Don Juan: A Fabulous Incident Which Befell a Travelling Enthusiast*, trans. R. Murray Schafer, in R. Murray Schafer, *E.T.A. Hoffmann and Music* (Toronto, 1975), 63–73. All subsequent references will be given in the text by page number to this edition. The phrase quoted in the title of this essay is from p. 67, the epigraph p. 69.

1. Julian Rushton, "*Don Giovanni*," *The Online Grove Dictionary of Music*, http://www.grovemusic.com/shared/views/article.html?section = opera.901351, 7.
2. Robert Pack, "Synopsis of *Don Giovanni*," in *Mozart's Librettos*, trans. Robert Pack and Marjorie Lelash (Cleveland, 1961), 218–219.
3. Aristotle, *Poetics*, trans. Richard Janko (Indianapolis, 1987), 14.
4. Søren Kierkegaard, *Either/Or*, part 1, trans. Howard V. Hong and Edna H. Hong (Princeton, 1987), 120.
5. Hoffmann's *Lebensansichten des Katers Murr* (Tom-Cat Murr's Views on Life) is alluded to in the phrase "Tested Advice for Authors" early on the second page of the main text of *Either/Or*. See *Either/Or*, 20, and editorial note 13, 606.
6. Ibid., 120.
7. David J. Baker, "Hoffmann's Night with Donna Anna," *Opera News* 60.8 (January 6, 1996), 25B.
8. Lorenzo Da Ponte and W.A. Mozart, "Libretto" to *Don Giovanni*, in *Mozart's Librettos*, 249.
9. Baker, "Hoffmann's Night with Donna Anna," 24C.
10. Ibid.
11. Da Ponte and Mozart, "Libretto," 223.
12. Rushton, "*Don Giovanni*," 6.
13. Da Ponte and Mozart, "Libretto," 245.
14. Kierkegaard, *Either/Or*, 62.
15. Rushton, "*Don Giovanni*," 6.
16. Kierkegaard, *Either/Or*, 119.

17. Da Ponte and Mozart, "Libretto," 299.
18. Ibid., 229.
19. Kierkegaard, *Either/Or*, 96.
20. Da Ponte and Mozart, "Libretto," 303.
21. Ibid., 245.
22. Kierkegaard, *Either/Or*, 71.
23. Ibid., 62.
24. Hoffmann, "Ombre adorata," trans. Schafer, in *E. T. A. Hoffmann and Music*, 55.

Four

Don Juan in Nicholas's Russia (Pushkin's *The Stone Guest*)

BORIS GASPAROV

DON JUAN AND ADOLPHE

On February 2, 1830, Alexander Pushkin wrote to Countess Karolina Sobanska:

> C'est aujourd'hui le 9 anniversaire du jour où je vous ai vu pour la première fois. Ce jour a décidé de ma vie. Plus j'y pense, plus je vois que mon existence est inséparable de la vôtre; je suis né pour vous aimer et vous suivre—tout autre soin de ma part est erreur ou folie; loin de vous je n'ai que les remords d'un bonheur dont je n'ai pas su m'assouvir. Tôt ou tard il faut bien que j'abandonne tout, et que je vienne tomber à vos pieds.[1]
>
> (14:62–63)

Just a few months later, in the fall of the same year, Pushkin wrote his own version of Don Juan's story, a drama in verse entitled *The Stone Guest*.[2] The play carried the epigraph from Mozart/Da Ponte's opera: "O statua gentilissima del gran' Commendatore! . . . Ah, Padrone!" However, its plot somewhat deviated from the opera's. Pushkin retained the Commendatore's old age but made him Donna Anna's husband rather than father. This gave Don Guan, as he called his hero,[3] an inspiring challenge, namely, to seduce the widow of the man he had killed and preferably at the site of his grave to which she was assiduously paying visits.

Don Guan's principal means of seduction are arduous monologues, addressed to Donna Anna, first in disguise as a shyly worshipping "Don Diego," then, as he felt that success was near, under his real name, revealed in a daring stroke of eloquence. A remarkable feature of these monologues is their close kinship to Pushkin's letters to Sobanska (there were two, written the same day).[4] In the general strategy of approaching his addressee, as well as in the concrete language he employs, Don Guan closely follows Pushkin's own passionate effusions. Both Don Guan and his creator confess, as if almost against their will, to being completely transformed by the experience of meeting the object of their passion. Both lament bitterly, albeit vaguely, about transgressions of their past that now seem to make their happiness impossible. As Don Guan puts it, pendant to Pushkin's unspecified "remords": "[My] tired conscience is burdened by many evil deeds" (7:168). Both dismiss preemptively their own eloquence as a flop (AP: "Si jamais vous lisez cela, je sais bien ce que vous penserez—que de maladresse" [14:64]; DG: "[Have I forgotten] . . . that my sinful voice should not resound so loudly in this place?" [7:155]). Yet somehow this does not preclude either from retaining hope against hope that he will be allowed to dwell in silent adoration at his idol's feet, which now apparently is his only purpose in life.

Pushkin's first brush with the characters, made so vivid in the consciousness of the time by Mozart's opera, occurred in his teenage years. In 1817, while still a student at the Lyceum in Tsarskoe Selo, a young woman named Mary Smith stayed with the family of the Lyceum's director, Yegor Engelhardt. She had just lost her husband, with whom she expected a child. The situation inspired the seventeen-year-old Pushkin to write a poem, "To a Young Widow" (a subject explored earlier by his literary idol of that time, Voltaire). Clearly addressed to Mary Smith, albeit in the disguise of the conventional literary name "Lila," Pushkin's poem exhorts the addressee not to be timid in giving herself up to their—presumably mutual—passion. The ghost of her late husband is not going to appear from beyond the grave to interrupt their happiness. Pushkin had the impertinence to push the poem under her door, causing the grieving woman yet more distress.

Another reminder of the opera comes from Pushkin's pen more than a decade after this early mishap and in a situation nearly as ambiguous. This time Pushkin returned to Moscow after six years of exile. He found there a new crop of teenage beauties, the trademark or "bride's market" of Moscow. He fell in love with them, one after another, writing gem after gem of lyric poetry into their albums, proposing, or nearly proposing, but invariably being rejected. Unlike Byron, he was unable to match the scandalous halo that surrounded his stormy years in the southern provinces either with his wealth, his high social standing, or his good looks. Assuming the posture of Don Juan—playfully ambiguous and superfluously passionate—he repelled even those who were otherwise appreciative of his genius and intelligence. So posturing, he wrote into the album of the sisters Ushakov a "list" of female names,[5] in teasing imitation of Leporello, something of course Don Juan would never have actually done himself. The "list" contained about thirty first names neatly arranged into two columns. Generations of Pushkin scholars have kept busy trying to dig up the identities behind each name and to understand the apparently pregnant significance of the division into two columns. The letters to Sobanska, which presaged the direct appearance of Don Juan in Pushkin's work, was a natural continuation of this chain of episodes whose inconclusive character was, after all, not unsimilar to what the operatic Don Giovanni himself experienced onstage.

It is time to explain who Karolina Sobanska was. Born in 1794 or 1795 as Karolina Tekla Rzewuska, she belonged to a family that occupied a high place in the ranks both of Polish nobility and the Russian imperial elite. Her father was the governor general of the Kievan district; her sister, Countess Eveline Ganska, married Balzac in the last years of his life. Sobanska was married at a young age by her family. Her husband, whom she soon abandoned, was almost thirty-five years older than she, a circumstance that connected her, albeit tenuously, to the Donna Anna of Pushkin's play. Beginning in the late 1810s, Sobanska became the maitresse of General Jan ("Ivan Osipovich") Witt, also much her senior. A thoroughly rotten character, universally feared and despised, Witt combined important official positions in the southern provinces with secret services as a highly placed informer. Among prominent subjects of his attention were Mickiewicz and Pushkin, both of whom lived at the time in Odessa. Sobanska helped the poorly educated general to write his reports to the secret police in St. Petersburg while serving as an irresistible magnet for their subjects. In particular, Mickiewicz had a stormy love affair with her, a fact that left significant traces in his poetry. He used to call her Donna Giovanna. Despite Sobanska's dazzling brilliance, beauty, and noble name, her position in Odessa society was precarious. She was not accepted in most of the best houses, compensating for this by being brilliant in vibrant, masculine company.

By the late 1820s Sobanska, who had moved to St. Petersburg, strove to obtain a divorce. She hoped to marry Witt, to whom she was completely albeit secretly devoted. The divorce was eventually granted in the mid-1830s, although by that time Witt had abandoned her. She married his adjutant instead, but he died a couple years later. Still later, already in her sixties, So-banska married Jules Lacroix, a prolific French writer. When she died in her nineties, none of Pushkin's letters (of which at least one she certainly received) were to be found among her papers.[6] We know only of the drafts that Pushkin kept in his possession.

Sobanska replied to Pushkin with a brief note whose scornfully teasing attitude was transparently veiled by immaculately wrought conventional expressions of devotion. Pushkin's response looks even more impulsive and desperate than his previous letter. (We do not know whether he eventually polished its draft or even finished it). Like Mickiewicz before him, he ap-pealed to her with a highly charged literary name. The name, however, comes from a seemingly unexpected quarter, which makes it stand out against the aura of Don Juan's courtship hovering over the whole exchange. Pushkin calls his addressee not Donna Giovanna but Ellénore:

> Chère Ellénore, permettez-moi de vous donner ce nom qui me rappelle et les lectures brûlantes de mes jeunes années . . . et votre propre existence si vio-lente, si orageuse, si différente de ce q'elle devait être.[7]

> (14:64)

The burning reading experiences ("les lectures brûlantes") allude, of course, to Benjamin Constant's *Adolphe*, a novel that, after its appearance in print (in 1816), created a tremendous and instant resonance in Russia and throughout Europe. It was *Adolphe*, alongside Byron's *Childe Harold's Pilgrimage* and *Don Juan*, that diminished Pushkin's teenage infatuation with Voltaire.[8] Sobanska's precarious societal position, together with her high personal qualities, made the comparison to Constant's heroine pertinent, but the symbolic situation projected by Pushkin's letters was immediately recast. Evoking Adolphe seemed self-defeating: it "lay bare" Don Juan's de-vices of seduction by tacitly acknowledging the Adolphian inner alienation that makes the writer incapable of a passion as all-consuming as his own let-ter claims. At the same time, casting off Don Juan's mask and revealing the writer's (presumably) "true" identity constitutes a logical next move in the strategy of seduction. This is in fact what Pushkin's Don Guan does when he eventually reveals his true identity to Donna Anna. He pretends to believe that with this move he ruins all his hopes for happiness, when in fact it as-sures his success.

This close cohabitation of Don Juan and Adolphe in Pushkin's letter is illu-minating. In my view, it offers a clue to the extraordinary fascination that the Romantic age felt for the character of Don Giovanni/Don Juan/Don Guan.

What made Constant's *Adolphe* such a revelation for his contemporaries was its portrayal of the abyss between the external "appearance" of the hero's words and actions and the "true" essence of his feelings. The split between how the hero speaks and acts and how he reflects upon his speaking and acting poisons all his experiences. It makes him desperate about his ability for any genuine feeling, a perpetual self-doubt that, by paralyzing his will to act, becomes a self-fulfilling prophesy. When Adolphe resolves to make Ellénore his lover, he seems to think about his task cynically, in Don Juan's manner. But unlike the genuine Don Juan who launches into every amorous enterprise with a full spontaneity, Adolphe's plans for seduction are cold and calculating to the point of exaggeration. Even when he threatens to take his life because Ellénore will not give herself up to his passion, he does so with full awareness of his inner coldness. Eventually Adolphe ruins his career prospects, and abandons all his former plans and occupations, solely because he is unable to extricate himself from the self-perpetuating progress of his love affair. Ironically, his behavior looks like that of an infatuated lover. Yet the deeper Adolphe plunges into social and emotional circumstances created by his own actions, or rather his inaction, the more acutely he feels the debilitating inner alienation, that stands at the core of that very inaction.

Constant succeeded in casting the fundamental Romantic dilemma—the irresolvable contradiction between the subjective and the objective—into the shape of a modern social novel predicated on contemporary psychological and social conditions. More than any other early nineteenth-century literary hero, Adolphe, alongside the Romantic image of Hamlet, could be held responsible for the progeny of literary characters afflicted by self-reflection, in novels by Stendhal and Balzac, George Sand and Musset, Pushkin, and Lermontov.

Where was Don Juan's place in all of this? I believe that Don Juan or, more specifically, Mozart's Don Giovanni, fascinates Adolphe's soul mates in the 1810s through 1820s by his total obliviousness to their predicament. He is the last person to be asked whether what he strives to attain is really what he yearns for. Even more important, he knows no worry as to whether his words truly reflect his inner feeling. The Enlightenment believed in the ability of language adequately to express thought. Romanticism scorned that complacency, simultaneously reveling and despairing at its discovery of a fatal crevice between the former and the latter. But Don Giovanni, a character emerging at the fault line between the two epochs, simply ignores this controversy. He is as alien to the rationalist ideal of coherence as he is to Romantic contradictions and self-doubt. He is spontaneous and calculating, passionate and cynical at the same time, without reflecting on those inconsistencies or being disturbed by them. In effect, Don Giovanni's deceptions cannot be named as such since there is no discrepancy between his goals and means. At any particular moment, he acts and speaks as he feels, or feels as he acts and speaks, even if his actions and words fully contradict one other. His protean personality transforms itself to meet the demands of every new situation, his art of seduction bending entirely to these transformations. He is pastoral in his duet with Zerlina, cynically jocular with Leporello, mockingly deferential to Ottavio, alternately cunning and audacious in his confrontations with Donna Anna, banal—one could even say provincial—in his mandoline serenade to Donna Elvira's maid.

In an age of self-reflection and brooding subjectivity, Don Giovanni emerges as an unattainable ideal figure of the harmonious unity of the subjective and objective, of the inner state and its externalization. In this respect he presents a figure similar to that of the "naive" poet of the past—Homer, Tasso, Racine—in his opposition to the "sentimental" poet of the modern age. According to Schiller, the naive poet's writing reflects the perfect harmony between his creative mind and the world. Every phenomenon that comes to the poet's attention naturally becomes a source of his inspiration and turns into a poetic work of art. The sentimental poet, on the other hand, lives in a time both enriched and afflicted by reflection. This renders his artistic self both contradictory and unaccomplished. He strives but never attains his ideal. Contrary to the organic wholeness of naive poetry, the work of art created by a sentimental poet is incomplete and fragmentary. But it is exactly these self-defeating qualities that give the latter its depth.

The sentimental or Romantic artist comes to terms with his self and his art by comparing himself with his naive antipode. He needs the presence of the latter to reveal, by contrast, the origin and the nature of his own strengths and weaknesses. Likewise, the "modern man" of the Romantic age needs Don Giovanni's company for his self-cognition. Hence the widespread fascination with Don Giovanni. Like everything about the Romantic age, it is neither simple nor wholesome, but rather dialectical. By observing his counterpart with a mixture of envy, delight, and scorn, the Romantic subject becomes aware of the contradictions that torment him. Adolphe's initial posturing as a winsome seducer demonstrates his unsuitability to assume Don Juan's role. This demonstration is instrumental to his eventual understanding of what he cannot and ought not be.

An implicit dialogue between the naive hero and its sentimental counterpart can be seen in early nineteenth-century works with the theme of Don Juan. Byron's title character, at least at the beginning, lives in every moment as fully as Mozart's Don Giovanni. The Adolphe element, however, is represented in Byron's story by the voice of its narrator. Byron's narrator parades his subjectivity, which is contradictory and inconsequential to the point of capriciousness. He ridicules everything including his own scorn. At every moment he is ready to undermine his reader's expectations, only to subvert his own game the next moment by laying it bare. For better or for worse, Byron's narrator is everything his title character is not.

Particularly fascinating is the treatment of the theme in E. T. A. Hoffmann's novella *Don Juan* (1813). It features Donna Anna, rather than the title character, as its principal hero. The story's narrator conveys his discovery of what, he feels, is the hidden meaning of Mozart's opera. He claims that Donna Anna pursues Don Giovanni not to avenge the death of her father but because she has fallen in love with him, although she cannot acknowledge her true feelings, not even to herself. That is why she repeatedly seeks confrontations with Don Giovanni, which always end up inconclusively; that is why she keeps postponing her wedding to Don Ottavio, under the pretext of her still unaccomplished mission of revenge. When, at the opera's finale, after Don Giovanni's disappearance, she asks her fiancé to postpone the wedding for yet another year, she is confident that she will never belong to her "cold, unmanly, ordinary" suitor. Her kind of love, which ravages her with an all-devouring flame ("die im Innersten ihres Gemüts in verzehrender Flamme wütende Liebe")[9] that is literally tearing her apart, makes her into a quintessentially Romantic figure. Donna Anna's secret passion exemplifies the irresistible attraction that brings a Romantic subject to a character such as Don Giovanni to the point of self-destruction.

Pushkin's case occupies a peculiar position in this broader context. His art and personality exemplifies not an opposition between Don Giovanni and Adolphe or, by the same token, between the naive and the sentimental artist, but rather a symbiosis. Unlike Byron, Hoffmann, or Kierkegaard, who viewed Don Juan from the Romantic perspective as a wonderfully extraneous phenomenon, Pushkin seems unable to choose between identifying himself with Don Juan's element or treating this emblem of "naive" spontaneity as his anitpode.

Pushkin's treatment of Don Juan's character reflects this duality. In Don Guan's monologues an artful rhetoric of seduction and the genuine passion (without which no rhetoric can succeed) are tightly intertwined. In the beginning Don Guan's behavior emulates that of the operatic character. He becomes instantly inflamed at the sight of Donna Anna at her husband's grave, finds, in a stroke of inspiration, the right mode of timorous piety and self-effacing awe with which she is to be approached, and proceeds with finely apportioned expressions of passion and reticence, keeping a sharp eye on his prey's emotional progress. Yet, after a while, he seems to be altered by his own game. After Donna Anna finally agrees to receive him in her house, he dutifully boasts about his new victory to Leporello, his record keeper. Yet when the latter initiates their habitual bantering with an exclamation of mock horror: "Oh the widows, this is what all of you are!" Don Guan responds with an unexpected eagerness: "I am happy! I want to sing, I would be glad to embrace the whole world" (7:159). Mozart's Don Giovanni dies as he lives. He deals with the ultimate horror of the Commendatore's appearance with the same full involvement with, and possession of, himself that he brings to every situation, be it a passionate pursuit, cynical bantering, or a dangerous game. But Pushkin's Don Guan eventually loses track of whether it is his novel experience of genuinely falling in love that makes him surpass himself in his art of seduction or his subsequent eloquence that sweeps him, alongside the object of his adoration, into the conviction that he has indeed fallen in love. When the Stone Guest appears, Don Guan's last thought is directed to Donna Anna: "I am perishing—this is the end—oh Donna Anna!" (7:171). The self-absorbed wholeness of Don Guan's personality seems to crumble, revealing the genuine care for the other, a crucial sign of "dialogical" openness. His last words, with which the drama ends, offer a note of ambiguity: is it indeed possible that Don Guan fell in love for the first time? What were his feelings in the last moment? And could he have given an account of them? Had he lost his fundamentally "naive" nature? Like Adolphe, Don Guan perishes with the name of a woman on his lips without offering any answer to these questions. For the reader, however, the questions remain.

The ambiguity of Pushkin's Don Guan is emblematic for Pushkin's entire art. Much has been written about an "archaic" streak in Pushkin's personality, a contradiction between his acute awareness of the psychological and aesthetic tremors of his time, on the one hand, and the polished reticence and studied casualness of salon culture that he cultivated as his literary posture, on the other.[10] He seems never to have adapted to the advent of the nineteenth century. The texture of Pushkin's poetic discourse is extremely dense. It absorbs within itself a cacophony of diverse voices representing contradictory feelings and attitudes. Yet somehow all this density is packaged so as never to lose an appearance of polished yet casual lightness. It is the posture of a well-mannered relic from the ancien régime who shies away from the bourgeois eagerness of Romantic spirituality and its disheveled discourses. Pushkin's manuscripts reveal a tremendous and never ceasing struggle with the word.[11] However, his final product always poses as something that costs neither effort nor care to its creator. He claims to be oblivious to the cardinal Romantic dilemma, that of the discrepancy between language and thought or deed. According to Pushkin, "a poet's words *are* his deeds."[12] Let despicable "prose writers" have their vulgar worries about how to convey their thoughts; the poet has his winged words ready for whatever thought may occur to him.[13]

This posture of refined aristocratic artlessness and reticence rendered Pushkin impervious to the directly ideological discourses of Romanticism. He absorbed ideas of Romantic metaphysics and philosophy of history implicitly through the medium of his characters and narrative. The ambiguity about his age kept him alienated from the intellectual tides of Romantic nationalism and spirituality and, eventually, after those tides had risen high in Russia in the 1830s, from the public itself.

Ironically, however, it is exactly Pushkin's inability to put himself unequivocally on the side of either the naive or the sentimental artist, of Don Giovanni or of Adolphe, that makes him a quintessential Romantic. His inner contradictions turn out to be even more dramatic than those within the Byronic subject or Constant's hero. We may be assured that the contradictions and self-subverting irony that tear apart the Romantic subject *are* in fact the essence of his subjectivity. With Pushkin one can never be sure with whom one is dealing. One does not know whether his contradictions reflect the subjectivity of a "modern man" or are an artful salon game. Nor does one know whether he bares the outmost depths of his soul to his readers or is just making fun of them. Pushkin's elusiveness makes his confessional moments particularly acute. They are subversive to a point of self-destruction. His merciless playing with paradoxes reminds one more of a sharp and relentless Modernist subjectivity.

There was a price to pay for this noncommittal attitude toward his time. The further Pushkin developed as an artist and a person, the more acutely pessimistic and fatalistic he felt about the world and himself. This inner development is symbolically expressed by rethinking Don Juan's story in a way that emphasizes the inevitability of Don Juan's final defeat. Gradually the Stone Guest steps into the foreground of Pushkin's consciousness, pushing Don Juan to the margins, diminishing him to the role of an opponent who never really had any chance. The development of this lugubriously fatalistic attitude goes hand in hand with the darkening of the political and spiritual climate in Russia through the first decade of Nicholas' reign.

As to the "Sobanska moment," it did not leave any traceable consequences in Pushkin's life other than in Don Guan's monologues in *The Stone Guest*. Apparently she was not a woman to be added to Pushkin's list. A month after his passionate epistolary effort, Pushkin traveled to Moscow, where he resumed his courtship of the seventeen-year-old Natalia Goncharova to whom he had proposed unsuccessfully a year earlier. He made a formal proposal (via her mother) once again on April 6, and this time it was accepted. Pushkin wrote

The Stone Guest while making preparations for his wedding, which took place early the next year. It was near that time that Pushkin's perception of Don Juan and his story began taking a new, more gloomy and pessimistic turn.

THE STONE GUEST AND THE BRONZE HORSEMAN

While still a youth, Pushkin had often based his narrative poems on versions of a conventional triangular scheme of the love affair. Its invariable features comprised a young and beautiful woman and her two suitors, one old, ridiculously ugly, and physically feeble but given formidable institutional power; the other, young, attractive, and aspirant. The old suitor claimed the beauty as his, yet his frailty made him unable to enjoy his possession or to make her happy. The young suitor made a valiant attack on the old man's power and received triumphantly the "sweet reward" for his victory. At this early stage the traditional, even old-fashioned scheme had little in common with the story of Don Juan. Instead it smacked of a neoclassicist comedy. The young Pushkin made it provocatively fresh, first, by using rather explicit sexual language, and second, by spicing its meaning with daring allusions. In his mock fairy tale *Ruslan and Ludmila* (1817–1820) the evil magician Chernomor abducts Ludmila right from her nuptial bed. Ludmila preserves—or endures—her virginity, thanks not so much to her virtue or resourcefulness (as would be the case in the harem operas of the time) as to Chernomor's laughable impotence. What made the story particularly amusing to contemporary readers was a number of cunning allusions to modern Petersburg life in the portrayal of Chernomor's castle and its sinister splendor. These allusions made readers wonder about the identity of the decrepit enchanted realm and its sovereign that were portrayed in the story. (Alexander I was notorious for his affairs with young women, some of whom Pushkin had a chance to observe when as a teenager he studied near the emperor's summer residence.) When Ludmila's bridegroom Ruslan eventually raises her from the enchanted sleep into which she has been plunged by the evil magician, the scene resounds with Pushkin's political exhortations, especially with his poetic epistle "To Chaadaev": "Believe, O friend: the dawn of a wondrous happiness will rise. Russia will awake from her sleep, and our names will be inscribed over the ruins of the autocracy."

Even more daring was the treatment the theme received in *The Gabrieliad*, the poem Pushkin wrote a year later. This time, it was the heavenly power that posed as the lascivious yet grotesquely feeble authority. According to the poem's mock version of sacred history, God sent the archangel Gabriel to the beautiful Mary to convey his desires and repel Satan, who was also inflamed by the charms of the "young Jewess." Gabriel dutifully fought Satan and performed the Annunciation. However, he and Mary could not resist their mutual attraction. They accordingly became a happy, albeit shadowy, couple in an equally happy world—or so the "official" story was told. Pushkin nearly paid a very dear price for this risky exercise, whose Voltairean mockery struck an oddly discordant note at a time of the rising tides of state-sponsored and personal piety. In the late 1820s, when Pushkin was already back from his exile, an official investigation of the poem's authorship began after some soldiers complained about their officer's reading blasphemous verses to them. Pushkin attempted, in vain, to attribute the poem to Prince Dmitry Gorchakov, a well-known libertarian and a minor poet who had recently died. Eventually he was forced to admit his authorship in a private interview with Nicholas, the details of which remain secret. After that the emperor wrote on Pushkin's file: "The affair is known to me in full, and considered terminated." This episode, together with the fact that it was Nicholas who returned Pushkin from what appeared to be an interminable exile, was instrumental in cementing Pushkin's personal loyalty to the new emperor.

The early incarnations of the triangular scheme demonstrated that the figure of the old authority had nothing to do with the beauty he claimed as his possession. His impotence, revealed by the affair, portended his quick demise. All the young suitor had to do was make one daring assault on the imposing yet false love. His victory, and ensuing "wondrous happiness," were all but assured. A crossing of this master plot with the Don Juan theme occurred in the poem "To a Young Widow," which treated Don Juan's story in the same boisterously optimistic vein. The poem's lyrical subject is confident that the object of his passion rightfully belongs to him and that the gloomy shade of her dead husband has no power to reclaim his old rights. The whole situation is viewed, as it were, from Don Juan's perspective. Don Juan is shown at the moment of his triumph, and the statue appears as a petrified relic of the past that will no longer have any hold over a blissful future.

A turning point in the development of this master plot occurred in December 1825. Repercussions of the Decembrists' uprising, and its precipitous and catastrophic outcome, were to be felt in several of Pushkin's major works of the late 1820s. The traces are particularly poignant in the last chapter of *Eugene Onegin*, which Pushkin wrote also shortly before he was married. In it the novel's hero is shown returning to St. Petersburg after years of wandering. Here he encounters Tatiana, now a married woman and grande dame of Petersburg society. Now it is Onegin's turn to fall in love with her. He writes her a letter whose topoi and phrasing vividly recall Pushkin's own letters to Sobanska. A stormy interview in Tatina's private chamber ensues. She admits that she still loves him but professes her eternal faithfulness to the man to whom she "was given." After she leaves, her husband, the "fat General" (whose remoteness is emphasized by the fact that he remains unnamed in the story) suddenly appears at the scene, his spurs clinking. In this "evil moment" the narrator opts neither for a scandal or a duel; he rather leads his story to a morally good ending.

An interesting detail of *Eugene Onegin*'s finale is the suddenness of the general's appearance at the scene and the ominous clang of his spurs, an allusion to the Stone Guest's thunderous steps. The unexpected, catastrophic character of the triangular scheme's outcome had long fascinated Pushkin (since, indeed, December 14, 1825). Yet the further he evolved his triangular scheme, the more this sudden outcome looked inevitable—and therefore right, if we follow the rising patterns of historical determinism in the consciousness of the time. Pushkin's sympathies and nostalgic admiration may still have remained on the side of the defeated suitor; the woman's decision to remain in the possession of the old authority to which she was "given" may have left her quite unhappy. But the established order persists, as in Mozart's opera, after having shown its ability to repel its assailants. The eighteenth-century comedy about a duped old suitor/husband and a triumphant young couple gradually turns into the story of Don Juan's defeat in which, finally, the Stone Guest assumes the commanding role.

When, in his epochal *History of the Russian State* (1816), Karamzin put forth his vision of Russian autocracy as a representation of the essence of Russian national character and historical mission, the young Pushkin reacted with sarcasm and indignation, and this despite all the admiration he had for the author. In one of his epigrams of that time he dubbed Karamzin an enlightened champion of autocracy and an admirer of the charms of the whip. Pushkin, like Karamzin, was here perceiving Russian autocracy as a historical inevitability. Three major historical debacles, Napoleon's invasion of 1812, the Decembrists' aborted coup, and the brutally suppressed Polish uprising of 1830–1831, seem to have convinced him of the unshakable nature of Russia's autocratic order and the futility of all efforts to assault it.

This submission was not a happy one. Pushkin's eyes remained open to the gloomy nature of the unshakable order. Its petrified immobility made its triumphs over its assailants sudden and catastrophic. The oppressive power was capable of coming to life only for a short critical moment; yet this was enough to assert its authority and repel each of its challengers. The Stone Guest thus retained his gloomy and immobile appearance, even if this very immobility was perceived as a sign of destiny that made all attempts to shake the Stone Guest's power futile.

The climax of this development was reached by Pushkin in his narrative poem, *The Bronze Horseman* (1833). As in his novel in verse, his hero is named Eugene. This Eugene, however, is greatly diminished in stature. He is a petty official whose only aspiration is to marry a young girl from Petersburg's suburbs. In this he almost succeeds, though his now uneventful existence is interrupted by the catastrophic flood of the fall of 1824. The rising tides of the Neva ferociously assault the river's granite embankments in a frenzied attempt to overthrow the city built by Peter the Great. The city withstands the assault, but Eugene's bride drowns, and he loses his mind. One night, wandering through the city, he arrives at the site dominated by Peter's equestrian statue. In a sudden revelation he perceives the ultimate source of his misfortune in the iron will of an emperor who founded his city on the banks of a tumultuous river. In a pathetic imitation of Don Juan's defiance of the statue, Eugene raises his voice in a threat to "the idol" who destroyed his life. In full accordance with the prototypical story, the statue suddenly comes to life. Eugene's defeat is instant: he flees in horror, hearing the thunderous clang of the bronze horse's hooves behind him.[14] The founder of the city has taken Eugene's bride from him; he was certainly not going to give her back.

Pushkin's oeuvre of the 1830s was interspersed with various incarnations of this gradually developing master plot. The outcome of these incarnations all point to the reassertion of authority and order, which come at the very last moment, often as a result of a catastrophic turn of events. The fatalism of the Stone Guest's triumph, solemn and horrifying, inevitable and precipitous, reflects Russia's peculiar historical experience in the first third of the nineteenth century: its triumph over Napoleon's invasion, its resistance to the rise of revolutionary tides in the late 1810s and the 1820s, and its ascendance, after initial trials, to the heights of a seemingly unassailable power during the first decade of Nicholas's reign. Pushkin's gradual shift from the perspective of Don Juan to that of the Stone Guest reflects the development of Romanticism, a development that led to its eventual demise. For it shows a transition from the uncertainties of the individual subject to a more dangerous preoccupation with national character and its preordained historical destiny.

NOTES

1. "Today is the ninth anniversary of the day I have seen you for the first time. That day decided my life. The more I think about it, the stronger I feel that my existence is inseparable from yours; I was born to love you and to be your servant—all my other ambitions are nothing but either an error or the folly; without you, there is nothing but the remorse for happiness that I was unable to consummate. Sooner or

later, it must happen that I abandon everything, and come to prostrate at your feet." Pushkin's works are cited from A. S. Pushkin, *Polnoe sobranie sochinenii*, vols. 1–19 (Moscow, 1994–1997).

2. The somewhat unusual title of the story might be borrowed from a Russian translation of Molière's play as suggested in B. V. Tomashevskii's commentary to *The Stone Guest* in A. S. Pushkin, *Polnoe sobranie sochinenii*, vol. 7 (Moscow, 1935), 55. This, however, seems unlikely, first, because Pushkin knew Molière's works in the originals, and second, because that particular Don Juan had no significant impact in his own treatment of the theme.

3. The name Pushkin chose for his hero sounds as unusual in Russian as in any other language. Apparently he wanted to avoid the conventional Russian pronunciation of the name, *Don Zhuan*, borrowed from French. Pushkin's intention must have been to come closer to the original Spanish sound of the name. However, he mistakenly took Spanish "j" for an English- or German-like "h," a sound that Russian does not have, which in the Russian pronunciation of foreign names is habitually rendered as "g": *Gegel'* for Hegel, *Gamlet* for Hamlet, etc. (Russian does have "kh," a sound roughly corresponding to Spanish "j"; its use has eventually become the norm for pronouncing Spanish names: *Khuan, Khose*, etc.).

4. For a detailed analysis of the parallels between the two plays and the letter, see L. I. Volpert, *Pushkin i psikhologicheskaia traditsiia vo frantsuzskoi literature* (Tallinn, 1980), 102–124.

5. Pushkin had an intense relationship with one of the sisters, Ekaterina.

6. *Materialy k letopisi zhizni i tvorchestva Pushkna, 1826–1837. Kartoteki M. A. i T. G. Tsiavlovskikh*, vol. 3.2 (Moscow, 1999), 421.

7. "Dear Ellénore, allow me to give you this name that reminds me both the burning reading experiences of my young years . . . and your own existence, so violent, so stormy, so different from what it should be."

8. Anna Akhmatova, "Adol'f Benzhamena Konstana v tvorchestve Pushkina," in A. Akhmatova, *O Pushkine* (Leningrad, 1977), 50–88.

9. *Hoffmanns Werke* (Berlin: Aufbau, 1979), 2:28.

10. Iu. N. Tynianov, "Arkhaisty i Pushkin," in his *Arkhaisty i novatory* (Leningrad, 1929), 87–227; V. V. Vinogradov, "O stile Pushkina," in *Literaturnoe nasledstvo*, vol. 16–18 (Moscow, 1934), 135–214; B. Gasparov, "Pouchkine et le romantisme européen," in *Histoire de la littérature russe*, vol. 2 (Paris, 1997).

11. A fascinating picture of Pushkin's creative process can be seen in a recent facsimile edition of some of his notebooks: Alexander Pushkin, *The Working Notebooks*, vols. 1–8 (St. Petersburg, 1995).

12. In his essay "What Is the Word," included in the book *Selected Passages from the Correspondence with Friends* (1844), Gogol testified on this pronouncement by Pushkin, ostensibly made in a conversation: N. V. Gogol, *Sochineniia v odnom tome*, ed. N. S. Tikhonravov and V. I. Shenrok (St. Petersburg, 1901), cols. 1381–1384.

13. See the poem "The Prose Writer and the Poet" (2:391).

14. The connection was made in Jakobson's famous article, "Pushkin and His Sculptural Myth" (1935), in Roman Jakobson, *Selected Writings*, vol. 5 (The Hague: Mouton, 1979), 237–280.

Five

Mörike's Mozart and the Scent of a Woman

HANS RUDOLF VAGET

ZITTO: Mi pare sentire odor di femmina . . .

According to Edward Dent, the "perfect" twentieth-century English Mozartian and author of a classic study of *Mozart's Operas*, *Don Giovanni* was "completely misunderstood" throughout the nineteenth century. Dent was by no means alone in dismissing the interpretive efforts of a Hoffmann or a Kierkegaard—to mention only two of the most famous—as hopelessly subjective, arbitrary, and Romantic. Alfred Einstein, that other "perfect" Mozartian, was hardly less censorious about those two seminal readings of Mozart's puzzling *dramma giocoso*. In his masterly *Mozart: His Character, His Work*, Einstein considered the Danish philosopher's passionate engagement with *Don Giovanni* politely but almost dismissively as merely "Søren Kierkegaard's fantasies on *Don Juan*." And, for Hoffmann's take on this "opera of all operas" in his fascinating early story *Don Juan; or, A Fabulous Adventure That Befell a Music Enthusiast on His Travels*, which turns on the assumption that Donna Anna is secretly in love with her (would-be) rapist, Einstein had no patience at all, rejecting it out of hand as "nonsensical."

Bashing nineteenth-century views of Mozart has long been a commonplace with the perfect and not so perfect Mozartians of our time—so much so that one is tempted to call for a moratorium on all facile dismissals and thus for a reconsideration of these and similar received opinions. Such a reconsideration would be based on the careful acknowledgment that our current views of any classic work, including Mozart's great opera, are formed not via direct communication with the mind of its creator, but as a result of a highly complicated process of appropriation from our predecessors—those legions of interpreters and readers preceding us who, it behooves us to assume, were no less intelligent and sensitive than we are. Let it be mentioned in passing that some of the popular twentieth-century views of Mozart, which appeared plausible when they were first aired—Peter Shaffer's *Amadeus* (1979), for example—are hardly less fanciful than Hoffmann's, or Kierkegaard's, but have already acquired a thick patina of datedness.

Neither Einstein nor Dent commented on Eduard Mörike's novella of 1855, *Mozart's Journey to Prague*—a work that has come to be regarded, at least in the German-speaking sphere, as the most subtle and sublime of all the nineteenth-century literary reimaginings of this composer. The novella describes how Mozart, on his way from Vienna to Prague for the premiere of *Don Giovanni* and during an unplanned stay at the estate of a nobleman, becomes inspired to complete a still-missing part of the first act of the opera. David Luke's recent translation of this gem of a story should prove a great help in remedying the relative neglect of this work in the literature in English. Even in Germany, though, Mörike's reputation as a major poet, which today is secure, was late in arriving. In fact, it was Hugo Wolf, the most discriminating among the masters of the German lied, who definitively secured the author's place in the pantheon of German literature when in 1889, fourteen years after the poet's death, in a stunning eruption of his own creativity, he set to music no fewer than fifty-three Mörike poems. It was through music that Mörike was brought to the attention of a wider public both in Germany and abroad. It seems somehow appropriate, then, that it was his novella about Mozart rather than his more ambitious, but ill-fated novel, *Nolten the Painter*, that captured the imagination of posterity. The charm of his narrative derives as much from the nostalgic evocation of the waning phase of the rococo period as from the intimate portrait of Mozart, who is fashioned here as the very exemplar of that culture. It is this subtle blend of the Mozart cult with the nostalgia for the lost world of the ancien régime that made the provincial but civilized world of Mörike's fiction seem especially attractive when, after the catastrophe of 1933—1945, Germans were searching their past for shreds of an uncompromised, usable history. For many Germans Mörike represented an unsullied piece of their past. This new appreciation of the poet, born from a profound spiritual need, is most evident in Benno von Wiese's landmark book on Mörike of 1950. One of the leading figures of German *Germanistik* of the postwar period and himself politically compromised, von Wiese set the tone for much of the deliberately nonpolitical cult of Mörike in the Adenauer era. In his preface, pointedly dated "Easter 1950," he called attention to the "purity" and restorative quality of Mörike's poetic world and declared it to be his intention to "show the healing powers that flow for us from this quiet source still today." In much of the recent German commentary on our novella this belief in the restorative power of Mörike's work still resonates.

However, for today's reader, Mörike's portrait of Mozart elicits different responses, generating different questions of a purely historical sort that concern Mörike's place on the map of Mozart's bewildering literary afterlife. To locate that place we shall look at *Mozart's Journey to Prague* through some neglected lenses that can bring into focus certain underexposed aspects of the perception of Mozart in the nineteenth century. And we shall compare Mörike's reimagining of Mozart not, as is customary, with the composer's biographical record but rather with his work—*Don Giovanni* itself.

We take our first cues from Nietzsche, whose preoccupation with Wagner seems, for most commentators, to have obscured the fact that he was also an ardent Mozartian. It comes as somewhat of a surprise, therefore, to find that Nietzsche was among the first to question the widespread tendency to demonize the creator of *Don Giovanni*. In an aphorism of *Human, All Too Human*, published in 1880, Nietzsche comments disapprovingly on the general privileging of the "music of the stone-guest," i.e., those portentous D-minor moments associated with the spectral, "talking" statue of the Commendatore and its uncanny appearance at the Don's last supper. To Nietzsche's way of thinking, these moments, usually played as though they "leaped from the wall in order to frighten the audience and put them to flight," had been given disproportionate weight. He brands this "a sin" against the spirit of Mozart, which was "gay, sunny, tender, and lighthearted" and, in its serious vein, was good-natured (*gütig*) and not frightening (*furchtbar*). Nietzsche's Mozart is characterized above all, as he observes in *Beyond Good and Evil*, by that most un-Wagnerian quality of "Höflichkeit des Herzens"—courtesy of the heart.

This sounds suspiciously as though the author of *Human, All Too Human*, who actually did not care for Mörike's poems, had *Mozart's Journey to Prague* in mind when he penned these remarks. But we have no record of his having read Mörike's novella. Mörike, for his part, would have found much to agree with Nietzsche's general perception of Mozart. The courtesy of the heart that Nietzsche sensed in Mozart's music comes over loud and clear in Mörike's novella. And what Nietzsche saw in Mozart's work as a whole—that it represents the coda of a great era of European taste—is prefigured in how the poet from Swabia situated Mozart in the twilight of the ancien régime.

On the other hand, Nietzsche's antennae would certainly have registered with disapproval the privileging in Mörike's story of what one might call the apocalyptic dimension of *Don Giovanni*. For such privileging was part of a certain demonizing tendency focused on the theme of mortality that was completely in line with the image, dear to the nineteenth century, of Mozart the tragic, unappreciated *Wunderkind* cut down at the height of his creative power and dumped into an unmarked grave. This apocalyptic tone in Mörike's novella is heard most emphatically in the narrator's reference to the statue's entrance in the churchyard scene at "Di rider finerai pria dell' aurora." Here, Mörike's language for the first time strikes that ominous and solemn tone that will dominate the remaining part of the novella and culminate in the concluding poem ("Ein Tännlein grünet wo"), which summarizes the many premonitions found throughout the narrative of Mozart's early death: "As from some remote stellar region, from silver trumps the notes dropped, ice-cold, piercing the marrow and shivering the soul, down through the dark blue night." Mörike's "silberne Posaunen" refer to the three trombones prescribed in Mozart's score, but beyond that they invoke the otherworldly call to Judgment Day in the Apocalypse, which the standard German translation has executed by trombones, the English by trumpets.

It is illuminating to see that Nietzsche, dissenting from the Romanticizing and demonizing trends decried by Einstein and Dent, had, unbeknownst to him, an unlikely but in many ways like-minded French ally. That ally was Hector Berlioz, who, as an opera composer, is generally known to have admired Gluck far more than he admired Mozart. In 1826, as a budding musician, Berlioz composed a set of variations (now lost) on "La ci darem la mano," the seduction duet from act 1 of *Don Giovanni*. Over the ensuing years, as Hugh Macdonald has reminded us, the creator of *Romeo et Juliette* and of *Les Troyens* developed a great love of Mozart. In a letter of 1856 he confessed; "J'adore Mozart," and ten years later he attended no less than eight performances of *Don Giovanni* at the Theatre Lyrique in Paris. However, the French composer and music critic seems to have been constitutionally incapable of admiring anything unreservedly and without a grain of critical salt. Thus Berlioz vehemently censored Mozart for Donna Anna's second act aria "Non mi dir, bell' idol mio" for its old-fashioned ornamental style, and he chided him for using just one trombone in the "Tuba Mirum" of the *Requiem*, when in his own *Grande Messe des Morts* he called for a total of sixteen trombones and sixteen kettledrums. Nonetheless, his admiration for *Don Giovanni* was deep and sincere throughout his life. He praised this opera for its felicitous form, characterizing its graceful style as "Raphaelesque." And in a review of 1839 he confessed: "Never have I felt such admiration for the creative power of

Mozart's genius nor for the constant lucidity of his mind. There is something despairing, I was almost going to say vexing, about this unfailing beauty, always calm and sure of itself." Like Nietzsche, Berlioz was averse to the sort of demonization of *Don Giovanni,* both as opera and as figure, we find, on the intellectually highest level, in Kierkegaard. And when in a somewhat different context he complained about the "trombonization" of Mozart, he may well have had in mind the same general phenomenon as did Nietzsche.

Mörike's emphasis on the theme of mortality was, however, no mere matter of intellectual or musical fashion. It had tragic biographical roots. He was a twenty-year-old university student at Tübingen when, in the company of his favorite brother, August, he attended for the first time a performance of *Don Giovanni* at the Stuttgart Opera. A few days later, quite unexpectedly, August died from a cerebral hemorrhage—a cruel twist of fate that could not have failed greatly to reinforce Mörike's overwhelmingly tragic perception of Mozart's work. Almost thirty years later, after a series of professional and personal disappointments, and living with persistent doubts about his religious shortcomings as a man of the cloth, he returned to the subject of *Don Giovanni.* Writing to his wife, Margarethe, in the summer of 1852, he reported that during a journey to visit friends he fell to fantasizing about Mozart. He divulged nothing about the content of the story that began to take shape in his mind, hinting only that it would feature "silberne Posaunen"—the very instruments that would occupy such a conspicuous place and have such an ominous role in his finished work. This is the first document we have that touches upon the novella's genesis. It is safe to assume, though, that Mörike had been contemplating a story about Mozart well before 1852.

In *Mozart's Journey* a grand counterpoint to the theme of mortality is provided by the broadly and lovingly spun out theme of creativity. In fact, it is precisely the psychologically probing representation of the creative process that constitutes the chief reason for the high esteem in which Mörike's novella is held today. His notions of creativity are archly Romantic and strongly reminiscent of Goethe. Mozart's extraordinary creative force is viewed here as death bound, for with every work into which he pours his inner self he moves closer to his own end. Mörike's Mozart and Mozart's Don mirror each other in their more or less reckless proclivity to squander the gifts with which Nature endowed them. This is the crucial point that is understood by Eugenie, Mozart's fictionally idealized soul mate: "The conviction, the utter conviction grew upon her that here was a man rapidly and inexorably burning himself out in his own flame; that he would be only a fleeting phenomenon on this earth, because the overwhelming beauty that poured from him would be more than the earth could really endure." Surely, we are meant to connect this declaration to the image that Mörike uses for the fiery end of the Don himself, which is likened to a "magnificent spectacle" such as the "burning of some splendid ship." These are familiar tropes from Romantic speculations about the artist. They are best encapsulated in Goethe's *Torquato Tasso* (1790), the first work in German literature to thematize the tragic fate of the artist in the modern world. Given Mörike's well-known admiration for Goethe, it is safe to assume that Tasso's famous speech, in which he likens the poet to a silkworm, was not far from Mörike's mind when he was fashioning his own vision of Mozart:

> Verbiete du dem Seidenwurm zu spinnen,
> Wenn er sich schon dem Tode näher spinnt:
> Das köstliche Geweb' entwickelt er
> Aus seinem Innersten und läßt nicht ab,
> Bis er in seinen Sarg sich eingeschlossen.

(GOETHE, *Plays*, v. 3075FF)

> Forbid the silkworm to continue spinning
> Though it is spinning on to its own death!
> It will evolve its precious weft from deep
> Within its inner self and will not cease
> Till it has cased itself in its own coffin.

Generally speaking, the representation of the creative process is at the epicenter of all literary portraits of the artist, and, as in so many other cases, here, too, we have to ask whether that portrait bears a greater resemblance to the sitter of the portrait or to its painter. Mörike had no scholarly ambitions. To be sure, he was familiar with Alexander Oulybishev's monumental work on Mozart's life and works, written in French, the German translation of which had appeared in 1847. Oulybishev was Mörike's chief source for the biographical information that went into the making of the novella. But when it came to recreating the beloved figure of the composer—to make him come alive as a creative artist—Mörike drew on his own resources, relying on his profound empathy with Mozart and on his chameleonlike adaptability. It goes without saying that the resulting work is a double portrait of the creator of *Don Giovanni* and of Mörike himself. However, the question remains to what extent Mörike was able to capture the peculiar mode of Mozart's musical creativity and to render that essential sexual energy that characterizes both the opera's libertine hero and his creator and that is particularly suggested by the Don's animal-like ability, demonstrated in act 1, scene 4, to pick up the mere scent of a woman.

Mörike offers the reader glimpses of the composer at work, in a series of episodes distributed over the course of his ingeniously devised narrative, that leave us with a nicely detailed image of Mozart the artist. This portrait is completed with skillfully interwoven retrospective inserts that reveal, through the eyes of his wife, Konstanze, Mozart the private man. We witness a day in the life of Mozart as he travels with Konstanze from Vienna to Prague to supervise and conduct the premiere of *Don Giovanni*, the opera's score still incomplete. This much is based on the historical record; the rest is more or less Mörike's invention.

On the third day of their journey, at midday, the Mozarts stop to escape the heat in their coach, which is relieved only temporarily when Mozart accidentally spills a flask of eau de cologne. With Konstanze resting at a nearby inn, Mozart wanders onto the grounds of a nobleman's estate complete with an Italian-style country house and, tucked away, a trellised arbor, which he enters in order to ponder his unfinished opera. He absent-mindedly plucks an orange from a carefully nurtured orange tree, blissfully unaware that this precious, memory-filled family heirloom is meant to serve as a present from the owner, Count von Schinzberg, to his niece, Eugenie, whose engagement is to be celebrated that very day. Instead of being reprimanded for trespassing, Mozart is invited to stay and grace the festivities. To the delight of the ladies of the house, all of them admirers of the composer, he accepts and, with customary artlessness, joins the music making, the dancing, and the general merriment. Acceding to his hosts' pleas, Mozart, assisted by Konstanze, performs for the distinguished assembly some of the completed parts of the opera, including the scene of Don Giovanni's demise. By this everyone is deeply moved, including the composer. The morning after, the Mozarts continue their journey in an elegant new coach, a present from the count, while Eugenie is overwhelmed by premonitions of Mozart's early death.

In the course of one day we are made privy to the three basic stages of the creative process: of inspiration and conception; of critical self-reflection; and of the culminating first performance. Astutely, Mörike chooses a brief, self-contained piece for demonstrating and illuminating Mozart's creativity, the bridal song in act 1, scene 7, which involves Zerlina, Masetto, and a chorus of peasants—and he succeeds brilliantly without recourse to the hackneyed conceit that most writers employ when faced with the task of rendering the creative process: invoking some transcendent agency. Mörike's Mozart—and this, above all, constitutes the essential modernity of his procedure—draws exclusively on inner sources buried in the depths of the composer's psyche and memory.

Earlier in the day, still in the coach, Mozart's thoughts had already turned to the one lacuna in the otherwise finished first act of his new opera. It was to be "an easy little number . . . : a duet and chorus for a country wedding . . . a simple childlike melody, bubbling over with happiness." He recalled the text of that song with its plain eroticism and unaffected anticipation of sexual pleasure ("Giovinette che fate all' amore"), but on that occasion was unable to develop a "musical idea"—one, that is, that would match the erotically charged mood of the words. A more propitious moment arises now in the secluded arbor, next to a softly splashing fountain in the count's garden, a scene that is staged as a traditional *locus amoenus*, an earthly paradise, where the fortuitous visitor is greeted by a veritable overload of sensual stimuli. The sight of the orange tree transports his thoughts to Italy and evokes the memory of an enchanting musical spectacle, witnessed long ago, performed by a Sicilian troupe of actors, the Figli di Nettuno, on boats in the Gulf of Naples. Lost in daydreaming, he reaches for an orange, plucks it, and begins to twirl "the scented fruit from side to side under his nose, while his lips silently toyed with a melody." Erotically stimulated on multiple levels—by the juicy, plump fruit he is fondling; by the memory of those beautiful Italian youths; and by a subconscious relapse into the blissful contentment of the infant at his mother's breast—he is suddenly seized by an idea, tentative at first, that crystallizes a few moments later when, still daydreaming, he cuts the orange in two halves. Inhaling "the fruit's exquisite fragrance," he puts the two halves very gently together, takes them apart, then reunites them once again. Although Mozart is interrupted at this climactic moment by the count's stern gardener, his conceptualization of the bridal song is achieved, and as soon as the disturbance has passed the composer has no difficulty drafting the melody of "Giovinette che fate all'amore." There is probably no other work in all of literature in which the exact moment of musical inspiration is staged with equal felicity and conviction.

At this point of the narrative we do not as yet fully comprehend what triggered the surge of inspiration. We are offered further insights into the inner sanctum of the artist in the second stage of the creative process when, a few hours later, Mozart reflects on what actually took place earlier in the arbor by reconstructing in considerable detail the scene in the Gulf of Naples that he had witnessed, when traveling in Italy with his father as a thirteen-year-old boy. This occurs in the conversation over dinner when the enthusiastic composer, as if to probe the suitability of his melodic invention, treats his hosts and the other guests to an enraptured description of the charming but somewhat enigmatic spectacle performed by that Sicilian troupe. Three elements of his recollection render perfectly transparent the connection, established through preconscious association, between the Sicilian-Neapolitan pantomime and Zerlina's bridal song: first, the orange-colored balls tossed to and fro between the boats of the Figli di Nettuno, which mnemonically materialize before Mozart's inner eye at the sight of the orange tree in the garden; second, the all important musical memory of that scene—a medley of "Sicilian airs, dances, *saltarelli, canzoni a ballo*" that obviously account for the lively rhythm of the bridal song in six-eight time; third, the young "princess" for whose favors the two groups of the Sons of Neptune playfully compete. She was "a sweet innocent creature of about my age . . . nodding her head very nicely in time to the music; to this day I can still see her smile and [remember] her long eyelashes." In retrospect, Mozart realizes, "I clearly saw Zerlina dancing there before my eyes, and in a strange way that laughing landscape of the Gulf of Naples was there as well." Zerlina stands revealed as the recreation of the thirteen-year-old Mozart's early erotic encounter.

Once again we note a striking similarity between Nietzsche's and Mörike's visions of the creator of *Don Giovanni*. The following observation from *Human, All Too Human* could easily serve as an apt gloss on Mörike's novella. Speaking of the special character of Mozart's melodic inventions and distinguishing them from Beethoven's, Nietzsche observes: Mozart "finds his inspiration not in hearing music but in gazing at life, the most animated life of the South. He was always dreaming of Italy when he was not there."

The first try-out of the new musical number occurs after dinner. The "company now with one accord demanded to hear the duet sung by the composer" and Eugenie, with the count taking the part of the chorus. So infectious is the gaiety of the piece that the entire company breaks into dance and other merrymaking. This unforced, self-assured, and elegant interplay between the von Schinzbergs and Mozart serves as a perfect illustration of the ideal symbiotic relationship between artist and society that Mörike nostalgically—or rather as a utopian vision—projects upon his protagonists. At an earlier point in this festive and progressively more joyful gathering, Eugenie had sung Susanna's act 4 aria "Deh vieni" from *Le Nozze di Figaro*; there followed a movement from one of Mozart's piano concertos, executed by the composer. With the impromptu performance of the spanking new bridal song, the gaiety of the company reached its high point—only to be overshadowed in every sense of the word later that evening by the first performance of additional passages from the opera with which this one day in the life of Mozart comes to a somber close. Performed in the dark, by candlelight, Mozart's playing of *Don Giovanni* reestablishes the primacy of the theme of mortality not only in the opera itself but also in Mörike's discerning portrait of the artist. In fact, by having the performance culminate in the Don's descent into hell, rather than in the cheerful sextet with which the opera closes, Mörike reveals once more the Romanticizing and demonizing bent of his recreation.

By focusing on Zerlina and the Don, Mörike placed himself at a safe distance from Hoffmann and created a space for himself where he was able to develop his own vision of the opera. It is a vision in which Donna Anna, Don Ottavio, and Donna Elvira—the representatives of the nobility—are relegated to the background. As we have seen, this Zerlina is very much Mörike's own creation, born of a typically German and Romantic nostalgia for Italy and from a distinct predilection, likewise Romantic in character, for the child-bride, familiar from Novalis and other Romantics. However, by connecting his Zerlina to a fictitious erotic encounter of the pubescent Mozart, Mörike divests the opera's Zerlina of some of her essential qualities: her unabashed physicality and sexual forwardness. In Mörike's child-bride we find no hint of Zerlina's outrageous readiness to allow herself to be seduced on the very day of her wedding to Masetto. Nor is there any trace of that sexual curiosity that, even though it is thwarted, imparts to her the unaffected vivacity and undamaged humanity that raise her indeed, as the Don asserts, above her modest social standing. In Mörike's soft-lens vision of *Don Giovanni* there seems to be no place for the kind of creature that Mozart and Da Ponte envisioned—a young woman perfectly capable of fending off her attacker when the Don attempts to rape her, a fair-minded bride who asks for a sound beating from Masetto in order to repair their relationship, a self-confident partner who uses her body to define the terms of marital peace. And, for good measure, a lover who appears masochistically capable, as Theodor W. Adorno fantasized in his gushing "Huldigung an Zerlina," of turning pain into pleasure.

Mörike's softening of the contours is more pronounced in the case of the Don himself, who in Mozart's and Da Ponte's conception is a young noble-man of extreme licentiousness—*estremamente licentioso*. But in Mörike's out-line of the opera Don Giovanni's outrageous dissoluteness remains a matter of rumor; here the Don attains his heroic stature and measure of greatness solely through his courage in the face of death. The sexually animalistic side of the man (inseparable from his courage) is obscured by the ominous mood of his impending death through divine intervention. Nowhere in the opera is the predatory sexuality of this erotic anarchist articulated more succinctly than in act I, scene 4. Having just killed Donna Anna's father, Don Giovanni prepares to tell Leporello of his encounter with a new *bella donna* but interrupts himself with the remark: I seem to smell the scent of a woman—"mi pare sentir odor di femmina." Ironically this is Donna Elvira, the prototypically aban-doned woman, but this surprise in no way lessens the impact of this instance of the Don's animal-like sexuality, which is epitomized in his uncanny ability to pick up the scent of the opposite sex. It is revealing to note that Mörike, too, uses olfaction in his reimagining of Mozart. But in that trifling incident in the coach at the outset of the story, when Mozart spills the content of a flask of perfume, the fragrance is employed to relieve the discomfort of over-heated travel; and when we see him smell an orange, his sense of smell serves uniquely to tease new musical inspiration from his memory. Nowhere in Mörike's novella do olfactory sensations take on the sexual connotations that they have in the opera. In Mozart's and Da Ponte's conception it is just that strong animal instinct for the next sexual prey that lends urgency to the Don's devastatingly seductive charm. It also fuels his delight in the good life that so intrigued Mörike's contemporary, Kierkegaard. Obviously, Don Giovanni the compulsive pursuer of women lay outside the radius of Mörike's sensibility.

Nietzsche was probably correct in believing that Mozart dreamed all his life of Italy. It is crucial to note, however, that Mozart's vision of the South has greater depth than Mörike allows. It comprises not only the predictable clichés such as that idealized rococo scene enacted by those Sicilian actors in the Gulf of Naples but also a precise sense of what makes life under the southern sun different: a freer, less inhibited relationship to sexuality, as embodied in Don Giovanni, as well as a freer, less fraught relationship to the body, as personified in Zerlina.

Perhaps the most enigmatic moment of Mörike's entire novella occurs right after the scene in which Mörike describes Mozart's own playing through of parts of the opera. Here Mörike has Mozart report that at an earlier stage of the composition he was haunted by the fear of not being able to complete *Don Giovanni*—the fear, more precisely, that some lesser contemporary—"perhaps even some sort of Italian"—would complete the work and "cheat me of the honor due to me." Continuing this line of thought he wonders about the prospects of his opera in the future, for he seems to sense that "in the next sixty or seventy years, long after I am gone, many a false prophet will arise." What is he referring to? How are we to make sense of this? How seriously are we to take the biblical reference (Matthew 7:14)?

"Sixty or seventy years" after *Don Giovanni* would take us to the years of the novella's genesis, the 1840s and 1850s. Since it is utterly improbable that Mozart himself would have had any such premonitions, we must assume that, clumsy though this procedure may be, Mörike is here venting his own concerns about the future of opera and the future of music. Could it be, given the biblical allusions, that we are to think of Meyerbeer's *Le Prophet*, a spectacular and wildly successful *grande opera* in the Parisian style, which began its triumphal round of the opera houses of Europe in 1849 and would have left Mörike unimpressed? Or more likely, is it that Mörike alludes here to Wagner, and perhaps also to Liszt and the entire *neudeutsche* movement? Mörike disliked Wagner's music, and it seems quite plausible that he perceived in Wagner's Romantic operas—*Das Rheingold* and the works thereafter could not, of course, have been known to him—a threat to the unique standing of Mozart at least in the German-speaking sphere and to the entire culture to which *Mozart's Journey to Prague* pays homage. However this may be, the jarring remark about the false musical prophets who will arise in the nineteenth century indicates a keen awareness on Mörike's part of the precariousness of his Mozart project as a whole and of its historically questionable nature.

Mörike's vision of Mozart and of rococo culture is very much the product of a retrospective glorification of Vienna and Weimar classicism that was typical of nineteenth-century Germany, especially in the aftermath of the failed revolution of 1848. The untimeliness of Mörike's vision became fully apparent in the twentieth century, as a brief comparative glance at Bertolt Brecht reveals. Writing in his *Journals* (*Arbeitsjournal*), Brecht deplored the lack of a refined erotic culture in Germany, but he allowed for two exceptions: Goethe and Mozart (March 8, 1941). It is doubtful that he would have looked at Mörike's historical nostalgia with favor; most likely he would have frowned at the uncritical representation of the relationship between artist and society in the ancien régime as symbiotic. Like Mörike, Brecht viewed *Don Giovanni* as a "peak" of German achievement, reached early in the history of bourgeois culture and never subsequently equaled (June 8, 1943). In Brecht's view this peak was reached because of a decisive aspect of *Don Giovanni* that remains obscured in Mörike's novella: the fundamentally emancipatory spirit of the operas in the early revolutionary phase of the middle class. As well as in *Don Giovanni*, Brecht finds that spirit embodied most clearly in *Le Nozze di Figaro*, *Die Zauberflöte*, and *Fidelio* (April 29, 1950).

Be that as it may, it should be obvious that the perception of *Don Giovanni* in the nineteenth century was neither so monolithic nor so arbitrary as Edward Dent's blanket dismissal suggests. Read closely and in context, Mörike's novella reveals the existence of a discourse on Mozart beyond Hoffmann and beyond Kierkegaard, a discourse that aligns itself most readily with the views of Nietzsche and Berlioz. But Mörike's great accomplishment remains: his pioneering representation of the creative process, based on a subtle analysis of the interplay of sensory stimuli and memory that anticipates the insights of Freud in his essay *Creative Writers and Daydreaming*. To this day the sophistication and elegance of Mörike's reimagining of the creator of *Don Giovanni* remain unmatched.

REFERENCES

Braungart, Wolfgang. "Eduard Mörike: 'Mozart auf der Reise nach Prag.'" *Erzählungen und Novellen des 19. Jahrhunderts.* Vol. 2. Stuttgart, 1990, 133–202.

Dent, Edward J. *Mozart's Operas: A Critical Study.* New York, 1991 [1947].

Dieckmann, Friedrich. *Die Geschichte Don Giovannis. Werdegang eines erotischen Anarchisten.* Frankfurt am Main, 1991.

Einstein, Alfred. *Mozart: His Character, His Work.* Trans. Arthur Mendel and Nathan Broder. New York, 1945.

Goethe. *Plays.* Ed. Frank G. Ryder. New York, 1993.

Immerwahr, Raymond. "Apocalyptic Trumpets: The Inception of 'Mörike auf der Reise nach Prag.'" *Publications of the Modern Language Association of America,* 70 (1955): 390–407.

Klose, Dietrich, ed. *Über Mozart. Von Musikern, Dichtern und Liebhabern. Eine Anthologie.* Stuttgart, 1991.

Kreutzer, Hans Joachim. "Die Zeit und der Tod. Über Eduard Mörikes Mozart Novelle." In *Obertöne: Literatur und Musik. Neun Abhandlungen über das Zusammenspiel der Künste.* Würzburg, 1994, 196–216.

Macdonald, Hugh. "Berlioz and Mozart." *The Cambridge Companion to Berlioz.* Ed. Peter Bloom. Cambridge, 2000, 211–222.

Mahlendorf, Ursula. "Eduard Mörike's 'Mozart on the Way to Prague': Achievement of Integration Through Mastery of an Oedipal Crisis." In *The Wellsprings of Literary Creation: An Analysis of Male and Female "Artist Stories" from the German Romantics to American Writers of the Present.* Columbia, SC, 1985, 67–84.

Mörike, Eduard. *Mozart's Journey to Prague: Selected Poems.* Trans. and intro. David Luke. London: Libris, 1997.

Oulybysheff, Alexander D. *Mozarts Leben nebst einer Übersicht der allgemeinen Geschichte der Musik und einer Analyse der Hauptwerke Mozarts.* Für deutsche Leser bearbeitet von A. Schraishnou. 3 vols. Stuttgart, 1847.

Prawer, Sigbert S. *Mörike und seine Leser: Versuch einer Wirkungsgeschichte. Mit einer Mörikebibliographie und einem Verzeichnis der wichtigsten Vertonungen.* Stuttgart, 1960.

———. "The Threatened Idyll: Mörike's 'Mozart auf der Reise nach Prag.'" *Modern Languages* 44 (1963): 101–107.

Wiese, Benno von. *Eduard Mörike.* Tübingen and Stuttgart, 1950.

Six

The Gothic Libertine: The Shadow of Don Giovanni in Romantic Music and Culture

THOMAS S. GREY

So Don Juan is an image which constantly appears, but does not gain form and substance, an individual who is constantly being formed, but is never finished, of whose life history one can form no more definite impression than one can by listening to the tumult of the waves.

—Kierkegaard, 1843

At the conclusion of Mozart and Da Ponte's 1787 opera, Don Giovanni disappears amidst the red flame of the D-minor allegro, with its unseen chorus of infernal spirits and the brief flicker of a descending chromatic tetrachord before the jaws of hell finally close around him. A befitting end, as the rest of the cast moralizes upon hearing Leporello's stuttered account of it: "E de' perfidi la morte alla vita è sempre ugual" ("The sinner's end is always in keeping with his life"). More fitting, perhaps, than his antagonists quite realize. While for them it merely licenses the *lieto fine* they have gathered to enact, Don Giovanni's end is also a prophecy, a vision of the Romantic future whose pale fires might already be dimly glimpsed on the cultural horizon. Don Giovanni's operatic life and death aptly foreshadow a dawning future of transgressive passions, antiheroes at odds with the social order, fulsome orchestrations, D-minor *agitato*, chromatic harmonies, indulgence, blasphemy, and, not least, a penchant for melodramatic "red-fire" finales.

The anticipation of Romanticism in Don Giovanni's final moments is a familiar point, even a truism of musical and cultural history. But, aside from these generalized augurs of Romantic temperament and practice, what becomes of Don Giovanni himself after his infernal descent? In what sorts of musical, dramatic, or other cultural guises does he return? Beyond the critical reception of Mozart's paradigmatic classic itself, the posthumous career of its title figure (and/or "Don Juan" more generally) remains a rich field of inquiry.[1]

The happy ending celebrated upon the site of Don Giovanni's fiery end is premature. (Perhaps some sense of this, and not just an emergent taste for the Gothic, influenced the suppression of the concluding ensemble after 1800.) In answer to the question posed by Elvira, Zerlina, Ottavio, and Masetto ("Where has he gone, the perfidious scoundrel?"), Leporello describes, or gestures at, the events he has just witnessed: the flaming abyss, the living statue, the infernal din, Giovanni's disappearance. Elvira confirms Leporello's fractured testimony, remarking that this apparition must be the "shade" she encountered on fleeing the house some moments ago ("Ah certo è l'ombra che m'incontrò!). Clearly he does return, continually, and in various guises. For, if the shade of the Commendatore can continue to walk the earth in search of vengeance, who is to say that Giovanni's own ghost will not find a way back, inhabiting other bodies or characters with echoes of his former music or else finding new musical strains to animate his form, and to continue his never finished business of seduction. As an archetype Don Juan is, in Kierkegaard's words, "an individual who is constantly being formed, but is never finished." At the time Kierkegaard was writing, around 1840, the unhallowed specter of the ancient libertine had been haunting the Romantic imagination, as musical spirit and poetic archetype, for several decades. Not until the end of the century, if even then, would he be put to rest.

RÉMINISCENCES DE "DON JUAN"

Franz Liszt's ambitious and grandiose piano fantasia of 1841, *Réminiscences de Don Juan* (published 1843), is perhaps the central monument of the Romantic reception of Mozart's opera and its title figure. Predictably, it is framed—overshadowed, one might say—by the music of the marmoreal specter and of Don Juan's damnation, both proportionally amplified well beyond their role within the opera itself. In his deployment of the D-minor "infernal" music vis-à-vis the other themes borrowed from the opera (the duettino of seduction, "Là ci darem' la mano" and the so-called champagne aria, "Fin ch'han dal vino"), Liszt might be heard to reenvoice the spectral music as an emanation of Don Giovanni himself, as if Liszt were calling him back from the fires of hell to enact a new, Romantic fantasy scenario through the medium of Liszt's own pianistic virtuosity (and reflecting his own Don Juan-like persona, as *poète-musicien maudit*).

As a musical sketch of the opera, Liszt's fantasy is programmatically over-shadowed by the music of the Commendatore's ghost. Rather than quoting the introduction of Mozart's overture, Liszt begins with the stentorian admonitions from the graveyard scene: "Di rider' finirai pria dell'aurora" and "Ribaldo! audace! Lascia a' morti la pace." In the Romantic spirit of organic musical and dramatic integration, the Commendatore's warning voice intrudes on the other emblematic scenes of pastoral seduction ("Là ci darem' la mano") and orgiastic revelry ("Fin ch'han dal vino"), casting shadows not directly seen, or heard, in Mozart. Yet if we adjust our listening to the piece somewhat along the lines of Kierkegaard's contemporaneous literary "fantasia" on Mozart and the Don Juan theme, we will hear all its musical energies as defined by the single all-consuming, all-controlling axis of Don Giovanni himself. As Kierkegaard insisted, all the characters and all the music of the opera are ultimately projections of the vital force that is "Don Juan." Or, to read it from another historical-narrative perspective, we can hear the fantasia as a kind of musical séance (as early piano recitals were sometimes titled), in which Liszt the musical sorcerer-priest calls up the spirits of Mozart's opera from the tomb of the past to reanimate them, like the sinister gesturing portraits of Gothic melodrama. Don Giovanni steps back into our presence (as Liszt's au-ditors) through those same infernal fires into which he disappeared at the opera's end, a Gothic revenant called back from his purgatorial half-life to reenact his pleasures and crimes in pantomime for the wondering audience of a later era, the miraculous waxwork figure of a famous "historical" character.

The possibility of identifying Don Giovanni with the demonic music of the overture and finale, as here rearranged and intensified, comes into an au-dible focus at the climax of Liszt's introduction. At the last and fiercest of the piano's heaving chromatic surges (recall the "tumult of the waves" to which Kierkegaard likens the intangible image of the hero's "life history") the heavy tread of the opening music yields to a lighter measure, at first gently yearning (*dolce teneramente*) and then tripping (*delicatamente*) by way of transition to the reenacted scene of Zerlina's seduction: the transcription and variations of "Là ci darem' la mano" that form the core of the fantasia. In this approach to the duet tune we can imagine Don Giovanni as one of the new generation of Romantic vampires rising from the grave or descending from a blood-soaked, rocky eminence by moonlight to seek out his next virginal victim, whom the vampire greets with the same flattering civility as Don Giovanni does the peasant bride. Imagined this way, the gently impassioned urgings of "Là ci darem' la mano" recall the suave entreaties with which the vampire finally wears down its victim's powers of resistance.

As Liszt lingers on and embellishes the musical moment of seduction, it starts to lose its original air of pastoral innocence. The first variation of the duet unfolds *elegantemente*—florid, leisurely, and structurally complete. The second is more texturally fragmented; it skips and leaps about as if avoiding a hot surface. This time, well before the thematic model reaches the phrase of mutual accord ("Andiam, andiam mio bene"), the variation process is interrupted by a Lisztian development, the melodic petals of the original Mozartean flower scattered by gusting chromatic scales in octaves, sixths, and thirds. In the revised score of 1877 this darkly occluded developmental idiom leads into a lengthy preluding to the finale-section of the fantasia (based on "Fin ch'han dal vino"), introduced by an apt echo of the Commendatore's line "chi si pasce di cibo celeste" with which he declines to partake of Don Giovanni's proffered feast in act 2. Throughout this "prelude" to the last section, the oracular monotone of the Commendatore continues to cut through the edgy, impatient preparations for the "champagne" aria theme, whose motif is sequenced through various minor keys. As choreographed by Liszt, these "reminiscences" of Don Giovanni's characteristic moments of seduction and frantic revelry thus absorb the shadow of the libertine's dark end. The music nominally pertaining to the Commendatore and his ghostly monument is applied to a broader character portrait of Don Giovanni, tempering his aristocratic charm and his unbridled, hedonistic exuberance with new Byronic shadows. The fire, smoke, and thunder of his last moments are variously projected back onto his character and his career as a whole. The musical portrait that emerges is suffused with a newly Romantic chiaroscuro.

Liszt's musical portrait exhibits, as we could expect, affinities with other "reminiscences" of Don Juan, in various media, from E.T.A. Hoffmann to the middle of the nineteenth century and beyond. Richard Wagner carries the brooding Byronization of the Don Juan figure to an extreme in the person of his Flying Dutchman, the doom-driven spectral seducer in search of redemptive quiescence. Other versions, however, did not discard the elements of wit, cunning, and aristocratic breeding that had been essential to the character's amorous conquests form the beginning. Even Richard Strauss's *Don Juan* of 1889, after Nikolaus Lenau, recuperates some of those original ingredients, although in a language that looks ahead to the cinematic persona of Errol Flynn more than it recalls Mozart's *Don Giovanni*. The aristocratic Don Juan, a product of the feudal ancien régime, increasingly loses his social bearings in the nineteenth century, but his spirit finds a home in two newly enduring cultural tropes who maintain significant musical presences: the vampires of popular fiction and drama, on one hand, and the embodiment of restless Romantic subjectivity in Faust, on the other. At the same time, the Don Juan character and its variations respond to a continual, latent pressure of bourgeois domestication, just as Romantic music comes to depend, in a sense, on the foil of Biedermeier stolidity and normality in preserving its own transcendent identity and ambitions. This dialectic of the numinous and the domestic is prominent in a work like Wagner's *Flying Dutchman*, but it was already native to German Romantic opera from the beginning, from the time that a "vampiric" variation on the Don Juan figure emerges most distinctly. A contrary (or dialectical) impulse to domesticate, to neutralize, or to simply eradicate the Romantic and demonic elements of the Don Juan figure accompanies its metamorphoses throughout the nineteenth century.

GIOVANNI THE VAMPIRE

Considering the overwhelming impact of Lord Byron's literary oeuvre and persona on the collective cultural imagination of Europe in the 1810s and twenties, it is only to be expected that these would play a role in reshaping the image of Don Juan for a new generation. Byron himself was too conscious of his natural affinity with the figure not to treat it with a certain ironic literary detachment in his own epic-satiric poem, *Don Juan* (one of his few major works entirely unsusceptible to dramatic or operatic adaptation). In a different way, he kept his literary distance from a character more genuinely of his own creation: the vampire Lord Ruthven. Ruthven was developed by the poet's estranged physician-valet John Polidori in his tale *The Vampyre* (1819), after Byron's own fragmentary sketch deriving from the famous ghost-story "workshop" at the Villa Diodati, on Lake Geneva, in the early summer of 1816. The name Ruthven, which continued to be the favored vampire appellation until Bram Stoker's *Dracula* of 1897, did not originate with Byron's fragment, however, but as the name of the Lord Byron figure in Lady Caroline Lamb's roman à clef, *Glenarvon* (another product of the year 1816)—thus a sort of signpost pointing back to the Byronic persona as such.[2] Lord Ruthven feeds as much on the character and reputation of Polidori's master, his own progenitor, as he does on the female victims devised for him by his literary mediator, Polidori.

Thanks in part to this Byronic genealogy, the vampire became the principal Gothic-Romantic reincarnation of Don Juan for about half a century following the French Revolution. Though still vaunting a suave aristocratic finish, as he would continue to do into the era of Dracula, the Romantic vampire's campaign of seduction depends less on social standing or the droit du seigneur. As with Don Juan, the fatal fascination he exercises over his victims is both sexual and social, but it now involves an uncanny, mesmeric quality that was only latent in his ancien régime counterpart. The consequences of his predatory behavior are of course more drastic, as well as more psychologically and metaphorically fraught. And while the vampire generally dispenses with old-fashioned courtship formalities such as moonlight serenades, both music and moonlight remain for him potent vehicles of seduction.

Polidori's Byronic *Vampyre* traveled quickly to the continent and back, insinuating himself into the popular consciousness as the demonic protagonist of several successful melodramas. Charles Nodier initiated the process with a three-act *mélodrame* for the Théâtre de la Porte-St. Martin, *Le Vampire*, with music by the prolific purveyor of melodramatic scores, Alexandre Piccini, and stage sets by Ciceri, designer of carefully wrought historical panoramas, elegant *féeries*, and the like for the Paris Opéra.[3] (As if to boost the Romantic credentials of the vampire and to infuse the figure, so recently minted, with some mythographic dignity, Nodier provides a visionary prologue in which the vampire haunts the inside of Fingal's Cave off the Hebridean coast, where he contests with several Ossianic shades for power over the fate of the heroine Malvina as she lies sleeping atop a rough-hewn ancestral tomb.)[4]

Nodier's melodrama premiered on June 13, 1820, a little more than a year after Polidori's story was first published in the *New Monthly Magazine*. Less than two months later, James Robinson Planché had translated and adapted the piece for London's Lyceum Theater (currently styled the "English Opera House") as a two-act "Romantic melodrama," *The Vampire; or, The Bride of the Isles* ("Overture by Mr. Reeve," with other music by a Mr. Moss and a Mr. Hart). Planché's prefatory gloss on modern vampire mythography is suggestive with regard to the figure's kinship with Don Juan (his "supernatural powers of fascination") and the subsequent impulse to domesticate both of them (the otherwise unusual "marriage clause"):

> This Piece is founded on the various traditions concerning the vampires, which assert that there are *Spirits*, deprived of all *Hope of Futurity* by the Crimes committed in their mortal State—but that they are permitted to roam the Earth . . . with *Supernatural Powers of Fascination*—and, that they cannot be destroyed, so long as they sustain their dreadful Existence, by imbibing the blood of female victims, whom they are first compelled to marry.[5]

Not long afterward a German adaptation by Heinrich Ludwig Ritter was staged in Karlsruhe (*Der Vampyr, oder die todte Braut*, March 1, 1821), the immediate source of W.A. Wohlbrück's substantially reworked opera libretto for his brother-in-law, Heinrich Marschner (first performed Leipzig, March 28, 1828).

At the same time that these early vampire dramas were reaching the stage, *Don Giovanni* was enjoying a particular spate of attention in London. (In Germany the canonic status of the opera was well established; E. T. A. Hoffmann's famous tribute, the novella *Don Juan,* was published in the *Allgemeine musikalische Zeitung* in 1813). The opera received its London premiere to great acclaim at the King's Theater in April 1817. In the custom of the age, several of the "minor theaters" paid homage to this success with a series of burlesques. The popular young singer-actress (and later theatrical manager) Lucy Vestris personated Mozart and Da Ponte's protagonist as a trouser role in a "comic extravaganza" concocted for the Olympic Theater by William Moncrieff, *Giovanni in London; or, the Libertine Reclaimed* (December 26, 1817), in which the Latin rake is eventually reformed into a respectable English husband.[6] The piquancy of a transvestite Don Juan must have appealed, for another *Don Giovanni* parody, the "Comic, Heroic, Operatic, Tragic, Pantomimic Burletta-Spectacular-Extravaganza" by Thomas Dibdin, *Don Giovanni; or, A Spectre on Horseback,* first produced at the Surrey Theater in 1817 with a Mr. Short in the title role, was revived at the Adelphi Theater in April 1821 with Mrs. Harriet Waylett as Don Giovanni, and then again at Drury Lane in 1829 with an aptly named Miss Love in the title role. Shortly before Mrs. Waylett represented Dibdin's Don Giovanni at the Adelphi, she created the dual title role in yet another related burlesque, *Giovanni the Vampire,* by the industrious playwright, librettist, dramatic adapter, and historian of costume, James Robinson Planché (the same who had adapted Nodier's vampire melodrama for the English Opera House the previous year). Lord Ruthven's resemblance to Don Juan apparently struck a chord from the very beginning of the vampire's career.

The complete text of Planché's burlesque was not printed, only a prologue involving the "Spirit of Burlesque" in conversation with the "Genius of Imagination," along with the cast list and lyrics of the musical numbers. The affinities between Don Juan and the recently popularized vampire are articulated clearly enough, though, in the title itself (in full: *Giovanni the Vampire; or, How Shall We Get Rid of Him?*) and in Planché's prefatory note. "The Public," he submits, "will readily acknowledge the wonderful resemblance which exists between the notorious Don Giovanni, and the supernatural being aforesaid; not only, in their insatiable thirst for blood, and *penchant* for the fair sex, but in the innumerable resuscitations that both have, and still continue to experience."[7] Planché was not especially in earnest in claiming as the goal of his satire "to put this libertine entirely *hors de combat*—to clap, as it were, an extinguisher upon his burning passions," for he did not hesitate to arrange Heinrich Marschner's 1828 vampire opera for the English Opera House the year after its Leipzig première. The cultural careers of both characters had yet to run their course.

The notion, in these several *Don Giovanni* parodies, of representing the legendary seducer by an actress in male costume was presumably inspired foremost by Planché's "Spirit of Burlesque" (the term itself becoming eventually associated with cross-dressing as well as undressing). In the case of Lucy Vestris's Don, Rachel Cowgill mentions also the motive of exhibiting to better effect the actress's much admired legs (although the engraving she reproduces of Vestris in this role shows them clothed only in loose-fitting breeches). The travesty casting of Moncrieff's *Giovanni in London*, Cowgill concludes, was of a piece with the play's comic thrust, with the hero forced to exchange his philandering for marriage and domestic routine, a milder alternative to infernal damnation. Lucy Vestris's own reputation as a loose-living, unconventionally independent woman of the theater cast a further layer of irony over this treatment of the character. The female Don of the burlesques by Dibdin and Planché, Mrs. Harriet Waylett, was the object of a more poignant irony: at the very time she was playing these roles she was also the victim of a failed actor-husband who preyed on her earnings and, to that end, libeled her in anonymous pamphlets and newspaper items. While the female casting of Don Giovanni is necessarily a parodistic gesture, the dual role played by Mrs. Waylett in Planché's *Giovanni the Vampire* also points (however inadvertently) to a future development, the female vampire, beginning with Sheridan Le Fanu's Sapphic *Carmilla* in the 1870s and flourishing through the fin de siècle.[8] The "punishment" of Don Giovanni through an imposed marriage, in *Giovanni in London*, anticipates, on the other hand, the impulse from the middle to the end of the century to neutralize the Don Juan figure by means of domestication. Meanwhile, burlesque remained the more limited vehicle of woman's revenge on these predatory male characters.

The early vampire melodramas, like these *Don Giovanni* burlesques or "burlettas," contained a generous amount of comic and sentimental song and atmospheric stage music, but, as we could expect, it was the fully operatic treatment of Polidori's Byronic vampire story by Heinrich Marschner that most thoroughly developed Lord Ruthven's kinship to Mozart's Don Giovanni. Engravings of the climactic infernal descent of both operatic characters published by H. Ramberg in the 1820s (see figures 6.1 and 6.2) present them as veritable twins, in aspect as in circumstance (though this may also reflect a schematic element to the artist's technique). At any rate, it is indeed the characters' final punishment, and not least its musical realization, that most effectively focuses attention on the parallels.

FIGURE 6.1. Mozart, *Don Giovanni*, final scene (engraving by J. H. Ramberg, Leipzig, 1824).

In Marschner's opera the interrupted banquet is that celebrating Malwina's midnight wedding to the satanic Lord Ruthven, which includes its own citation of a "too familiar" song: the pastoral chorus of homage, "Blumen und Blüthen in Zephyrgeköse," with which Malwina was already serenaded at length in the finale of act 1. (This is likely the parodic target of the itinerant and generally tactless bridesmaids' chorus in Gilbert and Sullivan's *Ruddigore,*

FIGURE 6.2. Marschner, *Der Vampyr*, act 2 finale (engraving by J.H. Ramberg, Leipzig, 1831).

whose Sir Ruthven Murgatroyd sends up a long line of demonic villains from Planché and Marschner/Wohlbrück to Dion Boucicault's vampire *Phantom* of the 1850s and his animated ancestral gallery.)[9] The D-minor agitation here begins well before Ruthven's moment of damnation, starting with the hero Aubry's Elvira-like intrusion on the scene, and so Ruthven's *Höllenfahrt* is more curtailed than Don Giovanni's—just a quick, syncopated chromatic descent and half a dozen measures of crashing cadential confirmation, illuminated by a last flash of the diminished-seventh woodwind "laughter" motive that has shadowed the vampire's evil career throughout the drama. (The musical gestures of Ruthven's final damnation and the isolated wisps of musical smoke accompanying the hushed amazement at his disappearance through the "vampire trap" all recall, too, Alberich's curse-laden departure from Walhalla in the last scene of *Das Rheingold*, reminding us of what the villain of the *Ring* still owes to the melodramatic demons of the recent past.)

In addition to the seduction of an impressionable peasant girl on her wedding day and the consternation of her bumptious bridegroom (a *Don Giovanni* moment already replicated in Nodier's original vampire melodrama), Marschner was provided by his librettist Wohlbrück with a Donna Elvira figure in the character of Janthe (Polidori's Greek-oriental beauty Ianthe, repatriated to Scotland), who dotes on the dark nobleman from the outset, as well as a Donna Anna analogue in Malwina, the vampire's principal aristocratic victim present in all versions. The roles of Janthe and Malwina do not strictly follow the models in Mozart/Da Ponte, of course, and the sequence of numbers involving the seduction and murder of Janthe (Duet, no. 3–Chorus with solos, no. 4–Melodrama, no. 5) presents rather a partially inverted variant of the introductory ensemble of *Don Giovanni*. In place of the comic servant standing guard we have a spectral choral ensemble-introduction to set the scene. Following that, an A-major andantino duet (perhaps a nod to "Là ci darem' la mano") effects the seduction of Ruthven's first victim. Her cries of distress are greeted by the arrival of her father, Lord Berkeley, and henchmen, but in the ensuing duel it is Ruthven, the seducer, who succumbs. Finally, in place of the fragmentary F-minor trio during which Mozart's Commendatore expires by the light of the rising moon, Marschner's Ruthven is rather *revived* from his wounds by moonlight in the short D-minor "Melodram," the chromatic lines ascending as Aubry carries the body to the appointed hillside clearing. For this new macabre transformation of the libertine seducer, carnal fulfillment and death are proximate experiences, as in the metaphorics of Renaissance poets. After each *petite mort* he suffers (or enjoys), this Gothic Don Juan rises again with a postcoital frisson, as we hear in the strings accompanying Ruthven's revival during the Melodram. Previously, Don Juan's "eternal recurrence" had depended on revival at the hands of new authors and actors; but once his spirit inhabits the vampire's body, sexual conquest, death, and rebirth become linked in a cycle that may persist within a single dramatic or narrative frame.

VARIATIONS ON "LÀ CI DAREM' LA MANO"

The fatal turn of Don Giovanni's attempt on Donna Anna at the opera's opening and its later nocturnal consequences (the graveyard encounter with the Commendatore's monument, the banquet scene, and Don Giovanni's final reckoning) provide significant atmospheric and situational links to the character's vampiric "reincarnation" or metamorphosis in the earlier nineteenth century. The dramatic momentum of the opera, like that of dramatizations of the vampire story, depends on the ultimate frustration of the seducer's enterprises, hence of the appetite that sustains him at the expense of an endless series of victims.[10] Precisely what occurs in Donna Anna's chambers we never know for sure, although she assures Ottavio that she recognized the impostor in time. The seduction of Zerlina begins smoothly, but is elaborately foiled in the finale to act 1. Giovanni's last target, Donna Elivra's maidservant, never so much as appears within his reach. Along this trajectory of declining success, however, it is the Zerlina episode that emerges as the central, emblematic scene of seduction, and the one most recognizably emulated by Don Giovanni's Gothic kin.

Thus, it is no accident that the musical homages to *Don Giovanni* by the greatest "poetic" virtuosi of the Romantic era, Liszt and Chopin, both revolve around variations on the Giovanni/Zerlina duettino. The straightforward descriptive title of Chopin's op. 2, "Variations sur 'Là ci darem' la mano' de *Don Juan* de Mozart," also speaks to a broader pattern of Romantic *Don Giovanni* reception and interpretation, as a series of meta-variations on this signal moment of seduction. What Chopin adds to the variation process, by way of fantasy, is above all a largo introduction that meditates at great length on nothing more than the opening notes of the melody, "Là ci darem' . . . ," at most reaching out to "la man–," but no further. Chopin's introduction is a nocturnelike reverie embellishing these few notes in a lush, moon-drenched ambience of purling *fioratura,* halting chromatic runs, and sixteenth-note triplet figurations gently leaping or cascading over sustained dominant pedal tones in the strings. In short, Chopin's introduction provides, in place of the ordinary countrified festivities of Masetto and Zerlina, the perfect site of Romantic seduction.[11]

Although devoid of the demonic element characteristic of other transformations of Don Giovanni, Chopin's variations might nonetheless suggest why the Zerlina-Giovanni encounter is the crucial "moment" for the opera's Romantic reception. It is the only extended example of Don Giovanni's seductive endeavors we actually witness in the opera, even if foiled in the end, like the rest of them. The fascination of "Là ci darem' la mano," its power as an emblematic musical moment, rests also in its delicate, quintessentially Mozartian counterpoint of fresh melodic innocence with intimations of sensual experience. The contrast between Chopin's two fantasia introductions (first to the whole opus and later to its finale/coda) and the prevailing Biedermeier insouciance of the variations "composes out" a dialectic manifest in the contrast between the balanced diatonic phrases of the duet's first period and the simple chromatic appoggiaturas that portray Zerlina's eroding will power in the face of this "supernatural" charisma ("Mi fa pietà Masetto! . . . Presto non son più forte!"). Where Liszt's more multifarious fantasy emphasizes the shadowy abyss that threatens to engulf the seductive idyll of "Là ci darem'," Chopin's variations magnify the seductive charms within the Mozartean idyll itself, cultivating the sentimental seeds latent in that naive pastoral garden.

The variations wrought by Marschner's *Vampyr* on the subject of the Zerlina/Giovanni duettino, as a musical model and as a situation, involve similar negotiations of the naive and sentimental. Ruthven's duet with his first victim, Janthe (no. 3: Andantino, A major, 6/8) seems to take "Là ci darem' la mano" as a point of departure, as suggested before, even if her character is rather an analogue to Elvira. In the initial andantino section, Janthe voices remorse over deceiving her parents and the bridegroom they have chosen for her. Ruthven urges his suit in a contrasting phrase, whose accompaniment portrays his "beating heart." As in Mozart's duet, this leads to a second, more animated section in which the girl capitulates to the false promises of the seducer and joins with him in misguided harmony. In Marschner this second section includes its own harmonic-developmental contrast, where the hint of a tango rhythm in the bass (Janthe recalls how she first recoiled at Ruthven's advances: "Als du dich zuerst mir nahtest bebte ich entsetzt zurück") is obviously an unintended irony. More villainous and less suave than Giovanni, Ruthven expresses his satisfaction in gloating asides before dragging Janthe off to a nearby cave to complete the fatal seduction. The more complex formal design of the duet, the increased role of harmonic contrast and development, and its integration with the following scene (involving the offstage murder) contribute to a consciously modern, Romantic, or "sentimental" musical conception, in contrast to the exquisitely studied naïveté, as it were, of "Là ci darem' la mano."

Emmy, the true Zerlina analogue in the opera, is "sentimentalized" in several senses: as a character as well as in the dramaturgical and musical expansion of her role. Malwina, the Donna Anna figure, remains the crucial victim in a strict dramaturgical sense, as in most versions of the Polidori prototype, since it is Ruthven's interference in her liaison with Aubry (Ottavio) that precipitates his downfall. (Aubry mistakes Ruthven for a friend and benefactor at first, as Ottavio does Don Giovanni.) Yet, just as Zerlina becomes the more potent emblem of Don Giovanni's libertine predations, it is the peasant bride Emmy, the second in the vampire's ritual triad of victims, who emerges as structurally and psychologically central in *Der Vampyr*. Emmy's role derives not from Polidori but from the 1820 Parisian melodrama of Nodier (et al.) where—as "Lovette," the daughter of the manager of *château* Marsden—she is affianced to Edgar, the valet of "Sir Aubrey."[12] The song with which Nodier's old Ossianic bard "Oscar" tries to warn Lovette about the danger of vampires ("O jeune vierge de Staffa . . . gardez-vous, jeune fiancée, de l'amour qui donne la mort") is given in the opera to Emmy herself, who entertains her wedding guests with a vampire ballad ("Sieh' Mutter dort den bleichen Mann") at the very moment she is about to become a victim herself. In Planché's adaptation of Nodier the peasant bride is called Effie; she also unwittingly draws the vampire nigh with a song, a kind of Scottish barcarolle to the tune of "Ye Banks and Braes" followed by another folk tune addressed to her absent fiancé ("There's nae luck about the house . . . when Robert's far awa'"). Marschner's Emmy similarly sings of her forlorn state apart from her bridegroom ("Dort an jenem Felsenhang / Lauschte ich den Weg entlang, / Georg zu erspähen"), before instructing her guests about the ways of vampires. In all of these cases song casts a melancholy veil over the peasant bride (in contrast to Mozart's Zerlina), anticipating her doom and warning the audience of the danger that approaches.

Emmy's brief lied, "Dort am jenem Felsenhang," and her longer strophic vampire *Romanze* are at once naive and sentimental gestures. Their melodic lines are simple and devoid of ornament, and their range small (the lied spanning no more than on octave). Both emulate a declamatory, syllabic style of folk song, rejecting operatic elaboration. The irregular grouping of ¾ and 2⁄4 measures in the lied "naively" mirrors the irregular alternation of four- and three-stress lines, but with a self-consciously hesitant, "sentimental" result. Similarly, the *Romanze* invokes a traditional mode of balladic recitation but almost suggests the use of musical setting as a means of artificial ethnographic "transcription" of a spoken delivery, reproducing rhetorical inflections of recitation in details such as sudden breaks in the melodic line ("weich schnell von ihm zurück!") or the gradual rise by half-step of the "reciting tone" toward the end of each solo verse. (This generates a chromatic harmonic progression that would have no place in conventional folk song.) The element of sympathetic identification in Emmy's account of the "pale stranger" and the mesmerizing effect he exerts locate the singer rather closer to Wagner's Senta (whose ballad has traditionally been identified with Emmy's *Romanze*) than to Mozart's Zerlina. Yet where Senta yearns for the advent of her mysterious phantom, Emmy is only passing the time, waiting for her delinquent fiancé. Despite a propensity to Romantic melancholy, she is still a regular village maid.

Emmy's songs are atmospheric preliminaries, however, to Marschner's amplification of the "Là ci darem' la mano" moment, which is spread across two numbers: an extended trio (no. 13), with the outraged bridegroom Georg looking on from the wings, and an A-minor/-major duet (no. 16), in which Ruthven carries out the second seduction of the stipulated three. The trio, "Ihr wollt mich nur beschämen," is an ambitious, flexibly constructed ensemble that anticipates the famous quartet from Verdi's *Rigoletto* in elements of situation and musical design. The triplet motion that initially conveys Ruthven's importunate desires subsequently infiltrates the reaction of the concealed, helpless spectator Georg, as it does Emmy's own responses, at first demure in duple eighth notes and quarters, but then rhythmically flustered as Ruthven manages to extract a kiss.

The faltering of Zerlina's resolve, so economically drawn by Mozart, is rendered more gradually in Emmy's case, but also to good effect. When she first resists the petition for a kiss, she manages to reprise her diffident principal phrase ("Ihr wollt mich nur beschämen, so eitel bin ich nicht") back in the tonic, but her voice grows faint (*pianissimo*), and the previously solid accompaniment melts into Ruthven's gently palpitating triplets (example 6.1a). When some twenty measures later Ruthven achieves the kiss, these "seductive" triplet rhythms totter to a halt, echoed in fluttering diminution by the woodwinds, until Ruthven turns aside to proclaim his triumph to the descending D-minor signature of his true demonic nature (example 6.1b).

Presently Georg emerges from the shadows. As Georg argues with Emmy over the intentions of the new, unduly solicitous lord of the manor, Marschner tosses in a Mozartean turn of phrase that echoes, deliberately or not, appropriate moments of *Don Giovanni*: Masetto's angry "Ho capito, Signor, sì!" and the collective ire directed at Giovanni in the stretta of the act 1 finale (example 6.2a, example 6.2b, example 6.2c) The ensemble concludes (Allegro) with Ruthven gloating over his success, Georg seized by a cold sweat and premonitions of disaster, and Emmy vacillating between "fear and love" ("My mind misgives and yet rejoices; some sweet, mysterious impulse draws me to the stranger"). When Ruthven extracts the kiss, after a phase of erotic deferral,

Marschner, *Der Vampyr*: Trio, Act 2, "Ihr wollt mich nur beschämen"

EXAMPLE 6.1a. Marschner, *Der Vampyr*: Trio, act 2, "Ihr wollt mich nur beschämen."

Marschner, *Der Vampyr*: Trio, Act 2, "Ihr wollt mich nur beschämen"

EXAMPLE 6.1b. Marschner, *Der Vampyr*: Trio, act 2, "Ihr wollt mich nur beschämen."

Marschner, *Der Vampyr*: Trio, Act 2

EXAMPLE 6.2a. Marschner, *Der Vampyr*: Trio, act 2.

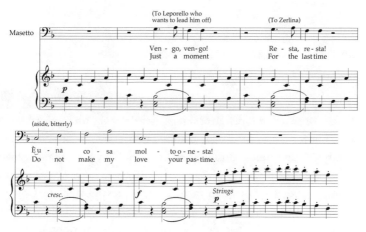

Mozart, *Don Giovanni*: Aria, Act 1, "Ho capito, signor, sì!"

EXAMPLE 6.2b. Mozart, *Don Giovanni*: Aria, act 1, "Ho capito, signor, sì!"

Mozart, *Don Giovanni*: Finale, Act 1

EXAMPLE 6.2c. Mozart, *Don Giovanni*: Finale, act 1.

his sudden shift to a demonic musical register briefly gestures toward the consequences; but for the most part no distinction is drawn in this ensemble between Ruthven's attentions to Emmy and those a Don Juan character would
show to any peasant bride on his list. From Byron to early Wagner, interest
in the vampire seemed to remain focused on his resemblance to Don Juan,
the vampire's "Supernatural Powers of Fascination" (in the words of Planché's
gloss on the figure) rather than on any strictly ghoulish attributes.

Only afterward, between the trio and the completion of Emmy's seduction
in the duet, no. 16 ("Leise dort zu jenem Laube"), does Ruthven give full vent
to his ghoulish condition, in his "Grosse Szene" with Aubry (no. 14). Here,
he also conveys the pitiable, unwilling nature of his condition in a way wholly
at odds with Don Juan's unwavering belief in the "principle" he represents.
These revelations cast a shadow on the subsequent duet. Like Don Giovanni,
Ruthven urges the girl to follow him to a private spot. But the innocence

EXAMPLE 6.3. Marschner, *Der Vampyr:* Duet, act 2, "Leise dort zur fernen Laube."

of "Là ci darem' la mano" is exchanged for a quiet note of agitation, the gently pulsating Andantino triplets of the earlier trio, and even a faint echo of Schubert's uncanny Erlkönig (example 6.3). Zerlina's fleeting hesitations are multiplied, modulated, and sequenced in Emmy's part, as are Giovanni's importunate urgings in Ruthven's. When Emmy finally yields ("Wohl, es sei, ich folge dir!") it is with more a sigh of resignation than the pleasurable cadential yielding of Zerlina's "Andiam'!" The faster second section, expressing the couple's newfound unity of purpose, is actually a variant, initially *maggiore*, of the softly agitated first section, the pulsing triplets now *un poco più mosso*. As they depart, with no Donna Elvira to stop them, the music sinks back to the quiet A-minor agitation of the beginning. The matrimonial idyll proffered by the libertine is nowhere in evidence now. The young woman is lead on to destruction only by the anxious, inchoate desire stirred up in her by those "Supernatural Powers of Fascination" she cannot understand.

I have so far focused on the Marschner/Wohlbrück *Vampyr* because its synthesis of the Don Juan figure with the earlier Byronic vampire is most explicit here, and the variations or paraphrases it executes on Don Giovanni's (attempted) seduction of Zerlina confirm the centrality of this "moment" in the Romantic consciousness of Mozart's opera, especially as juxtaposed to the demonic element of the avenging statue and Giovanni's end. As in *Don Giovanni*, the simple peasant girl or bride continues to provide a foil to more socially exalted victims, probably because she most persuasively combines traits of purity, innocence, helplessness, but also inner strength and indestructible moral fiber—traits that generate a dynamic counterpoint to the pleasure-seeking, reckless, godless, power-abusing, decadent, amoral seducer. Music remains a vessel of pleasure and eros (as Kierkegaard argues) and an agent of seduction, but in a new Romantic turn it is now just as crucially allied with divine and redemptive powers, moral purgation and spiritual elevation.

The period of cultural ferment in Paris in the years around 1830, remarkably fertile in the operatic field, seems to have been a moment of particular resonance for *Don Giovanni*, to mention just one such moment between the Byronic decade of the 1820s and the moment of Liszt, Kierkegaard, and Wagner's *Flying Dutchman* at the beginning of the 1840s.[13] The title figures of Meyerbeer's *Robert le diable* (1831), Hérold's *Zampa* (1831), and Auber's *Fra diavolo* (1830)—immensely popular works throughout the nineteenth century—each embody traits of the Don Juan figure as demon, outlaw, and seducer, whether comic, earnest, or flamboyantly melodramatic.[14] Unlike Marschner's Ruthven and his baritonal Byronic brethren in Germany up to Wagner's Dutchman, these French roles are tenors (Zampa's part traversing both baritone and tenor territory), perhaps better suited to conveying the comic and ironic elements present in all of them—even Meyerbeer's Robert, whose Mephistophelian companion, Bertram (originally a baritone, revised for bass Nicolas Levasseur), takes over the expression of darker, more explicitly diabolical accents.

Robert is the bad seed of a nameless demonic father who seduced a fair and chaste princess of Normandy. Both he and Hérold's dashing Byronic corsair, Zampa, find themselves challenged by a saintly woman named Alice. Robert's Alice is a demure peasant maiden raised from infancy with him as his *soeur-de-lait* and thereby placed beyond the pale of his reckless, pleasure-seeking impulses. (The princess Isabelle is the object of his erotic affections, but one whose devotion, along with Alice's encouragement, eventually reforms Robert.)

Zampa's Alice is a high-born beauty, Alice Manfredi, seduced and abandoned by Zampa a dozen years earlier, before he embarked on his career of piracy. Dead from grief or shame, this Alice returns as a marble effigy of her former self, animated by a mission of righteous vengeance—thus a synthesis of Donna Anna and the Commendatore. When the *main glacée* of Alice's statue seizes Zampa at the opera's climax, dragging him down through flames and a chromatic chordal shower, she rescues the heroine, Camille, from his devouring embrace. Regendering the avenging monument as a female grants a kind of symbolic agency to the many victims of Don Juan's seductions, otherwise denied them in most versions of his career.

Scribe and Auber's Fra Diavolo is a bandit and con man who, if we read him as a Don Juan, robs the figure of his dignity and integrity. Charming and seductive, his nobility is a mere sham (his incognito as the "Marquis of San Marco"). His victims include the conventional pairing of noble and peasant, the English traveler Lady Pamela and the innkeeper's daughter by the name of Zerline, but Diavolo is only interested in Pamela's diamonds and Zerline's hard-won dowry. He manages to turn the head of the English lady by engaging her in a pleasant barcarolle *à deux*, but Zerline, as if in defiance of her Morzartian namesake, evinces no interest in the mysterious marquis or his songs. Worse, perhaps, than infernal damnation is this Don Juan's loss of those "Supernatural Powers of Fascination," to be exposed as a mere poseur, convicted as an ordinary felon, and thrust without ceremony or special effects into a provincial jail.

DON JUAN UND FAUST

Of those three French Romantic cousins to Don Juan, Robert "the devil" is the only one to repent his ways and to achieve redemption, thanks to the faith of a simple, honest girl and a posthumous letter from his mother denouncing the wiles of his diabolical father. The triangle of Robert-Bertram-Alice unabashedly replicates that of Faust-Mephistopheles-Gretchen, and thereby reminds us of another important line among Don Juan's Romantic descendents.[15] As Kierkegaard put it, Faust "reproduces" Don Juan; "Don Juan . . . is the expression [of] the daemonic determined by the sensuous; Faust its expression as the intellectual or spiritual."[16] Naturally, the line is a principally German one, investing the figure with Romantic yearnings, a poetic appreciation of nature, and a previously unknown penchant for moral reflection. If Don Juan was potentially rendered impotent by burlesque, travesty, and the good sense of a comic heroine at the hands of the English and French, an equal threat to his identity was posed by German metaphysics. The late Romantic poet Nikolaus Lenau, best known for his own large verse drama on the Faust theme, illustrates this point in his shorter *Don Juan* ("dramatic scenes," 1844; published 1851), where a reflective monologue on the unappeasable nature of desire marks the beginning of the character's decline. He thinks (or thinks too much) and ceases to be.[17]

The potential affinity of Don Juan and Faust for the Romantic sensibility is most overtly signaled by the title of a tragedy in four acts, *Don Juan und Faust*, by Christian Dietrich Grabbe, a member of the "Young German" generation.[18] Symptomatic of the encounter between the two mythic figures is the shift of genre from comedy to tragedy: Faust's earnestness trumps, and ultimately extinguishes, Don Juan's hedonistic joie de vivre. Grabbe's Don Juan unwittingly articulates a sense of this threat to his identity near the beginning of the drama, when he tries to divert suspicion from himself to another figure with designs on Donna Anna. "Know ye not that a great *magus* has come from northern Germany's frozen wastes to Rome, spreading here his pestilential air? In a black cloak, with pallid face, as if the sun had never shone upon it, he creeps about the Aventino."[19] Don Juan paints Faust as a vampire from the "Gothic" North, shadowing his steps and pursuing his women. The real threat posed by this Faustian vampire is, paradoxically, to Don Juan himself. It is not women's blood but Don Juan's own élan vital after which Faust thirsts.

In a scenario that ultimately comes across as more farcical than tragic, Grabbe pits Faust and his Mephistophelian cicerone (an unnamed black knight) against Don Juan and Leporello in a contest to win Donna Anna away from her betrothed, Don Ottavio (here, Oktavio). Faust spirits Anna away to a magical palace conjured high on the slopes of Mont Blanc. At the end of act 2 Anna's father, Don Gusman (the Spanish envoy to Rome) teams up with Don Juan, oddly enough, in order to reclaim his abducted child, just moments after Don Juan has killed Oktavio in a duel. No sooner is the curtain up on act 3 than Don Juan is dueling with the "Gouverneur," Don Gusman, whom he kills and who swears the usual vengeance from beyond the grave. This new, nature-loving Don Juan savors the trek up Mont Blanc (while Leporello complains) and discovers Faust and Donna Anna arguing over Protestant versus Catholic doctrines. Don Juan and Faust follow this with a proto-Shavian argument over ideals of the *menschlich* versus the *übermenschlich*. Don Juan taunts Faust's failure with women, for all his *übermenschlich* accomplishments in philosophy and science; Faust in turn magically transports Don Juan and Leporello back to the Roman cemetery containing the remains of Don Gusman and his avenging monument. In a short subterranean interlude reminiscent of scenes from Louis Spohr's Romantic opera *Der Berggeist* and Marschner's *Hans Heiling* (and composed in a similar vein by Lortzing), Faust consorts with mining gnomes and solicits from them a mysterious, fatal brew of tears shed by his first wife, Amalia, whom he murdered by a spell cast in his passion for Donna Anna. (Despite his Protestant theology he seems not to have considered divorce.) Arguing afterward with the intractable Donna Anna, he likewise fells her, accidentally, with an angry word uttered too rashly. The drama concludes with Grabbe's rewriting of the banquet scene, presided over by the Mephistophelian "knight." With only an hour left on his infernal contract, Faust appears to inform Don Juan of Anna's demise. Faust is dispatched to the infernal abyss by the "knight," and soon the statue of the Gouverneur arrives, with the usual consequences: Don Juan promptly joins his erstwhile rival, Faust, in hell.

In this concluding scene of Grabbe's tragedy, Don Juan greets the news of Anna's death dispassionately but agrees to a duel with Faust as a matter of principle. We might say that he agrees also to a duel "of" principles, for, as in nearly all Romantic versions of the material, Don Juan becomes the embodiment of an egoistic, life-affirming principle in contest with apparently irreconcilable religious and ethical ones. The morality play toward which the subject always tended is transformed into Romantic allegory, in the manner of Goethe or Byron, as Don Juan struggles to maintain his "naive" instinctive impulses from the philosophical incursions of a Faust or Manfred. The Faust character, in turn, tries to appropriate from Don Juan those attributes he has bargained for with the devil: youth, energy, and the "Supernatural Powers of Fascination" that had also served the Romantic vampire. In this, however, Faust is true to his origins, the protagonist of the late sixteenth-century *Faustbuch*, who is rather more concerned with achieving a life of Don Juan-like debauchery than experience and wisdom.

The first operatic Faust, Louis Spohr's of 1816 (revised 1818 and 1852, text by Josef Carl Bernard), largely bypasses Goethe in favor a slightly earlier novel/drama hybrid by the Sturm und Drang writer Friedrich Maximilian Klinger (*Fausts Leben, Thaten und Höllenfahrt*, 1791) and the Viennese traditions of magic play and didactic spectacle. Even closer in the background is *Don Giovanni*. Klinger's Faust was a Diogenes-like seeker after virtue but at the same time a reckless seducer, ever subject to the whims of his own passions. Spohr's Faust likewise paves his path to hell with good intentions, along with the bodies of lovers and rivals. Like Don Giovanni, this Faust divides his erotic attentions between a simple, honest peasant girl (Röschen) and a high-born beauty (Kunigunde). Here too, the peasant girl is more susceptible to his charms and wiles than the noblewoman. At the opera's outset Faust, another conflicted baritone, is already intent on rejecting the cloying surfeit of pleasures his bargain has won him (duet, "In Sinnenlust so sinnlos leben"), and on turning his ill-gotten powers toward the benefit of others. But by the end of the first act the Don Juan impulse overcomes his virtuous resolutions. [20]

With the help of Bernard's libretto, Spohr contrives to rewrite Don Giovanni's infernal descent in *both* his act-finales, with Faust at first on the side of virtue but eventually consigned to the devil. The act 1 finale finds him seconding the attempts of a Count Hugo to rescue his bride, the fair

Kunigunde, from the clutches of the rapacious melodramatic villain Gulf. Divine thunderbolts and Mephisto's infernal connections conspire to plunge Gulf into a fiery abyss, where he is welcomed by a chorus of demons à la *Don Giovanni*. (Spohr does not even scruple to reproduce Mozart's D-minor to major tonal trajectory, with similar gestures of mounting distress and hellish triumph in the accompaniment.) Hell's flames seem to ignite Faust's baser instincts: in the act of rescuing Hugo's finacée, Kunigunde, from Gulf he is seized with a passion for her and pursues her to the brink of his own perdition in the following act. Like Giovanni and Ruthven, this Faust cannot resist the opportunity of spoiling a wedding. Thus, as the Donna Anna and Don Ottavio characters (Hugo and Kunigunde) are celebrating their marriage, Faust slips Kunigunde a love potion. While engaged with Faust in a dignified polonaise, she begins to submit. Meanwhile Röschen, the Zerlina/Gretchen figure (disguised in male attire) looks on distraught, Gilda-like, at the libertine's infidelity. As with Gilda or Gretchen, her devotion proves her undoing. Kunigunde, on the other hand, recovers her senses and plots revenge. In the end Faust's belated penitence does not save him from the dramaturgical imperative of the subterranean chorus.[21] Despite his fundamentally Mozartean musical temperament, Spohr's "bookend" infernal finales to acts 1 and 2 pay homage to a Romantic conviction that "red fire" and damnation should have the final word, and that catharsis needs no *lieto fine*.

Or does it? However satisfying Don Giovanni's final moments seemed to the Romantic temperament, and however obsolete the subsequent ensemble tidying up the consequences in piecemeal fashion, something of the impulse of *Don Giovanni*'s classically moralizing conclusion lived on. If tragedy issues in catharsis and comedy in marriage, then Mozart and Da Ponte's *dramma giocoso* called for a synthesis: a matrimonial happy end sprung from the ashes of the libertine's damnation. Spohr's somewhat tepid duplications of the infernal descent were perhaps only a first, incomplete stage in the Romantic response to the opera's ending. The more genuinely Romantic response would appreciate the potential for merging *both* endings in a broader synthesis: Don Giovanni's punishment and the matrimonial rewards of the virtuous. For Don Juan *marriage* would be the punishment to fit the crime.

THE MARRIAGE OF HEAVEN AND HELL

While Zerlina and Masetto head home to dinner at the end of *Don Giovanni*, the marriage between Don Ottavio and Donna Anna is left problematically deferred: Donna Anna wants a year of solitude to recover from recent events, perhaps (who knows?) to get over some conflicted feelings toward her father's murderer. The suspicion lingers that divine vengeance has not restored her peace of mind, that she will never be quite content with Don Ottavio. At the end of the performance described in E. T. A. Hoffmann's *Don Juan* Donna Anna appears "wholly transformed," her face "pale as death," her eyes blank, and her voice "trembling and uneven." Donna Anna is, in Hoffmann's eyes, the only character to grasp Don Juan's significance as a Romantic "principle." Her conventional obligation to destroy him, as her would-be seducer and her father's killer, conflicts with another impulse, to understand and to "redeem" him. "What if," muses Hoffmann, "Donna Anna were appointed by heaven to reveal to Don Juan through [her] love, love that Satan's art had heretofore defiled for him, his latent divine nature, and to rescue him from the desperation of his pointless strivings?"[22] Hoffmann's nameless narrator, a composer, hears in the score the exact relation of these "two conflicting natures," Don Giovanni and Donna Anna.[23] Had he written the opera, perhaps this Hoffmannesque composer would have realized the Romantic redemption of Don Giovanni that he briefly hypothesizes. Instead, following Mozart and Da Ponte, he sees Anna become a victim of Don Giovanni—not so much of Don Giovanni the seducer and murderer as of a "principle" that ignites and consumes her, in conflict with her obligations to a murdered father and a pallid, ineffectually virtuous fiancé. Hoffmann's Anna has glimpsed in her antagonist something of the lessons preached by the Devil in Blake's *Marriage of Heaven and Hell:* the inseparability of body ("energy") and soul ("reason"), that "Energy is eternal delight," and that desire, if restrained, becomes passive, "till it is only the shadow of desire." Driven to destroy Don Giovanni, she is herself destroyed by him (Hoffmann imagines), while a Romantic allegory would have united them—though perhaps with the same result.

The "conflict of principles" Hoffmann's musical narrator heard in the roles of Don Giovanni and Donna Anna resounds through the various operas mentioned in the foregoing pages, but is crystallized most clearly in Wagner's *Flying Dutchman*, which also provides the redemption imagined but left unrealized in Hoffmann's story. Wagner's overture immediately establishes the opera's genealogy in this regard: a demonically agitated main subject (D minor) contrasts with a beatific second subject (relative major) that emerges as a beacon of virtue. The restless, active "male" principle engages with the lyrical, resolute "female" principle, which proves the active one in the end, as it lights the way to triumphant resolution. Weber's *Freischütz* overture provides the prototype, followed by Marschner's *Vampyr* and *Hans Heiling* overtures (among others).[24] The Mozartean musical traces in Spohr's and Marschner's operas are essentially absent from Wagner's *Dutchman,* despite the musical genealogy. On a broader dramaturgical (and musical) level, however, *The Flying Dutchman* plausibly represents an end point of early Romantic responses to *Don Giovanni* and their revisions of the Don Juan figure, merging the predatory instincts of the vampire with the metaphysical angst and strivings of Faust.

Wagner's Dutchman embodies the character the Romantics imagined lurking beneath the gallant, old-style aristocratic exterior of Don Juan. He resembles Don Juan in the afterlife, as reemerging from the purgatorial fires in Liszt's fantasy, no longer the flippant adventurer but a newly Romantic subject burning with existential desire and not afraid to face his final moral reckoning. Like Don Juan, he exerts a mesmerizing fascination on his chosen victim (witness the beginning of his long scene with Senta in act 2), though it partakes more of the vampire's basilisk gaze than of the suave lyric charm of the original Don. The Dutchman demands absolute fidelity from his chosen women, a paradoxical antidote to his own and Don Juan's epic promiscuity. Failing the test, those women (Senta's hapless predecessors) are condemned, like the victims of vampiric seduction, to become like himself. (Hoffmann glimpsed something of this process incipient in the case of his Donna Anna.) The Dutchman seduces not through gallantry and serenades, but by exposing his victim to that unalloyed intensity of longing and desire that is his essential nature and that he expresses in musical form. The roiling D-minor music of Giovanni's damnation flows readily into that of the Dutchman's endless voyaging in Wagner's overture.

Despite its aesthetic appreciation of Don Giovanni's divine punishment, as realized by Mozart, the nineteenth century became more interested in saving than in condemning him. But "saving" Don Juan meant neutralizing or stabilizing his anarchistic, antisocial drives; in short, getting him married. Hence George Bernard Shaw's paradoxical inversion of the traditional scenario, with Donna Anna (Ann Whitefield, the "everywoman" and true Life Force) pursuing Don Juan (Jack Tanner) relentlessly, if obliquely, throughout the four long acts of *Man and Superman* (1903). Wagner's *Flying Dutchman* already points in this direction, without Shaw's ironic perspective, even though Heinrich Heine had made such a perspective readily available in his comic vignette on the Flying Dutchman story that first drew Wagner's attention to it. The Dutchman's perpetual cycle of courtship is motivated not by the desire for absolute pleasure but for an idealized state of domestic tranquillity.

This is what he hears in the siren refrain of Senta's ballad ("Doch kann dem bleichen Manne Erlösung einstens noch werden"), the promise she intends it to bear. When the theme of this essentially static refrain briefly "catches fire" in the excited coda to the ballad ("Ich sei's, die dich durch ihre Treu' erlöse!"), it is as if Senta's calm, domestic "principle" has been momentarily ignited by the rest-less passion she senses in the Dutchman, approaching her threshold even as she sings. Senta's quiet refrain is quickly consumed and extinguished by this sud-den passion. By the same token, the Dutchman understands that Wagnerian redemption means extinction, surcease. Arriving as the agent of a Romanticiced "Don Juan principle," voracious and volatile, his goal is only to extinguish this force, to end his cyclical vampiric half-life and to resolve his own musical iden-tity in the stasis of Senta's refrain as foreordained in the overture.

In transforming Don Juan into a demonic figure of unstable longing and desire, the Romantics demanded his marriage to a complementary angelic antithesis, following the dialectical imperative of the age. Or, to look at it another way, the Romantic principle that roamed free at the beginning of the century was to be subjected to a restraining Biedermeier or Victorian impulse as the century and its Romantic culture matured. Daland, the quintessential bourgeois spirit, does not perhaps misjudge the bond between the Dutch-man and his daughter so much as generally supposed. The music in which they commune in act 2 is sometimes shot through with transcendent fire, but much of it also speaks the melodic language of Daland. The Dutchman appears the demon suitor, as the Romantics made of Don Juan. But, unlike Don Juan, the Dutchman embraces monogamy and the image of domestic virtue with zeal.

Toward the end of the century Richard Strauss and George Bernard Shaw confirm the destiny of the Romantic-era Don Juan, rescued from his original fire-and-brimstone fate to face a more "philosophical" end: entropy, stasis, or domestication as the necessary antithesis to the unbridled dynamism of the Don Juan principle. In Shaw's *Man and Superman* this destiny is figured as the inexorable threat of marriage to Donna Anna. At the start of Strauss's 1889 tone poem, *Don Juan*, the musical protagonist is portrayed as a sort of Nietzschean "superman" of boundless energy and questing spirit (far more so than Shaw's phlegmatic Tanner). The entropy of his ending is however all the darker; following Nikolaus Lenau, Strauss represents a Don Juan literally "burnt out" by the force of his own passionate energies, facing not simply the stasis of domestication but a metaphysical void. Lenau's vision of Don Juan's end represents a characteristically Biedermeier or *Vormärz* synthesis of sentimentality and *weltschmerzig* resignation, which Dieter Borchmeyer identifies also with the ethos of Wagner's *Flying Dutchman*.[25] At the core of Strauss's tone poem is a lengthy episode in G major, grounded in tranquil *divisi* string writing and led by a long, wistful melody in the oboe. Lacking any clear programmatic reference, this episode expresses nonetheless that post-erotic domestic tranquillity, touched with melancholy resignation, toward which the Romantic Don Juan is inexorably drawn.[26] The musical dialogue of "principles" in Strauss's tone poem absorbs this antithesis of the original Don Juan character or principle through an "acceptance of *bürgerlich* stasis and conformity," in James Hepokoski's analysis, that signifies "not the destruction of the physical individual," despite the nihilistic gesture of the tone poem's conclusion, but the rejection of Don Juan's traditional male libertine persona for that of "middle-class heroic domesticity" and a stabilizing of the erotic impulse.[27]

The initial Romantic fascination with Don Giovanni's Gothic potential, the impulse to resurrect him as a phantom or a vampire, gradually yields to impulses both sentimental and philosophical. The vampiric transformation of the character demanded, in the end, not another consignment to the flames of hell but a more Wagnerian conclusion: not damnation but redemption. The process of cultural, philosophical, and musical reckoning to which the nineteenth century subjected the figure at first demonized him and then sanctified him, with the net result that his lurking, Gothic shadow is finally dissipated altogether. (Well, perhaps not altogether: he was to be briefly resurrected in a 1914 *dramma lirico* by Ettore Moschino and Franco Alfano aptly entitled *L'ombra di Don Giovanni*, in which he titillated a late-decadent generation by carrying on with a dark femme fatale at the foot of an altar, to judge by the Ricordi poster designed by Giuseppe Palanti; figure 6.3.) The revenant who had been continually recalled from the flames of hell since the beginning of the century is finally dispatched to heaven or at least to a quiescent Schopenhauerian nirvana. Quiescence, not hellfire torment, is the ultimate resolution of the Don Juan character, "resting in peace" his only definitive end. The stated aim of Planché's 1821 burlesque *Giovanni the Vampire*, "to put this libertine entirely *hors de combat*—to clap, as it were, an extinguisher upon his burning passions," is realized at last: cynically, but also philosophically, between Lenau and Shaw, and above all musically, between Wagner and Richard Strauss. All these post-Romantic versions of Don Juan manage to skirt damnation, but feeling a sense of cultural "lateness," perhaps, they voluntarily, even cheerfully, embrace their extinction.

FIGURE 6.3. Ricordi poster by Giuseppe Palanti for Franco Alfano's *L'ombra di Don Giovanni* (1914).

NOTES

1. For a recent survey of nineteenth-century performance and reception of *Don Giovanni* see Mark Everist, "Speaking with the Supernatural: E. T. A. Hoffmann, George Bernard Shaw, and *Die Oper aller Opern,*" in *Mozart-Jahrbuch 2002* (Kassel, 2002), 115–134; and the bibliography at http://www.soton.ac.uk/~me/pmr/prm.html.

2. Lamb's Scottish nobleman Ruthven Glenarvon projects Byron as "a heartless libertine . . . who, "after a vile career of preying on numerous women, is carried off by supernatural forces à la Don Giovanni." Roxana Stuart, *Stage Blood: Vampires of the Nineteenth-Century Stage* (Bowling Green, 1994), 37. Stuart's monograph provides an abundance of information on dramatizations of the vampire theme from the time of Byron and Polidori up to Bram Stoker.

3. The published text of this first vampire drama (Paris, 1820) also lists Pierre François Adolphe Carmouche and Achille de Jouffrey as collaborators, though Nodier seems to be the principal author.

4. Nodier's *mélodrame* is reprinted in Florent Montaclair, *Le Vampire dans la literature et au théâtre: Du mythe oriental au motif romantique* (Besançon, 1998),117–149, along with the texts of vampire dramas by Eugène Scribe (1820) and Alexandre Dumas (1851). Spelling of the names of characters drawn from Polidori varies between adaptations and is given here as it appears in individual sources cited.

5. The text of Planché's melodrama is reprinted in *Plays by James Robinson Planché*, ed. Donald Roy (Cambridge, 1986), 45–68. The prefatory note is cited by Stuart, *Stage Blood*, 75.

6. Rachel Cowgill investigates this burlesque and its surprising play on the gender identity of the legendary seducer in her essay "Re-gendering the Libertine; or, The Taming of the Rake: Lucy Vestris as Don Giovanni on the Early Nineteenth-Century London Stage," *Cambridge Opera Journal* 10 (1998): 45–66.

7. Quoted from Stuart, *Stage Blood*, 99.

8. On the female vampire and its frequent lesbian overtones in the later nineteenth century, see Nina Auerbach, *Our Vampires, Ourselves* (Chicago and London, 1994), 38–60. Auerbach notes a "domesticating" impulse toward the vampire figure (as I propose becomes applied to Don Juan in the nineteenth century) specifically in theatrical adaptations (e.g., chapter 1, 18–19, 21), but in contrast to the theme of Romantic male friendship as a vehicle of coercion, which she identifies as a more central motif.

9. Roxana Stuart clarifies the latter point of reference, which goes back to a vampire drama by Alexandre Dumas *père* staged at the Théâtre Ambigu-Comique in Paris in 1851, adapted by Boucicault first in 1852 (with the ghostly ancestral gallery) and revised (but without speaking portraits) in 1856. See *Stage Blood*, chapters 7 and 8.

10. Compare Don Giovanni's assertion to Leporello regarding women as his essential "nourishment": "Sai ch'elle per me son necessarie più del pan ch'io mangio, più dell'aria che spiro" ("You know they are more necessary to me than the bread I eat or the air I breathe"; act 2, scene 1).

11. The atmosphere of the introduction is recaptured in a later introductory passage, the fantasialike adagio in B-flat minor that leads, indolently, to the *alla polacca* finale/coda of variation 5. Otherwise the variations eschew romance for decorative Biedermeier ramblings.

12. Malwina's brother, as in Polidori, rather than her fiancé, as in Marschner/Wohlbrück. Wohlbrück confusingly makes "Edgar " the first name of his Aubry, while the peasant bridegroom (the Masetto figure) becomes "Georg."

13. Pushkin's homage to Mozart and Da Ponte, *The Stone Guest* (later composed by Darghomizhky as an experiment in operatic "realism") also originated in 1830, two years after the Russian premiere of *Don Giovanni*. See Boris Gasparov's essay in this volume.

14. The Meyerbeer grand opera and Auber opéra comique both have texts by Eugène Scribe; the text of Hérold's opera is a peculiar farrago of currently popular genres and motifs by an author of boulevard melodramas, A.-H.-J. Duveyrier, writing under the pseudonym Mélesville.

15. As discussed at more length in this volume by Ernst Osterkamp. Comparing *Les Huguenots* and *St. Paul*, Robert Schumann amusingly figures Meyerbeer as the Bertram (or Mephistopheles) luring modern music over to the dark side and Mendelssohn as the saintly Alice (or Gretchen) poised to redeem it: "*His* [Mendelssohn's] road leads to happiness, the other to evil"; *Robert Schumann on Music and Musicians*, ed. K. Wolf, trans. P. Rosenfeld (Berkeley and Los Angeles, 1983 [1946]), 199.

16. Søren Kierkegaard, *Either/Or*, trans. David F. Swenson and Lillian Marvin Swenson (Princeton, 1971), 1:89 (and cf. 98).

17. Prefacing his remarks on Don Juan and the Faust figure, Kierkegaard refers to the myth of a subterranean empire of the senses, a realm of pleasure (Wagner's Venusberg): "Not until reflection enters does it appear as the kingdom of sin, but by that time Don Juan is slain, the music is silent" (*Either/Or*, 1:88–89). Wagner, of course, would soon find musical inspiration in this very conflict that Kierkegaard saw as the death of Don Juan and the end of *his* music.

18. Produced in Detmold in 1829 with incidental music by Albert Lortzing. On Grabbe, see Ernst Osterkamp's essay on the interactions of the Don Juan and Faust figures in this volume

19. "Wißt ihr denn nicht, daß jetzt ein großer Magus, / Gekommen aus Norddeutschlands Eiseswüsten, / In Roma hauset und die Luft verpestet? / Im schwarzen Mantel, weißen Antliztes, / Als hätte nie die Sonne es gerötet, / Schleicht er am Aventin." *Don Juan und Faust*, act 1, scene 1; *Grabbes Werke*, ed. Albin Franz and Paul Zaunert (Leipzig and Vienna, n.d.), 21. Grabbe transposes the central action from Spain to Rome.

20. Leading bass-baritone roles in several other Spohr operas exhibit traces of the Don Juan figure in Faustian or otherwise demonic-supernatural variants. *Pietro von Abano* (1827, after the *Zaubergeschichte* of Ludwig Tieck), for instance, turns on the efforts of the medieval *magus* Pietro to seduce even *outre-tombe* the fair Cäcilie, daughter of the Paduan podestà, whose corpse he reanimates with his necromantic powers. *Der Berggeist* (1825, after the "Rübezahl" story of Musäus) transposes Pluto's rape of Proserpina into a German Romantic fairy tale: the ruler of the subterranean earth spirits abducts the heroine, Alma, on the eve of her marriage to the noble Oskar. Both scores seek to apply the ingredients of Mozartean lyricism and the "infernal" minor/chromatic vocabulary of the statue scene within extended or (especially in *Der Berggeist*) through-composed scene structures.

21. Perhaps sensitive to a possible charge of redundancy, Spohr makes rather short work of Faust in this second finale.

22. "Wie, wenn Donna Anna vom Himmel dazu bestimmt gewesen ware, den Juan in der Liebe, die ihn durch des Satans Künste verdarb, die ihm inwohnende göttliche Natur erkennen zu lassen und ihm der Verzweiflung seines nichtigen Strebens zu entreißen?" Hoffmann, "Don Juan," *Gesammelte Werke in fünf Banden*, ed. Martin Hürlimann (Zurich, 1982), 1:314.

23. "Sage ich dir mit wenigen Worten, wie mir in der Musik, ohne alle Rücksicht auf den Text, das ganze Verhältnis der beiden im Kampf begriffenen Naturen (Don Juan und Donna Anna) erscheint."

24. Wagner inverts this model, in a sense, in the *Tannhäuser* overture; there the active, sensual "principle" is represented by the Venusberg music (implicitly gendered female), while it is Tannhäuser's somewhat stolid song of resistance to Venus's charms that provides the second-subject "antithesis." In this case the resolution is provided by a musical third term, the Pilgrims' Chorus from the introduction, infused with the rhythmic gestures of the Venusberg.

25. Dieter Borchmeyer, "The Transformations of Ahasuerus: *Der fliegende Holländer* and His Metamorphoses," in *Richard Wagner: Theory and Theatre*, trans. Stewart Spencer (Oxford, 1991), 190–215. Borchmeyer refers to Lenau as "the *Weltschmerz* poet *par excellence*" (197).

26. The position of this tranquil episode parallels, serendipitously, that of the extended "dream sequence" in act 3 of Shaw's Don Juan play, which resurrects Mozart's (and Molière's and de Molina's) characters to discuss with the Devil, at leisurely philosophical length, the relative merits of hell and heaven and sundry other issues relating to man, woman, and modern European society.

27. Hepokoski argues that this transformation of personae is enacted at a formal level by a shift from a rondo principle to sonata-allegro, both characteristically "deformed" in the expressive-narrative process of the tone poem. Even if one does not accept the form-analytical premise (for my part, I don't detect any clear establishment of a rondo principle at the outset), the essay's sensitivity to a dialogue of gestural detail, formal-harmonic process, and narrative hermeneutics has much to recommend it: "Fiery-Pulsed Libertine or Domestic Hero? Strauss's *Don Juan* Reinvestigated," in Bryan Gilliam, ed., *Richard Strauss: New Perspectives on the Composer and His Music* (Durham and London, 1992), 135–176. In Strauss's own oeuvre, of course, the Nietzschean "superman" of *Also sprach Zarathustra* (or *Don Juan,* initially) is soon exchanged for the "domestic heroism" of *Ein Heldenleben* and the *Symphonia Domestica*.

Seven

Don Juan as an Idea

BERNARD WILLIAMS

*G*iovanni is Don Juan, but he does not have to bear the weight of all the significance which that mythical figure has come to express. Still less does Giovanni have to be pursued, as though by another Elvira, with every interpretation that has been given of Don Juanism as a psychological category: that it expresses latent homosexuality, for instance, or hatred of women, or a need for reassurance. Any of these may be true of the local womanizer, but he is not Giovanni, and these states of mind are not what *Don Giovanni* expresses.

Some later Don Juans, elaborated as they all are with a vast variety of metaphysical, social or psychological reflections, are closer relatives of Giovanni than others. Most remote are the negative, melancholic, or merely frantic embodiments of the hero: fleeing from exhaustion and inner emptiness, in Lenau's representation, or, according to George Sand and Flaubert, engaged in a despairing hunt for a genuine encounter with another person. These, at any rate, are not Giovanni, who is as unambiguously and magnificently removed from despair and boredom as it is possible to be. At the climax of the opera, his words are in praise of women and wine, "sostegno e gloria d'umanità" ("support and glory of mankind"), but his music encompasses a larger praise of life and humanity themselves.

This chapter is concerned only with Giovanni's closer relatives in the tradition. Moreover, it is interested in them only in so far as they seem to help in thinking about the opera. They are, of course, rarely independent of the opera. Later writers have not simply gone back to some archetype of Don Juan, or taken Mozart's opera merely as one previous embodiment of that character, but have in many cases been quite specially influenced by the opera. Indeed, nineteenth- and twentieth-century thoughts about Don Juan have been dominated by Mozart's embodiment of him. This is not merely because the opera is by far the greatest work given to this theme. It is also because the opera is in various ways problematical, and that it raises in a challenging way the question of what the figure of Giovanni means. Hence, not only is the opera the historical starting-point of many modern thoughts on this subject, but some of those thoughts lead directly back to the problem of understanding the opera itself.

What are we to make of Giovanni? The opera is named after him, it is about him, it is he who holds together a set of scenes in other ways rather disconnected. He is in a deep way the like of the opera, yet the peculiarity is that such character as he has is not really as grand as that implies: he expresses more than he is. He seems to have no depth adequate to the work in which he plays the central role. He has, in a sense, a character—to a considerable extent a bad one. But we are not given any deep insight into what he really is, or what drives him on. We could not have been: it is not that there is something hidden in his soul. It is notable that he has no self-reflective aria—he never sings about himself, as Mozart's other central characters do. We have no sense of what he is like when he is by himself. He is presented always in action—the action, notoriously, of a seducer. The facts that the opera is of great and unsettling power, that a seducer is at the centre of it, and that the seducer is virtually characterless, were brought together in one of the first and most important reflections on the wider significance of the work, Søren Kierkegaard's famous essay "The Immediate Stages of the Erotic, or The Musical Erotic". It was one of a set of essays that he published in 1843. They were not published under his own name; Kierkegaard appears under a pseudonym, and even under this he claims only to introduce two sets of papers, by authors "A" and "B." The papers of "A" present an aesthetic view of life, those of "B" an ethical view. The disjunction between the two views—the "Either/Or" of the book's title—is left before the reader. Through all this indirection, the account of *Don Giovanni* is of course Kierkegaard's; but the authorial evasions are important, and they encourage him, or permit him, to leave a central question unresolved.

It is important that Kierkegaard is writing about Mozart's opera, and not merely about the character of Don Juan in general. This is not simply because he regards Mozart's as the greatest embodiment of the character. Beyond that, he thinks that it is a basic truth about the character that this should be so, a truth which he tries to explain. Mozart's is the greatest embodiment because of a perfect match of medium and content—music is the most "abstract" of the arts, and is therefore ideally suited to express the abstract principle of sensual desire itself. And since that principle is what, above all, music expresses, *Don Giovanni* will also be the greatest work of music, a consequence which, amid a good deal of ironical self-reproof about the absurdity of such judgments, Kierkegaard (or rather his surrogate "A") more or less allows himself.

Giovanni is the spirit of sensuous desire. He is (in a characteristic phrase) "flesh incarnate." He represents the third, full, and final stage of three forms of sensual interest, each of which has been represented by Mozart. The first, "dreaming," is expressed in the tranquillity, the "hushed melancholy," of Cherubino's feeling; the second, "seeking," in Papageno's craving for discovery. Giovanni combines and goes beyond both of these attitudes, in full desire, in conquest. He is a seducer, yet it is not really he who seduces—rather "he desires, and that desire acts seductively." His is no particular or individual voice. It is the voice of all desire, and it speaks to all women: it is heard "through the longing of all womanhood." This is why Zerlina, the one woman whose attempted seduction is actually enacted for us, is rightly, and intentionally, an "insignificant" character. Yet this conclusion itself raises a doubt. Zerlina has less to her than the other two women, and what in her responds to Giovanni—to his charm, his desire, and, as is made perfectly clear, his rank and money—is nothing very deeply hidden. Giovanni had been called upon on other occasions, surely, to exercise that more searching appeal of the stranger, which is brilliantly evoked in the novel by John Berger called *G*, one of the latest re-enactments of the Don Juan theme—and also one in which the figure appears at his most anonymously impersonal:

> The stranger who desires you and convinces you it is truly you in all your particularity whom he desires, brings a message from all that you might be, to you as you actually are. Impatience to receive that message will be almost as strong as your sense of life itself. The desire to know oneself passes curiosity. But he must be a stranger, for the better you, that you actually are, know him, and likewise the better he knows you, the less he can reveal to you of your unknown but possible self. He must be a stranger.

In Zerlina it is no great distance to her unknown but possible self. It is a pity, one might feel, that Mozart did not enact for us the seduction of Donna Elvira—still more, of Donna Anna. According to E. T. A. Hoffmann's famous story, he did. Hoffmann represents Anna as actually seduced by Giovanni, and this fact as the ground of her response to him: "she was not saved! when he rushed forth the deed was done. The fire of a superhuman sensuality, glowing from Hell, flowed through her innermost being and made her impotent to resist. Only he, only Don Juan, could arouse in her the lustful abandon with which she embraced him. . . ." The idea that Anna succumbed to Giovanni had been anticipated by Goldoni; but the significance that Hoffmann gives to this idea, and the consequences of it for the character and power of Giovanni, are what make Hoffmann's tale more than an anecdotal extension of the traditional plot.

Kierkegaard writes:

But what is this force then by which Don Juan seduces? It is the power of desire, the energy of sensual desire. He desires in every woman the whole of womanhood, and therein lies the sensually idealizing power with which he at once embellishes and overcomes his prey. The reflex of his gigantic passion beautifies and develops its object, who flushes in enhanced beauty by its reflection. As the fire of ecstasy with its seductive splendor illumines even the stranger who happens to have some relation to him, so he transfigures in a far deeper sense every girl, since his relation to her is an essential one. Therefore all finite differences fade away before him in comparison with the main thing: being a woman. He rejuvenates the older woman into the beautiful middle-age of womanhood: he matures the child almost instantly: everything which is woman is his prey. On the other hand, we must by no means understand this as if his sensuality were blind; instinctively he knows very well how to discriminate, and above all, he idealizes.

The idea that Giovanni is in pursuit of the ideal was to have a good deal of later history; a similar representation of his aims was given by Théophile Gautier, who wrote, "It is not vulgar debauchery that drives him on; he seeks the dream of his heart with the obstinacy of a Titan who fears neither thunder nor lightning." It is one way of trying to express the true conviction that Giovanni, in his musical embodiment, means more than Giovanni, in his character as tireless seducer, could actually manage to be. But it does that in the wrong way. It betrays the opera by still resting firmly in the terms of masculine pursuit. The feminine appears still as an object, even though it is idealized—perhaps all the more so because it is idealized. That result cannot be adequate to Mozart's work. *Don Giovanni* is a story about a seducer, indeed about the seducer, and has him as hero, but no sensible person could think that it was a work that represented women as more passive than men, or as deriving the point of their existence only from being the object, especially the idealized object, of some essentially masculine principle. This is above all because it gives such a powerful sense of the individuality and the desires of the women in it.

The Romantic airlessness of "the ideal" suffocates both the individuality and the desires of women. It has been suggested, in fact, that there is just one respect in which the seducer—the real seducer, who pursues women and not the ideal—is one who himself affirms the liberty of women: though he exploits or even destroys them, he does decline to imprison them in a possessive institution. Although he "has" them or "makes" them, he does not make them his. The catalogue, as Jean Massin has said, is the negation of the harem.

If we are to give Giovanni his full stature, the erotic principle with which he is identified needs to be taken in some sense which is more general, and at the same time more honestly realistic, than the pursuit of the "feminine ideal." Kierkegaard himself seems to realize this, for later in his essay Giovanni is associated more generally with "exuberant joy of life." All the other characters have, compared with him, only a "derived existence": he is "the life principle within them." It is the idea of Giovanni as a principle of vitality which explains, for instance, Leporello's attachment to him: he is absorbed, involved, swept up by him. Some idea of Giovanni as embodying the "life force" is of course also what Shaw offers in *Man and Superman*; but in that enactment, seductive power and attractiveness have been replaced by a boundless loquacity, and the life force is extinguished among disquisitions on Darwinism and mournfully parochial paradoxes about the predatoriness of women. The Preface of the play is only too appropriately subscribed: "Woking, 1903."

Now that Giovanni has come to be identified with something as general as the living principle of all the characters, the centre of their vitality, a difficulty arises; and since that identification has something right about it, and expresses convincingly Giovanni's musical relation to the rest of the opera, it is a real difficulty, which everyone has to face. Has Giovanni any longer a relation to either the social order or an order of divine judgment? When he was just a finite and particular kind of sexual brigand, there was no mystery in the idea that he should be hunted, prosecuted, or damned; but when he has taken on this larger and more abstract significance, is there anything left to the idea of an order against which he is to be judged? In particular, what do we make of his end?

There is no clear or adequate answer to this question in Kierkegaard's own essay. He indeed notably plays down Giovanni's nastiness—he denies that he is really a schemer or even a deceiver, just because he is always energy in action, unselfconsciousness. When Giovanni becomes as idealized as this—so that he seems an innocent, the *Erdgeist*, a male, active, and unvictimized

Lulu—the question of the order that condemns him becomes a very pressing one. Kierkegaard tell us, in effect, only that Giovanni is opposed to the spirit of Christianity, which is also (by a highly Hegelian identification) reflective spirit. This leaves us with an excessively blank fact, that Giovanni is breaking Christian laws and that is why he is punished. But that hardly says enough, even to Christians, if Giovanni indeed represents everyone's living principle. Kierkegaard himself perhaps escapes this criticism because he offers us in the essay only the view of "A," the aesthetic view of life, and it is hardly surprising "that he gestures only remotely towards" the ethical. But the ethical will have to be got into closer relation to Giovanni than this, if Giovanni is everything that "A" says that he is.

In distinguishing Mozart's Giovanni from an intriguer, Kierkegaard explicitly distinguishes him from Molière's Don Juan. That figure is driven particularly by the fear of boredom, the attempt to overcome satiation. Molière is mainly responsible for the idea of Don Juan as the amatory strategist, the hunter who is above all concerned with the tactics of the chase. It was a theme taken up later by Stendhal, who himself, however, finally pronounced in favour of Werther as opposed to Don Juan, the sentimental rather than the strategic. Stendhal's contrast, of course, relates simply to love—as something made, at any rate, if not felt. But the ruthless pursuer of love can come to represent, rather than one type of lover, one type of pursuer.

Simone de Beauvoir has said: "If existentialism were solipsistic, the adventurer would be its perfect hero," and Giovanni is one type of the adventurer. He is a kind of nihilist, on this reading: one who indeed denies God and the fetishism of conventional moral approval and social rewards, and who lives through free action for its own sake. He represents "the union of an original abundant vitality and reflective scepticism," but unlike the genuine and committed existentialist hero he has no sense of freedom as something all should share, and hence, like an adventurer in another style, Pizarro, he has contempt for other people. At the same time, he is dependent, dialectically, on social institutions which he rejects—wealth, and the liberty given by class.

Da Ponte constantly reminds us that Giovanni is a member of the nobility and that he deploys his rank and, as he himself very explicitly reminds us, his money, to get what he wants. He belongs of course to the equally noble world of Don Ottavio and Donna Anna, but we are left in no doubt what his contempt is for such a world, as a social order. When Masetto sees Zerlina being taken away from him by Giovanni and is prevented by Leporello from following, his outburst combines the pains both of love and of social insult.

Formally there is a parallel here with the relations of Figaro and the Count, but there is also a basic difference. It is not only that Figaro is a complete person whereas Masetto is a more schematic and simpler character. Still less is it that Giovanni is the hero of his opera, while the Count is the villain of his—that oversimplifies our relations to both of them. Giovanni is not a hero we enter into, whereas, very strikingly, the point at which we are given the deepest and most sympathetic insight into the Count is in that aria ("Vedrò, mentr'io sospiro") in which he expresses the rage of baffled class power. The difference between the operas is that the Count and Figaro totally belong to the social world in which they are presented, and their motivations are naturally related to that world, whereas Giovanni is only making use of the social world in which he was born, and is basically a solitary figure who exploits but does not belong to his social surroundings. He is a brigand within his own country. He is at ease in being so, and Mozart is at ease in representing him so. While Giovanni is using his position, there is surely no ambivalence in it, or in the opera's attitude to it, such as Ernst Bloch suggested, who found in it the mark of "a strangely ambiguous titanism" (*eines merkwürdig gesprenkelten Titanismus*), and asked, "Is Don Giovanni, as Mozart shows him, a wolf or a human face under so many masks? Does he belong fully to the society of the Ancien Régime, as its most ruthless representative, or do we detect in him, in the erotic explosive rebellion, part of a return to nature?" Giovanni certainly lives off the land, but does so in an individual way that firmly refuses any such historical question. That he exploits others is identified by Simone de Beauvoir as a contradiction in the adventurer's situation—he both denies and affirms the need of his social background. But this is so, surely, only if he intends, or someone intends, his style of life to be an expression of freedom as something which everyone might try to follow. Giovanni himself entertains no such aspiration, nor does he reject it: he is not reflective in that style at all.

Nor in any other. It is this that marks him off from another great embodiment of reckless human energy with whom he has indeed been associated, Faust. A German author, Christian Dietrich Grabbe, produced in 1829 a play (*Don Juan und Faust*) which brought the two heroes together, a meeting which involves the following rather plodding exchange:

DON JUAN: Wozu übermenschlich
           Wenn du ein Mensch bleibst?
FAUST: Wozu Mensch
           Wenn du nach übermenschlichem nicht strebst?
DON JUAN: What is the point of the superhuman
           If you remain man?
FAUST: What is the point of man
           If you do not strive for the superhuman?

Such solemnities do not belong to the world of Giovanni. Even without them, Faust's undertaking, because it is essentially reflective, differs from Giovanni's. It is not merely that he is a scholar and an experimentalist, though that is true, and his attitude to Helen or Gretchen is of that kind—he loves or seduces as an experiment or an experience, in order to have done so, and that is the opposite of Giovanni, who simply says that he needs women "more than I need the food that I eat or the air that I breathe" (II.1). More basically, Faust's whole bargain—what makes him the over-reacher he is—is reflective: it is a product of the calculation of the values of finite and infinite, and that is not a kind of enterprise known to Giovanni. As Camus remarked, Giovanni does not really believe in the after-life, unlike Faust "who believed enough in God to sell himself to the devil."

But this leads us back to the questions about Giovanni's end; and whether it is, despite the opera's first title, *Il dissoluto punito*, a punishment. If the Commendatore is the veritable voice of Heaven, a Christian Sarastro, so to speak, then Giovanni's defiance of him, the refusal of repentance in the face of a manifest miracle, is awesomely perverse. The celebration of Giovanni as Promethean hero, or—as by Musset and by Baudelaire, for example—as a figure of fascinating satanic evil, will then be in place.[1] But Giovanni is not a satanic evil figure, and the extraordinary power his musical image expresses is not that of a tragic hero either. Camus is again to the point:

> Don Juan would find it natural that he should be punished. It is the rule of the game. And it is exactly a mark of his generosity, to have entirely accepted the rule of the game. But he knows that he is right, and that there can be no question of punishment. An inevitable end is not the same thing as a penalty.

If Giovanni's wilful defiance does not have a luciferian significance, then what he is defying cannot be God. The Commendatore in stone is on any showing an impressive figure: Shaw said that those trombones were "a sound of dreadful joy to all musicians". But his is not the voice of God. He is made of stone, and he does not come from Heaven (whatever he says about his diet), but from the churchyard where we first heard him. He is a terrible and unforeseen natural consequence of Giovanni's recklessness. He is indeed supernatural, but only in the sense of a realm of cause and effects which lie beyond the natural, not one that brings a new order of guilt and judgment. Giovanni's lofty refusal to repent when the statue demands that he should is not an ultimate offence to the cosmic order, but rather a splendidly attractive and grand refusal to be intimidated.

If Giovanni's refusal were to be Faustian *hubris* or Promethean defiance, as some Romantic writers wanted, it would have to be something that he had come to after consideration. Mozart's tempi reveal it as convinced, but not as considered. The Commendatore's andante gives Giovanni time to repent, but he does not give himself time, and could not do so. He is always in action; even when he is resting from one adventure, he is in flight for the next. His natural speed, throughout the opera, is that of "Eh via buffone" (rather slower than "Fin ch'an dal vino," a piece designed to show that even he can accelerate). That speed is not right for reflection; and no composer has ever found it the right speed for Faust. Shaw's Don Juan, by contrast, becalmed in that limitless lagoon of talk, loses his entire *raison d'être*.

The Commendatore does not need to be the voice of God; and the devils' chorus scarcely *could* be the sound of the Christian Inferno. The final sextet even refers to the place to which Don Giovanni has been removed, not by any Christian phrase, but in terms of the old creaking classical machinery of Proserpina and Pluto: Da Ponte attached no very great weight to that, no doubt, but it is quite right. Those old gods were themselves part of nature, and Giovanni's great virtue of courage, which he expressly boasts in his last moments, is displayed in a marvellous piece of consistency, of sufficiency, of bravado—a very proper and fine human reaction to something which, granted indeed his wicked life, is of the order of a vast and alarming natural consequence, rather than a transcendental judgment.

Curiously, each of Mozart's great Italian comedies has something unsatisfactory or problematic about its end. None of them perfectly solves the problem raised by its own depth—the problem of relating to the defining normality of comedy the intensity that the work has given to the irregular. Each promises a return to normality which it fails to define properly; each embodies some emotion which does not quite match the past or the future. In *Figaro*, there is the problem that at the end of the "mad day," the Count and the Countess express reconciliation and forgiveness in music of such rapturous beauty that it can only be saying that all will be well for ever, when we know, from everything we have seen, that it cannot be for more than a week. In *Cosi fan tutte*, everybody is rattled back to their right partners in a manner which, granted what we have just been shown, can only be totally heartless. In *Don Giovanni* the final sextet represents, very explicitly, a return to ordinary life. Should we take that to mean: a return to the ordinary as against the supernatural, which has just done its work? Or a return to the decent with the end of the wicked?

There is certainly a return to the expected, after the intervention of the extraordinary. But that return does not define what has disappeared as simply wicked, indecent, or unnecessary. In fact, the characters, with the exception of Zerlina and Masetto, scarcely do "return to normal," but rather try to stick something together from what is left now that Giovanni has gone. Life without him will not merely be life with the wicked satisfactorily punished. Although his punishment is the subject of the closing words of the finale, and the moral of its "antichissima canzon," Mozart has already shown us that life without Giovanni will be life that has lost a very powerful and single-minded embodiment of qualities which are indeed human. Because he was just those qualities, he himself lacked humanity—he was without love, compassion, and fairness, to mention only a few of the things that he lacked. But the relation of what he had to what he lacked cannot be adequately expressed simply in terms of vice and virtue, dissoluteness and punishment, and that is something that Kierkegaard's interpretation half sees—sees, one might say, with half of him; but his essay leaves us, inadequately, still with the punishment as a blank requirement of the Christian consciousness, besides contributing the ultimately sterile idea, favoured by some Romantics, that Giovanni's pursuit of women was more than it seemed because it was the pursuit of the ideal woman.

Contrary to that, other Romantics found his heroism in a displacement of ordinary virtue: face to face with the cosmic order, he defiantly, tragically, or even satanically, rejects it. That account of him both overestimates the transcendental character of what he confronts, and underestimates the simply human, recognizable, and invigorating quality of his attitude to that confrontation.

The sense of freedom that he expresses does not have all the metaphysical resonances that existentialist writers found in it, but it does have a significance which goes beyond an individual personal characteristic, and so does his recklessness. His single-minded determination to live at the fullest energy, at the extreme edge of desire, neglects consequences to himself as much as to others. Granted what makes life valuable to him, the ultimate consequences are irrelevant: cowardice, for him, would simply involve a misunderstanding of what was worth pursuing, just as considerateness (unless things happened to take him that way) would be a distraction. He understands perfectly well that society exists—he can skillfully negotiate its obstacles. He understands that other people exist—how else could he so unfailingly find the "unknown but possible self" of all those women? He has a perfectly clear idea of what might destroy him—his end was not just a mistake.

That end, however, and still more the essential closing bars of the opera that follow it, both affirm that there is no actual human life that could be lived as unconditionally as his. Those who survive Giovanni—not only the other characters, but, on each occasion that we have seen the opera, ourselves—are both more and less than he is: more, since the conditions *on* humanity, which are also the conditions *of* humanity; and less, since one thing vitality needs is to keep the dream of being as free from conditions as his.

NOTES

In an original note, Williams asked readers to refer to the well-known or pertinent books by authors named in his essay to avoid his continually having to interrupt his text with reference notes. For that note, please refer to Julian Rushton, ed., *W. A. Mozart. Don Giovanni*, Cambridge Opera Handbook, Cambridge University Press, 1981, p. 148 (from which the essay printed in this volume was copied by permission of Bernard Williams and Cambridge University Press. Certain formatting and stylistic changes were admitted into the reprint.).

1. See Charles Baudelaire, fragment of a scenario, *Le fin de Don Juan*, first published in *Oeuvres posthumes* (1887); Alfred de Musset, dramatic fragment, *La matinee de Don Juan*, first published in *La France littéraire* (1883).

Eight

Kierkegaard Writes His Opera

DANIEL HERWITZ

here are two operas. One is Mozart's *Don Giovanni*, the other is Kierkegaard's life. Each is about genius, each is filled with melodrama. The two are connected because, for Kierkegaard, *Don Giovanni* is the opera to end all operas, the one that sends him reeling into philosophy, the other with the power to reveal to him what opera is. Made delirious by this opera, Kierkegaard claims that it turned him into a young girl, infatuated, bowled over, in love both with the object of her love and with love itself. His response was not unrepresentative of the nineteenth century's reception of this opera. Bowled over by *Don Giovanni*, philosophers, composers, and poets adored and worshipped it, and in the end canonized it, a canonization that continues to this day. The seduction by this opera, the philosophizing and worshipping of it is my topic. I do not doubt the opera magnificent, but I do not write as a lover. Not quite anyway, for I intend to resist its seductive aura sufficiently to gain purchase on precisely that. Any opera that causes a man—and not just a man, a man writing autobiographically, and in the name of philosophy—to swoon into what he supposes is femininity, surely raises issues of gender. *Don Giovanni's* hypermasculine representation of the Don as a seducer of the grand (guignol) style is one reason why musicians and philosophers in the nineteenth century—with all its images of music, genius, and masculinity —adored it. Yet, what we need to understand is how this opera solicits philosophy from one of the great philosophers of the nineteenth century.

"I am still too much of a child, or rather like a young girl in love with Mozart, and I must have him in the first place, cost what it may," Kierkegaard announces in part 1 of *Either/Or*.[1] Published just less than sixty years after the Prague premiere of *Don Giovanni*, Kierkegaard goes on to say: "Immortal Mozart! Thou to whom I owe everything; to whom I owe the loss of my reason, the wonder that caused my soul to tremble, the fear that gripped my innermost being" (47). This exclamation, containing all the elements of a reaction to the sublime—elements of excitement and fear at being overwhelmed, of loss of reason and an inviting sense of wonder—brands this philosopher as one who responds to Mozart and his librettist as a young girl. In doing so, it raises the question of Kierkegaard's style of philosophical reasoning, which canonizes the masculine/seductive power of this opera. Responding to his sense of its aura with an essentializing philosophical language, Kierkegaard claimed that it was not only the greatest opera ever written but the greatest work of art ever. His philosophical apparatus may be worthy of deconstruction, his response to the opera may border on the obscene, but was he entirely wrong? Is this not one of the greatest works of art ever? If it is, then what power, what combination of love, seduction, and grace does it contain?

One must wonder about the character of Kierkegaard's seduction by *Don Giovanni* when he writes: "though otherwise I always thank the gods that I was born a man and not a woman, still Mozart's music has taught me that it is beautiful and refreshing and rich to love like a woman" (127). A young girl swooning over Mozart, now a woman ready to give "the full Monty," apparently there is a compensation to being a woman, even if the opera itself hardly contains role models of great and glorious female lovers. In fact, its women are uniformly passive; they become actors only when hysterical; they are self-important and repressed (which is to say upper class), the exception being Zerlina who, from the lower classes (in many ways the class of preference for both Mozart and Da Ponte) is given some of the Don's own wiliness. Zerlina's powers of seduction are clearly outmatched by the Don's, for he has wrapped her little finger around his big finger: she is after all a woman and he a man (and she is poor and he is rich). This opera gives women little representation of their own powers in love (this to some degree proves it to be a mirror of its time). So, if the opera instructs the philosopher that there is something wondrous about loving like a woman/female, then the source of this instruction must consist in the joyful abandonment to the passive position of listening, the turning of oneself into a receptacle for a joy that is perhaps otherwise unavailable to oneself in one's life, a joy in turn referred to the concept of "being a young girl in love." If the opera teaches this man to appreciate something about women he would otherwise not have known, then the question must arise why he would never, otherwise, have known it. This is a biographical question (about Kierkegaard's life), a cultural question (about his society and its times), and a question about opera (its construction of the relationship between musical joy and thematic material).

One could reverse the picture of the opera's sexism by saying that it is about a ranked ordering of castrati. The women all lack power: they are castrated (Zerlina being the partial exception). However, the males are also arranged according to orders of castration. Don Ottavio is a tenor lacking in what the Italians call *fegato.* Locked into his opera seria role, he waves his sword around like a hero to be but accomplishes nothing. Poor Masetto is a wimp, made even more hopeless by his low status as a ploughman, while Leporello is a mere sidekick and comic book image of the Don, leaving the field free for the Don's big voice and equally big sword. The Don's desire is limitless, uncontrollable, and wholly absorptive. It takes a statue to curb it, a statue that inhabits a cemetery—the land of the dead and the last judgment.

The Commendatore, the father figure, is the opera's central organizing force. His music is the first music to be heard in the opera's dramatic denouement (the opera's finale being read here as a dramatic aftereffect, a reinstatement of boring normality.) His famous words, uttered when he arrives in the penultimate scene to dine with the Don and condemn him to hell, are the most emphatic and tonally simplified in the entire opera, articulating as they do nothing more than the dominant/tonic relation of the opera's tonality: D Minor. ("Don Giovanni!/ a cenar teco/m'invitasti/ e son venuto.") In an opera whose mode is almost entirely major, an opera whose cheerful and caressing melodies are continually called on to seduce the object of desire, the music of this judging father has a basso insistence that grips one by the throat. Mozart is banking on the difference between the Commendatore's music and everyone else's, including the arias of its opera seria characters (all of which are either in the major mode or end in a reversion to the major mode) to make the Commendatore's music appear superhuman, statuesque, and indomitable. The music's form of declamation, standard rhetoric in opera seria, pronouncements by gods, divinities, and oracles, commands authority and insists upon commandment. It is a music that lays down the law through an oracular style whose melodic pattern is nothing but the statement of skeletal tonal relations.

In the opera's orders of castration, the Commendatore could not reappear as a Lazarus reborn in human form because no human can match the Don, not even a Lazarus. The Don's sword is unassailable. The father has, in his life as a mere man, already been vanquished by the Don; he can only defeat the Don, vanquish his powers, by becoming more than a person. He must become an artifact of justice as such, a larger-than-life representation of the IDEA of justice.

As such, he becomes the oedipal father par excellence, a man whose hold on the world—on his tremulous daughters and fearful young sons—is larger than life. The oedipal father is himself unkillable because he is *already dead* in the child's imagination, which means the child, having already murdered the father by wishing his death, is living on borrowed time, waiting for revenge from the father to take place in superhuman form. "Ah! tempo piu non v'e," the statue says before finally condemning Giovanni to the flames, "Ah there is no more time." Time borrowed is time lost: this is the moral prefigured in the overture, where the intensity of the minor mode was already suddenly and somewhat magically replaced by the irrepressible brightness of the major, as if the major stole from the minor and will live on borrowed time.

Should one wish to fill out the theory of the Don's oedipal drama, one would do well to consult the pages of the good doctor Freud, who in "The Dissolution of the Oedipus Complex,"[2] argues that the young child—by which he basically means the young boy—learns to give up his unbridled desire for the mother and to internalize the law of the father, when the reality principle finally takes hold of him and he realizes he can never out-compete the father. The father will always remain bigger than him; he will never win. This piece of knowledge becomes the basis for the child's relin-quishment of grandiosity, of his claim to Napoleonic grandeur in battle and unlimited territoriality in domain. Those who fail to internalize this lesson, those who, for whatever reason, refuse the relinquishment of their phallic grandiosity, will forever live their lives in incessant need to prove/confirm that they are stronger, better, and more adept than their fathers. They will never confront their own (phallic) limitations, nor will they ever succeed in proving that they are as grandiose in reality as they feel in fantasy. In short they will be consigned to the state of repetition compulsion, of doing the same thing over and over again in the hope that it will amount to victory and proof in the end.

This recipe for the accumulation of lists might seem just apt as a descrip-tion of the Don. The question then returns: why he, and the opera in which he stars, should have been singled out by "the nineteenth century" for canon-ization rather than *Figaro* or *Cosi*, both of which rival it in musical splendor, moral sophistication, and perhaps even musical seduction. For philosophers and Romantics, anyway, *Don Giovanni* was *l'ultimo* (at least until *Tristan* came along, and even then it remained in the pantheon of the few). What then of this canonization?

Kierkegaard believes *Don Giovanni* deserves canonization because it is the one opera that perfectly acknowledges the nature of the musical medium. In this work, Kierkegaard says, music finds its ideal vehicle for expression and self-representation and its ideal theme: the erotic-sensuous genius. "The most abstract idea—sensuous genius—is only expressible in music. . . . In the erotic-sensuous genius, music has its absolute object. It is not of course intended to say by this that music cannot also express other things, but this is its proper object" (62).

The perfect marriage between the medium of music and its theme makes *Don Giovanni*, according to Kierkegaard, not merely the greatest opera ever, but an opera of a different order than all other musical works. For the opera perfectly employs its musical resources to articulate its theme and then uses that theme to reflect back on the nature of music: music being the unique medium in which erotic genius flows. Kierkegaard's sensuous-erotic genius is the one whose principle of desire is free, whose creation cannot be fully analyzed in terms of rules, who causes delight, whose principle is universal in scope (embracing all humanity) and whose expression of desire has the appearance of inevitability, and whose force of will is indomitable—as if he could not but achieve what he achieves, as if his creative life has the force of necessity. The Don is nature incarnated as the genius of art, an art played out with the inevitability and finality of nature. The Don's principle is both natural and aesthetic: "erotic genius" is formulated through concepts appropriated from aesthetics (genius, artifice, and beauty), yet also in terms of natural inclinations and desire. This recipe for a paradigmatically male genius extends to the very concept of genius itself, which is encoded as male.

Hence the character of the Don symbolizes the opera itself and in so doing symbolizes all music and art. The Don is for the nineteenth century a symbolic incarnation of the principle of art. His seduction of women by dint of a voice that insinuates its aura around them, opening them toward a heightened state of delight, is an image of what music does to the listener. What the Don does to women is what the opera does to Kierkegaard: it feminizes him, showing him both how a woman can richly love and how it feels to be a young and hysterical girl who must "have Mozart at all cost." This conflation of sensuousness, seduction, and hysteria is almost a recipe for feminine love in the nineteenth century, a recipe described by nineteenth-century psychiatry, analyzed by Freud, and reinterpreted by Foucault. Indeed the very concept of the will, that correlate of the concept of genius, is equally male. The will is the source of musical and erotic indomitability. It is constrained by the forces of ordinary life and representation, desiring at all times to break out in song, perhaps, or in sex or in transgression. Music provides the occasion for liberation.

The nineteenth century was obsessed with this opera because it turned its listeners into females while simultaneously making them males. The male listener is feminized, yet also brought to identify so strongly with the Don himself that he ends up feeling more male than ever. He is afforded an experience that simulates the experience of both sexes or, better, both genders. His underlying experience is of bisexuality—more precisely, bigenderedness. *Don Giovanni* allows males who are out of touch with their capacity to be seduced by the world, who are out of touch with the richness of their own personalities, with their "feminine" sides, with their capacity to identify with women and hence to love them, to feel those things from the safety of what is in fact an increased sense of masculinity. The experience of *Don Giovanni* simulates the experience of wholeness, the experience of both genders, *while also keeping them clearly apart*, as if *Don Giovanni* is a meal where you can have your cake and eat it too. The misogynist can, through simulated identification with women, overcome his misogyny while reinforcing it through his identification with the Don.

This desire for wholeness, while preserving the rigid categories of gender, this desire for the simultaneous experience of both genders, runs deep in the nineteenth century. We surely inherit this today. One finds its inverse in Goethe's *Faust*, where Faust's essentially depressive male genius is saved by the eternal feminine. Goethe conceives of genius as essentially feminine, as a spirit that silently fills the composer's head, producing creation. Goethe's image of the mind as a space rather than as a pulsating capacity for Will bespeaks this conception. Yet, unlike Da Ponte and Mozart, Goethe understands that a culture split between rigid categories of gender signals a personal and cultural disaster in need of reparation.

Don Giovanni's music has the requisite Dionysian thrust to count as an expression of "sensuous-erotic genius," while the Don's character has enough lateral thrust to become symbolic of musical force as such. Romanticism rewrites the history of music, selecting those works from the eighteenth century with the right level of thrust as originators of a heroic-Romantic style that Romantic composers (Liszt, Berlioz, Wagner, and Mahler) then develop. *Don Giovanni* allows us to reconceptualize the Romantic (or one region of it) as a musical-aesthetic line with sources in Mozart and Beethoven that continue up to Wagner and Mahler. It is a male-centered line, heroic, embattled, mythic, quixotic. Its legacy is that of a character (the Don) transcribed into the music of Liszt and Wagner, indeed into the auras of Liszt and Wagner themselves.

And so a Titan is born and reborn who is capable, by dint of his genius, of blurring art and life, who lives as a *Lebenskunstler* in a special domain located somewhere between life and music, whose creativity and personal magnetism are the same.

But is this Kierkegaard speaking about Don Giovanni at all, this young girl swooning before Mozart's opera, learning to love like a woman? Can we properly infer a philosophical position about genius, opera, music from this famous poseur, this philosophical performance artist who rushes from role to role, ruse to ruse, ascending the ladder (if that is the right way to put it) of stages in life's way? It is well known that this philosopher's writing proceeds through the articulation of *positions*, each of which projects a complete worldview, a way of living and valuing, the point being to show the reader (you and me) that certain positions (of the aesthete, for example) are inadequate, and to do this not through argument or refutation (something Kierkegaard believes impossible) but instead through force of revelation. Kierkegaard's goal is to grip us with a picture, a truth, and then to unmask it. And so role is unrolled (rather in the manner of Leporello's list), with all its inviting seductiveness, and then unraveled. Following this procedure to its end, ought we not doubt that it is really Kierkegaard talking when he adulates *Don Giovanni* to the skies?

There is every reason to believe that the young woman in love is a pose rather than a signal of aesthetic truth. For Kierkegaard the philosopher makes clear that the aesthetic attitude (exemplified by the Don's way of living) is ultimately empty. To live like the Don is to live in the immediacy of the present. He is a metaphor for the aesthetic, its symbol. Since the aesthetic is nothing but immediate sensual gratification, it is inherently compulsive and cannot stop. When it stops , since it cannot reflect or understand itself to be part of a larger life narrative, it encounters only emptiness. So it is driven to accumulate experiences. If the opera is philosophically about opera, it is a philosophy, finally, about the emptiness of opera and the aesthetic, of a life lived without a sense of a larger life. Kierkegaard claims that there are three stages "on life's way," each of which supersedes the previous one: the Aesthetic, the Ethical, and the Religious. The first, the Aesthetic, sees an aesthete whose premoral existence amounts to a life of collecting, consuming, and discarding pleasures. In his relentless pursuit of pleasure, he devours the world. Like the Don, he is bulimic, since his life is empty when without the pursuit of pleasure. Because he cannot retain pleasures for risk of commitment, he must spit them out as soon as they are devoured. The aesthete is not refined but voracious, not a connoisseur but a consumer.

The second stage, the Ethical, encourages a larger concept guiding life. It shows a life in conformity to the rules of duty toward one's self, others, and the community. One who has reached the ethical stage recalls Hegel's ethics, whereby one internalizes the rules of morality and willingly acts in accord with their necessity. Bourgeois life, or *Sittlichkeit*, the life of marriage, family, and duty to the state—the world of hard Victorian work and making money—this is the world Kierkegaard both despises and envies. It sublates the erotic in a sustainable marriage, more or less the world of *The Marriage of Figaro*.

The third, the Religious, opens the door to fear and trembling. Here, in a leap of faith, one suspends both concepts and morality to find God in an existential gesture of irrational action. This stage is neither one of pleasure or morality but rather of a gesture of communion with God. Kierkegaard describes this stage of faith deliberately as the "suspension of the ethical." Since Faith demands such a suspension, the Ethical must be in place for the third and final stage to occur. Similarly, the Ethical stage requires the Aesthetic stage in order to be superseded, since moral duty is only understood as such according to the overcoming of inclination or desire.

For Kierkegaard one can never argue anyone out of their commitment to a stage. Any person must come, rather, to see for herself the ultimate emptiness or finitude of at least the first two stages. Kierkegaard's strategy for unmasking the emptiness of the aesthetic stage in *Either/Or* part 1 is to show, through his own masterpiece, *the Diary of a Seducer*, which appears in that text after his various adulations of the opera, that the life of the seducer is empty, antihedonic rather than enlivened.

However, here, in my argument, is where the second opera occludes the first. Kierkegaard's philosophical position is clear. The aesthetic life, typified by both the opera and character Don Giovanni, is an empty treadmill, inadequate to build a life on. However, if Kierkegaard entirely believed this, one might have thought that, fixated as he is on *Don Giovanni*, Kierkegaard would have wanted to show—perhaps through an appreciation of the opera's ending—the ultimate emptiness of the Don himself. But he does not do this, nor does he hardly ever mention the opera's end when the Don finally gets his "reward." Indeed Kierkegaard goes so far as to state that the very character of the Commendatore is unmusical and ought not really be in the opera, because it is either too intellectual or too moral. A bizarre idea, especially considering that his ultimate goal is not to advertise the joys of the aesthetic stage but to illustrate its emptiness. Indeed, again, his wild admiration for the opera is itself more or less unblemished by his philosophical position, which goes against it, an inconsistency that demands explanation.

My suggestion—my belief—is that he can't get away from the opera, can't allow it to end. My view, reading Kierkegaard against himself, is that the

adoration persists, desire persists, and is inconsistent with his avowedly philosophical position. Thus there are two ways to read the pose of the young girl
in love: as something Kierkegaard ultimately proves empty or inadequate and
as something he forever desires/believes in. He remains, therefore, seduced by
the opera, unable to extricate himself from adulating it.

This is exhibited, I think, in the way *The Diary of a Seducer* seems to
bounce off *Don Giovanni*. One would have thought that were it present to
prove the life of the Don unrewarding, then it would address that life directly. However, for Kierkegaard, *The Diary* is about a seducer, whereas Don
Giovanni is not. This requires some explanation. To be a seducer, Kierkegaard
says, requires a certain amount of reflection and consciousness; as soon as that
is present one may speak of cunning, intrigues, and crafty plans. Don Juan
lacks this consciousness, therefore he does not seduce. He desires limitlessly,
and this limitlessness is itself seductive. To that extent he enjoys the satisfaction of desire but no more; once he has enjoyed it he seeks a new object, and
so on, endlessly. He is therefore also a deceiver. It is the inherent power of his
sensuousness that deceives. To be a seducer, one needs time to plan, and time
afterward to reflect upon one's achievement. Don Juan has time on neither
side and therefore is not a seducer. Eloquent he may be, but seduction is a
different matter. For when he is eloquent, he ceases to be musical. Or so at
least Kierkegaard argues (97–98).

The Don is not a seducer because his principle of desire is too primordial,
too nonreflective and nonconceptual! Remarkably, genuine erotic genius is
not seductive, it is "genial" (ingenious, the product of deliberate planning
based in compulsive behavior, anything but musical). One may agree that the
sensuousness of the Don's eroticism outruns the merely seductive, but to deny
that it is *seductive* is amazing. Seduction is for Kierkegaard an intellectual
game, a game of art played out over people in which they are manipulated like
so many chess pieces on the chessboard coldly, analytically, and out of mere
passion for the game itself. This is how Kierkegaard thinks of his own seducer,
Johannes, the writer/protagonist of *The Diary of a Seducer*. Johannes is a man
who is truly misogynist; he views women in some Pushkinian fashion as mere
things to be undressed slowly and according to the minutest psychological
calculations. Johannes's diary, the text of the *Diary of a Seducer*, details in the
most tortured psychological language the dethronement of a young virgin girl
called Cordelia, whom Johannes meets and immediately decides to seduce.
This obsessive intelligence really does decide to stake out and seduce his prey.
He plays her moods, her motivations, her expectations like a violin. He is the
Sherlock Holmes of psychological intricacy, prefiguring her every response
with the next move in his language game. Johannes's compulsive art, played

out with little sensual enjoyment but with the greatest intellectual satisfaction, ultimately leads to Cordelia's seduction. Although, by the time he meets her in a hotel, the game is for him already over. He takes no pleasure in the ultimate act of sex and discards her promptly.

His brutality is made more intense by the facts of Kierkegaard's own life. He was engaged to a young girl in her teens called Regine or Regina (obviously close in name to Cordelia), whom in one mood (there are others) he hated for her average intelligence, immaturity, silliness, and bourgeois values. (She would end up married to a Danish diplomat in the Caribbean.) Why did he allow this engagement or encourage her? He even almost threw himself at her feet. What land of the neurotic did he inhabit? At the crucial moment he broke off the engagement, apparently in intense jealousy but with the greatest relief. Some say he was impotent, others that he simply hated women, still others that his own father had crushed his spirit of desire. (Was the Don's irrepressible spirit of desire a vicarious replacement of his own—is that why he refused to criticize that opera directly?) It is now known that the chief reason for relinquishing Regina was his own unmanageable manic-depressive illness, which prevented him from enduring her, rising to the occasion of her enjoyment, of *feeling* the joy in her company he so desperately wanted to feel. Added to this, he combined a deep and violent confusion of her with his also melancholic, hateful father and with the early loss of his mother. It was to Mozart that he turned in desperate search of pleasure (erotic pleasure), a joy that turned him into a young girl, allowed him a glimpse into the world of feeling he was not able to attain. The opera allowed him an identification with the lost and unattainable object of his desire (Cordelia/Regina) and, finally, allowed him simply to feel joy at something, *anything*, in life. It was to the world of the Don that he retreated, as if from the terror of a sustained erotic desire that would inevitably cash itself out in marriage, companionship, day to day lived reality (the thing he could not bear in his projected relationship with Regina). If opera is the paradigmatic object of appreciation for the mad, then the shoe fits. Kierkegaard never married and, it is widely assumed, had no other female love. He remained deeply guilty about Regina and took a significant interest in her later marriage.

Johannes's so-called diary was surely more personal to Kierkegaard than one might have thought, concerned as it was with a brilliant and perverse man who plays a young and silly girl like an accordion only to discard her, for Johannes was also a misogynist and perhaps even hated sex. One cannot help but wonder if the name for this fictional girl, Cordelia, is also meant unconsciously to recall Lear, bringing up the theme of banishment and refusal to recognize the one who loves you, resonating with his deep fury over woman and his deep guilt over Regina. The figure of Johannes is Kierkegaard rather than the Don, because it is the figure of a man bereft of the capacity to enjoy the sex he so skillfully plans (the figure of a frigid man). For Kierkegaard reflective seduction means seduction *without the capacity to enjoy women.* It means the replacement of sexuality by cruelty, the turning away from sex to a game of love that turns love into mere artifice. Johannes composes the affair like a master geometer, architect, or musician. But his musical composition little resembles the spontaneous outpourings of Mozart's compositional style or the stylish seductions of the Don that Kierkegaard refuses even to call seductions. His deepest longing is to recover what he never had, except in and through music: the immediacy of the erotic. Kierkegaard's seducer is a dead soul, just as his moral subject (married man) is a soul inhibited by an excess of "super ego." In spite, therefore, of a philosophical position that demonstrates the emptiness of the Don, the Don is reserved as a beneficent figure, capable of restoring life where it is socially and psychologically absent.

And so suddenly in *Either/Or* the line of reasoning changes. A text that ought to be there to get the reader off the aesthetic stage by proving it empty turns out 1. not to be about the pleasures incipient in that stage at all (those of Mozart's *Don*) but instead 2. about an unrelated item: the anhedonia of another being of Kierkegaard's own invention. We are left uncertain as to where Kierkegaard himself stands vis-à-vis the Don, and that is the point: he is as uncertain or ambivalent too. He shows us, on the one hand, the emptiness of a life when you try to live it as if in an opera and, on the other, the transition from the divine Mozart to he himself as the desolate and powerless Johannes.

Current scholarship suggests that Kierkegaard wrote and published the *Diary* to wean Regina from him by doing something that would (by humiliating her) lower her estimation of him, and was dismayed when after its publication she smiled as warmly as ever when they met in the street. Apparently he was playing erotic chess in reverse, aiming to lose his queen rather than checkmating his mate. Nevertheless, at the core was a deep incapacity to experience erotic pleasure in himself or to love as a form of social engagement. Now one can understand why Kierkegaard never discusses the end of Mozart's opera when the Don gets his reward and wishes to banish the Commendatore. Kierkegaard never wished the opera to end, since he associated music itself, the opera as symbolic of music, to a state of desire that exists psychologically prior to the devastating encounter with the great father, the one who thrusts one into the desultory position of a Johannes. This reading fits as well with the dissolution of the Oedipus complex and with the Don's refusal of it. Kierkegaard loves the Don's refusal of the law of the father because he hates the law as he hates the Ethical. He desires to inhabit the realm of the Don without termination, a realm in which he can take delight in sex through a sexuality that at once breaks through his misogyny and confirms it, that allows him to open himself to the capacity to be seduced, to identify with the women he otherwise detests by becoming one, and at the same time leaves the construction of gender intact. This is probably the only realm in which he can tolerate the sexual and the feminine in himself and thus in others.

To further pursue this line of reasoning, Kierkegaard's relinquishing of the aesthetic in favor of the ethical is conditional on the concept of a psychological and social world in which desire remains present (sublated) in marriage. The point is supposed to be that the joys of surrender or whatever are retained in married life. However, Kierkegaard, who detested the Copenhagen of his times, is dubious about whether this is so for bourgeois marriage, considered up close and personal. Copenhagen was for him a society regulated by moral masochism and hypocrisy. Morality was, when not considered abstractly but in practice, repression under another name, a world that had already won its victory over Kierkegaard's inhibited seducer Johannes, a world that produced people like him. I believe Kierkegaard's reading of bourgeois life (as it is rather than as it should be) reveals to him in practice a second stage of life so terrible that it is as if the Don, having been sent to the fires of hell, would find there not flames but a wife, children, a family, and a job, a stonelike fate worse than death.

And so, while the philosophical stance argues for relinquishment of the aesthetic in favor of the ethical, the Kierkegaardian heart remains wedded to the Don, the one continuing source of enlivenment for this desperate man. It is this conflict between Kierkegaard the philosopher and Kierkegaard the man, between philosophy and life, that makes the philosophy and the life operatic. From the conflict comes the second opera, which is played out over the first (*Don Giovanni*). Kierkegaard is and is not posing when he claims to be a young girl in love with this opera. Therein resides the melodrama. Therein philosophy becomes operatic.

I wish to return to Kierkegaard's analysis of the opera's philosophical power, an analysis relying on the concept of the erotic genius turns on a concept that conflates life and art. "Erotic genius" is a principle of human nature, also a musical force: it is found in both persons and works. This identification of life and art or persons and artworks is exemplified in the nineteenth century's elision with the character of opera as such, transubstantiating the Don into a musical principle and anthropomorphizing music into a kind of seductive and genial person(a).

In act 1, scene 4, the morning after his fight with the Commendatore, the Don and Leporello search for a lady who has fascinated the Don. In the first of a series of ensuing comic disasters, she turns out to be Donna Elvira, an ex-conquest whom he seduced through a proposal of marriage (the Don should have learned the truth in the country western song: "All my EXes live in Texas / That's why I live in Tennessee"). At a certain moment the Don stops intensely and exclaims: "Zito! Mi pare sentir odor di femmina" (Quiet, I sense the scent of a women); to which Leporello responds: "Cospetto, che odorato perfetto" (My god, what a perfect nose). The Don then adds, "All'aria, mi par bella" (To judge from the fragrance, she's lovely). Again Leporello: "E che occhio! Dico!" ("And what an eye, I must say"). This is comic, for Leporello's admiration of the Don's perfect nose and eye for women is somewhat ridiculous. Yet it is the Don's perfect nose or his perfect pitch that signifies his capacity to seduce women like an artiste. The perfect nose, the perfect pitch lies behind the power of Mozart's music to seduce us so beautifully. The music makes the Don's own nose sing. When we are aroused by the Don we are so because we are aroused by the music. The Don's seductive power lies in his voice, but also in his nose, giving the former thereby a phallic animation. We are seduced by the voice as Leporello's nose is aroused by the aroma of the Don's food, causing him to steal a few morsels and shove them in his mouth. This is surely an opera about consumption.

The activity of the nose is feminine for the listener, who picks up the aromatic flavor of the music and cannot contain him(her)self, but it is masculine for the Don, who is ready to follow the woman's scent as surely as he would hunt a deer. (Were the opera deeper in its representation of seduction, it would make much of the fact that the Don is himself seduced by the scent of women; *he* is the one who, like a young girl cannot stop and must have his prey at all costs.)

In the scene of eating and drinking, when the Don sits down to eat, he demands music and the on-stage band starts to play. They play first a tune from *Una Cosa Rara*, a well-known opera of the time whose libretto was composed by Da Ponte. Leporello responds: "Bravi! Cosa Rara," but then again when the Don asks what Leporello thinks of the music: "E conforme, e conforme al vostro merto" (It is worthy of you, it conforms to your worth). Here clearly we see that Da Ponte was proud that his libretti not only conformed to Mozart's worth but also facilitated Mozart's compositional style. The suggestion is that Leporello is being allied to Da Ponte himself through an in-joke.

In this exchange there is a rudimentary theory of opera, for if we are invited to think of Leporello's relation to the Don as we are to think of Da Ponte's to Mozart, then the relative weights of opera are being emphasized.

The libretto, while important, is ultimately subservient to the music, which, as Joseph Kerman argues in *Opera as Drama,* is the opera's central characterizing element, the thing that really animates the characters and establishes their narrative force. Let us not underplay the importance of the libretto, without a libretto there can be no dramatic organization. Hence, by associating himself with Leporello, Da Ponte is also joking about himself as the sidekick of the big man.

This association between the two pairs is yet further developed when the musicians turn to playing "non piu andrai" from *Figaro.* Now Leporello exclaims: "Questa poi la conosco pur troppo" (This one I know all too well). Again this is an in-joke both because the music is Mozart's own and because Da Ponte wrote the libretto. So, when Leperello says that he knows this one too well, of course, he does—he helped in his identification with the librettist to write it. In culinary terms a cook is not simply a musician who writes the musical reduction of the piece but the one with the magnificent nose.

The pairing, finally, invites us to reconsider the narrative of the opera and the interweaving specifically of music and seduction. Imagine this opera for the moment as an adventure in seduction by musical composition rather than by physique, wealth, and social status. Imagine the Don as a stand-in for Mozart, Leporello for Da Ponte, and their escapades in the land of women to be a stand-in for Mozart's and Da Ponte's own escapades in the land of opera. Imagine Leporello's list as this: a list of Mozart's own operas, chalked up one by one at a magnificent rate of success. And then Da Ponte himself, as an adventurer of the first order who ended up as the first professor of Italian at Columbia University, credited with his own list of Mozartian successes. Finally, imagine the Don's killing of the Commendatore and the Commendatore's ultimate haunting of him as Mozart's relationship to his own father Leopold. Or the Don's "gorgeous thirst" (to borrow a phrase from *The Philadelphia Story*) to be Mozart's own gorgeous appetite for musical composition. How does the opera look now?

Freud would refer to the transposition of seduction from life into musical composition as a case of taming and civilizing sublimation. The sadist becomes a great surgeon (or, better, a dentist), the strangler a kneader of pasta, the seducer a genius-composer. "The artist wins in reality what the neurotic can only win in fantasy," one can hear Freud saying, "fame, money and the love of women" (artists are apparently all of the male persuasion), and Mozart chalks up opus numbers at a rate dwarfing even Leporello's pen, charming all humanity, seducing the public with his music. Perhaps this is why he chooses the music from *Figaro* to be played while the Don enjoys his last meal: that music has become popular, a symbol of Mozart's and Da Ponte's own success in winning the whole public. The *whole public*, a list of admirers far greater than any mere Spanish *mille e tre*.

This opera is a celebration of the seductive/sensuous power of Mozart's own music. It is a music that Daniel Heartz, for example, has claimed is so aromatic that had "the censors . . . only known how suggestive of the erotic Mozart's music could be, they would surely have banned it."[3] The opera's seduction rests with its compulsive behavior focused on accumulations and lists. That is the point of the sublimation. It is only in music and other arts (and really only in the work of Bach, Mozart, Schubert, and a few others) that the constant accumulation of lists never ceases. There are always new projects of seduction, always the effortless and effervescent charm and originality of love. What is neurotic in life is acceptable in art. To recall, this is why Kierkegaard never wants to prove that the Don lives an empty life.

An icon of the male fantasy of seduction, the opera is a fantasy that turns seduction into a principle and makes artists out of men. But does the opera clear its name of the taint of sexism through this sublimation of life into art? Does the sexism so aestheticized become more natural or acceptable? Do Da Ponte and Mozart's rompings betray the sexism of their male fantasy? Or is Mozart's music *itself* therefore sexist with all its gorgeous melodies, forms, and textures?

The problem lies in identifying what one means by "Mozart's music itself." If one means hearing the notes not only independently of the libretto but independently of the whole pattern of eighteenth- and nineteenth-century music, then it is hard to imagine finding it sexist under such circumstances, music's being too abstract to speak of gender when removed from its libretto and cultural context. Yet few profess to hear music so purely. What would it mean to hear Mozart's music untainted by the entire history of Western music? Imagine someone hearing *Don Giovanni's* music on its own, without knowing anything about the history of the Don Juan myth. Would one find it sexist? Compared to Beethoven it might sound "feminine," compared to Schubert or *Cosi*, "masculine." Or perhaps no thought of gender would arise. But the music is not intended to be heard on its own. It is inextricably allied with its libretto, its narrative in such a way that the latter manifests itself in the aural texture of the former. The narrative speaks through the music. If the narrative is sexist, then the music is duly implicated. There is in *Don Giovanni* no "music itself."

However, what really lasts in this opera is "the (immortal) music." Mozart's music does not simply articulate the narrative, it overwhelms it. (This was the thought behind Kierkegaard's claim that in the opera *Don Giovanni's* music finds its perfect characterization.) Mozart's melodies ultimately color one's picture of who the Don is, as if he were the embodiment of an erotic music of spring. The sense that the Don is a mere symbol for absolute music (for "the musical erotic") is what Kierkegaard meant when he spoke of the Don as an incarnation. The Don is incarnated through an alchemy that makes him both man and music, which makes him both person and composer, both human flesh and figment of opera. The concept of the sensuous erotic genius is that of a metaphysical being eliding the very distinction between life and art, man and music.

Mozart's music—overwhelming the Don's character and glorifying it into a principle of incarnation—makes it less sexist, less the music of machismo. In loving the Don, we love him as a symbol of the incarnation of music in humanity/mankind. But at the same time the Don makes the music more sexist, because the Don is also a rapist, a bastard to women, and a man who beats up other men. But the music makes it seem as if everyone and everything comes up roses, smelling well. If this is not seduction, then nothing is.

We have arrived at the heart of the matter: a seduction by sensuous music that identifies the character of the Don with the music that characterizes him, which also conflates him with the composer himself. It is this transubstantiation of a seducer into an icon of music that prepares the fact of his canonization in the nineteenth and twentieth centuries. He becomes a cultural icon, an erotic-sensuous genius, because this is what is opera makes him. Mozart's music transfigures him. All we then need is Kierkegaard's concept of the "sensuous erotic genius" to instantiate him in the philosophical hall of fame. Here is the dialectic between concept and work: the music exemplifies for us what the concept in the end means, while the concept and the philosophical apparatus behind it dignify the music by canonizing it.

No wonder that there are two vastly different representations of the Don that no one can quite get straight: the one adulates him as an artiste and the other demystifies him as a neurotic. One might say that these two representations form an inherently unstable pattern of meaning for the opera. The audience is caught between viewing him as a killer and idealizing him as nothing less than the voice of Mozart himself. The levitation of human character by music is daunting and thrilling. But the occupation of that space comes at a price, the price of indifference to the human, to life lived on borrowed time that will either be annihilated by the father or end when the four hours of the performance are up. Then we will return to a life in which the Don can no longer function as an icon, a life in which one cannot sing one's way through the world, as if one were simultaneously to consume the world of people and compose the world as art. Does this return signal the end or failure of the Romantic identification of art with life? Is Don

Giovanni killed by the reality principle? Does the opera in the end know that the Romantic ideal is unsustainable and unattainable, as Wagner's operas also show? The Don's own escapades are purchased only on borrowed time. He will die in the end by the hand of the law. Put another way, the law of this opera is the law of life itself, the metaphysical design of a world in which the elision of life with music is in the end uninhabitable, except in the fantasy of those who refuse the reality principle, who refuse to learn what the Oedipus complex has taught them. The law is, when all is sung, said, and done, the reality principle.

Don Giovanni's life is not so much an empty life as an *uninhabitable* one. But, still, how inexorable is the reality principle? How often, and in what strange places, do we find ourselves humming passages from *Don Giovanni* as if we were kings and queens? How often and to what advantage do life and music converge into one? When do we enjoy the thought of seducing a world as if we had composed it? What are the traces of such phallic fantasies in our lives? And, finally, to what extent can we distinguish the sensuousness of Mozart's music from its seductive power? In these questions and in their answers lies the full power and significance of Mozart's opera.

For Kierkegaard these questions were too many and too pressing. He was constitutionally incapable of sustaining the poetry of desire in the face of his own beloved and fled from her *either* into a world of opera *or* into the stark world of his tortured Abraham. For Kierkegaard the philosophical urge to find answers all at once was little more than the bravado of the Don transposed into the conceits of the knowledge disciplines. Who could claim to have a philosophical capacity to descry the essence of this music and of music in general, to know how to canonize and to know what exactly is in the canon, to erect a system of life in which the aesthetic is rightly placed in relation to the ethical and the religious? This is a conceit worthy of the Don. It is also one at odds with the undigested ambivalences betrayed in Kierkegaard's own work. And so Kierkegaard lives and dies, writing his opera.

NOTES

An earlier and quite different version of this paper was published by the Musical Quarterly 78.1 (Spring 1994): 48–77, under the title "The Cook, His Wife, the Composer, and the Librettist." I wish to thank Janet Johnson, Michael Steinberg, Louise Stein, and Steven Whiting for helpful remarks.

1. Søren Kierkegaard, *Either/Or*, trans. Howard V. Hong and Edna H. Hong, *Kierkegaard's Writings*, vol. 4, part 1 (Princeton, 1988), 46.

2. Sigmund Freud, "The Dissolution of the Oedipus Complex" (1924), in *The Standard Edition of the Complete Psychological Works of Sigmund Freud*, ed. and trans. James Strachey (London), 173–179.

3. Daniel Heartz, *Mozart's Operas,* ed., with contributing essays, Thomas Bauman (Berkeley and Los Angeles, 1990), 189.

The Curse and Promise of the Absolutely Musical: *Tristan und Isolde* and *Don Giovanni* [1]

LYDIA GOEHR

There will never be more than one work of which it is possible to say that its idea is absolutely musical.
—Kierkegaard, *Either/Or*

In this essay I argue that Wagner's *Tristan und Isolde* draws upon an idea of the absolutely musical that is strikingly similar to that found in Kierkegaard's interpretation of Mozart's *Don Giovanni*. To acknowledge this similarity is not to deny in *Tristan* the indubitable presence also of Schopenhauer's ideas on music and the world Will. I just want to give credibility to the new and rather different thought that *Tristan* belies Kierkegaard's own claim that *Don Giovanni* is the only classic example of the absolutely musical. *Tristan* was coincidentally composed shortly after Kierkegaard's death in 1855. One wonders what Kierkegaard would have made of Wagner's bid for *Tristan* to realize so similar an idea.

To begin at the beginning, with Wagner's program note:

Yet what fate divided in life now springs transfigured in death: the gates of union are thrown open. Over Tristan's body the dying Isolde receives the blessed fulfilment of ardent longing, eternal union in measureless space, without barriers, without fetters, inseparable.[1]

Or to begin at the end: *Tristan and Isolde* closes with Isolde's transfiguration. Her song erotically and ecstatically brings her into Tristan's dying body. As she enters the Other, the Earth, the Will, she separates herself from the daylight or from the ordinary course of life's experiences that define her as individual subject and desiring self. Her song of transfiguration brings the work's action (*Handlung*) to the completion of what Wagner calls his "most full-blooded musical conception" (*vollblutigste musikalische Konzeption*), his drama absolutely musically conceived.[2]

Wagner's work shows a threefold interest in transfiguration: it has transfiguration as its *subject matter*, it is intended to *affect* its audience through transfigurative experience, and it brings about a transfiguration in the very *concept* of opera. To speak of transfiguration partially invokes the Christian idea according to which one is transported into a kingdom that is "not of this world." However, it also invokes an idea of immanence whereby the absolutely musical or erotic drive courses its way *through* the world transfiguring the world in the process. In the immanent view the absolutely musical drive is productive and destructive. It allows an escape from the world of constraint, yet favors an absolutist construction of aesthetic space. A space created entirely on the basis of erotic desire is one created under the double condition of utter liberation and complete control. The erotic and aesthetic space created by Tristan and Isolde's union is inseparable from the work's claim to be about the seductive character of music, for good and for bad.

The story of *Tristan* recalls a Celtic legend. In act 1 Tristan is escorting the Irish Isolde to Cornwall to marry his uncle, King Marke. Isolde is angry that Tristan has killed her fiancé, Morolt, and decides that he, and she, will die. They drink a death potion that turns out to be a love potion. In act 2 the lovers realize their love during the night. At daybreak the hunting party of the court returns. King Marke catches the lovers in embrace and accuses Tristan of disloyalty. Tristan throws himself on the sword of the jealous young soldier Melot. In act 3 Tristan lies wounded. He awaits Isolde's arrival. She arrives and Tristan is doubly released from his suffering: through love and through death. Isolde sings for him a *Liebestod,* which in the act of singing becomes her own:

Mildly and gently / see him smiling, / see his eyes / softly open! / Ah behold him! / See you not? / ever brighter / brightly shining / borne on starlight / high above? / see you not? / How his heart / so proudly swells, / full and bold / it throbs in his breast? / Gently breathing / stirs his mouth, / ah, how calmly / soft his breath:— / See him friends! / Feel and see you not? Can it be that I alone hear this wondrous tone / . . . / Shall I breathe them, / shall I hear them? / Shall I taste them, / dive beneath them? / Drown in tide of melting sweetness? / In the rapturous swell / . . . / I'm sinking, / I'm drowning / unaware, / Highest Love![3]

In a letter written on June 25, 1872, Wagner told Nietzsche that when attending a performance of *Tristan* he should remove his spectacles and listen to nothing but the orchestra. "Nun *Tristan* wird Ihnen doch interessant sein: nur: Brille ab! Nichts als das Orchester dürfen Sie hören."[4] Was Nietzsche being instructed here to listen to *Tristan* as a work of absolute music? Under one meaning of that phrase it seems he was. After all, it was through the separation of the ear from the eye that Nietzsche himself explained the origins of absolute music:

> It seems that in earlier times something must often have occurred much like what is now going on before our ears and eyes in the development of music; namely of dramatic music: while music without explanatory dance and miming (language of gesture) is at first empty noise, long habituation to that juxtaposition of music and gesture teaches the ear an immediate understanding of the tonal figures. Finally, the ear reaches a level of rapid understanding such that it no longer requires visible movement, and understands the composer without it. Then we are talking about absolute music, that is, music in which everything can be understood symbolically, without further aids.[5]

However, was Nietzsche speaking here of absolute music with its usual meaning, as designating a purely instrumental work of the symphonic genre? If so, why then was he speaking about developments in dramatic music? And why did Wagner himself deny that, in *Tristan*, as indeed in all his works, he was playing into the hands of an absolute musical working out?[6] To forestall confusion we need to distinguish the misleading conclusion that *Tristan* is *a work of absolute music* from the more tempting conclusion that *Tristan* is *an action of the absolutely musical*. To draw this distinction is to shift our attention in two ways, first, away from the idea of *absolute music* to that of *the absolutely musical*, and, second, away from the concept of a *work* to that of an *action*.

Wagner made these conceptual moves necessary if not fully explicit in the rationale he provided for *Tristan*'s genesis. In his writings Wagner rarely referred to the idea of the "absolutely musical" by this name, although he did often speak, albeit critically, of "absolute music" (a phrase he himself introduced into musical discourse). The general distinction here relies significantly on developments in nineteenth-century metaphysics and aesthetics. Following Carl Dahlhaus, the basic thought is that in *Tristan* there are two ideas of *the musical* at work, one having to do with *sounds* and one with *expression*, one *empirical* and one *metaphysical*.[7] Usually the phrase the "*purely*" or "*specifically* musical" refers to the sounding art of tone, and the "*absolutely* musical" to a broader, metaphysical conception, broader, first, because it accommodates the words and dramatic dimension of the work as well as its sounds and, second, because it extends the meaning of the music beyond the empirical domain into a so-described transcendent domain of expression. Still, the "absolutely musical" bears its name insofar as the sounding art of tone justifiably or unjustifiably assumes an aesthetic and metaphysical priority over the other mediums of art in order to give the overall work its meaning. At its core Wagner's aesthetic project was to restore to the idea of music, which in his judgment had become too narrow and formal, the broadest possible expressive and metaphysical significance. In other terms he intended to restore to "absolute music," negatively conceived as a merely sounding or formalist art of tone, its original expressive or absolutely musical character or, as he otherwise put it, to give back to the post-Beethoven symphony its drama. Indeed, the single way to become the one and only true follower of Beethoven, as Wagner aspired to be, was for absolute music to once more "become drama."

To focus on the metaphysical side of *Tristan* is not to dismiss the importance of the work's empirical or musical art of tone: the one account should be suitably compatible with the other. But here I give the metaphysical reading at least to placate the "skepticism" Joseph Kerman once expressed regarding the work's "purely musical claims" if, as he said they do, these claims imply that the unity of the work must be conceived independently of the drama.[8] To avoid this false implication, the so-called purely musical claim must be remade into a more fitting absolutely musical claim. In different terms, my reading provides some background to Virginia Woolf's remark of 1909 that, in *Tristan*, music reaches a point not yet reached by sound and to Patrick Carnegy's later employment of the phrase the "sheerly musical." Carnegy used this phrase to capture Paul Bekker's observation (although Wagner effectively said the same) that, in *Tristan*, sounds rather than people walk upon the stage.[9] Finally, I offer the sort of reading that further amplifies John Deathridge's interpretation of *Tristan* as a "monument to the supposed purity of music," where his "supposed" suggests that Wagner was concerned with far more than the "formalist" art of tone and where his "purity" suggests that Wagner was contributing to the development of a metaphysics of pure aesthetic experience of significant ideological import.[10]

As I develop my argument I pay much attention to Wagner's account of "an action." At this point I make brief use of Hans-Georg Gadamer's pertinent and concise description of the historical development of the concept of an *Erlebnis*.[11] My point in introducing this concept is only to show how well *Tristan* may be conceived of as an aesthetic lived-performance-experience in which the dramatic expression of the absolutely musical is rendered visible in both sensorial and cognitive terms. As "a deed [*Tat*] of music made visible" (to use Wagner's language), *Tristan* fits the aesthetic demands of an *Erlebnis*. The work *Tristan* does or the deed it performs is brought into close accord with the aesthetic experience it promotes. Otherwise put, I employ the concept of an *Erlebnis* insofar as it captures the character of an isolated, self-enclosed, and self-enclosing experience—and particularly an aesthetic experience into which both the lovers within Wagner's work and those in the audience who love the work are drawn. The lovers' experience is accordingly brought into tight analogy with that of the listeners. But, given this analogy, the argument tells us something also about the productive and destructive forces of aesthetic experience. For it lays bare the benefits and dangers of being pulled, drawn, or seduced into a world that is not real.

In describing this seduction I allow Adorno to enter late into my account as the Commendatore enters late into *Don Giovanni* to show that the aesthetic argument of the opera cannot be concluded without reminder also of its moral argument or, as in *Tristan*, without reference to the political tendencies of an emerging authoritarian state. For, in Adorno's view, the terms of absolute music are joined to the terms of an absolute society. I use Adorno's argument to expand my own, the argument concerning the claim that, in realizing Wagner's idea of the absolutely musical, *Tristan* brought about a profound transfiguration, if not also an end, to the very concept of opera. Some critics even claimed that the work brought an end to music too. What is obvious is that what we make of such proclamations usually depends on what we take to be at stake in the German tradition of music. What is not so obvious is how we resolve the conflict between the aesthetic and the moral that remains once we have decided what politically and musically is at stake.

Consider one of the "Either" options from Kierkegaard's *Either/Or*, namely, the musical or immediate stages of the erotic described by a self-confessed lover (named "A") of Mozart's *Don Giovanni*.[12] The first thing the lover claims about Mozart's opera is that it is and will remain unique among the classics of the fine arts because "there will never be more than one work of which it is possible to say that its idea is absolutely musical." In this work the music does not appear as an accompaniment to the text; instead it shows "its own innermost essence in revealing the idea." What does this lover of *Don Giovanni* mean by the idea of the absolutely musical? Apparently an erotic force expressed specifically in the Christian era as something sensuous and demonic. In the opera it is expressed through the figure of Don Giovanni, although *figure* is not really the right term. According to the lover, Don Giovanni is more than just figure; he is also the abstract metaphysical and musical movement of seduction. For the lover the movement sustains in the opera its absolutely musical inwardness and its absolute subject matter. Like Goethe's Faust, so the lover writes, Mozart's Don Giovanni "floats (*schwebt*) between his existence as Idea—which means Energy, Life, and his existence as an individual. This floating is identical to musical trembling or vibration."

For the lover the absolutely musical drive is nonpurposive, disinterested, unreflective, and ahistorical. It is without moral conscience. As primitive energy, it both expresses and is about the endless desire for satisfaction, where each satisfaction only gives rise to a new desire. (That sounds like Schopenhauer.) Don Giovanni acts seductively, although he is not a seducer. His individual conquests or extensive seduction might concern Leporello, the worried list maker, but from his perspective his seduction is intensive and intensional. In the intensive movement Mozart's opera shows its unity of musical mood, its single and overarching breath that constantly returns to the keynote. (That also sounds like Schopenhauer.) Don Giovanni is the keynote or the primitive element that is essentially life. "Don Giovanni is flesh incarnate," the lover says, "the inspiration of the flesh by the spirit of the flesh."

All the time one learns about the opera's interiority, how the absolutely musical expresses itself as sensuous medium and reveals itself as Idea. How does this revelation work? One might think it works through the opera's text or its visual dimensions. Yet the lover pays so little attention to these. All the time he asks his readers just to close their eyes and listen. But to what? Not to the words but to the sensuous force of Don Giovanni's voice, for this voice is the musical voice of seduction. Of course, another voice appears in the opera, the censorious voice of the Commendatore who, on that famous diminished seventh, begins to pull the voice of seduction into hell. Yet, even here, it is not the words of the moral judgment that count for the lover; it is rather the way the voice interrupts, limits, or even negates the erotic drive of the absolutely musical. The lover declares this negation of sensuousness an *unmusical* reassertion of the Christian spirit of life and reflective moral conscience. The reassertion is also a reincarnation, literally a vocal embodiment of the moral.

Seen from the exterior, the opera is about the relation Don Giovanni has as a self to other characters or selves. The opera is about that which one reads in its libretto. But for the lover who listens, this exterior perspective is set aside so that he may assume an internal perspective. Internally, he experiences the opera as an entire and immediate action, without plot, history, or temporal development. The absolutely musical has no past or future; it is always entirely present or contemporaneous such that the overarching *drive* is also the absolutely musical *moment*. This is intended to be true also of the aesthetic experience the work affords. As the lover tells us, his ecstatic listening, even if constituted over time, is experienced at every moment as atemporal, as here and now, as everywhere and nowhere.

> It is this musical life of Don Giovanni, absolutely centralized in the opera, which enables it to create a power of illusion such as no other is able to do, so that its life transports one into the life of the play. Because the musical is omnipresent in this music, one may enjoy any snatch of it, and immediately be transported by it. One may enter in the middle and constantly be in the center of it, because this center, which is Don Giovanni's life, is everywhere.

In this quotation the "musical" is referred to as omnipresent in the music; it is not identical merely to the sounding notes. Further, the lover identifies a structural analogy between his experience of everywhereness and the opera's structure itself. Elsewhere, he thus insists, the opera's overture must have the same content as the opera; it must be an interweaving of the themes and not a labyrinthine hodgepodge of associated ideas. It should be "concise, definite, strongly constructed, and, above all . . . impregnated with the essence of the whole opera." The overture should be related to the opera as prophecy, perhaps also as procreation.

Although there is no known or explicit influence of Kierkegaard's thinking upon Wagner's, the claims made on behalf of *Don Giovanni* fit *Tristan* too, or at least the statements Wagner made on the work's behalf. Wagner wrote that *Tristan* was consciously produced with *his* specific ideas in mind, although he was quick to add that the opera itself surpassed these ideas in its creativity and aesthetic result.[13] It might have been an *opus metaphysicum*, as Nietzsche famously declared it, but the opera was not itself reducible to or exhausted by a metaphysical treatise. The work remained and had to remain an entirely and deeply driven aesthetic deed of the absolutely musical, and that deed resisted any sort of complete articulation in words.

Wagner accordingly wrote that *Tristan's* outer face—the words, the plot, and visual gestures—receives its significance entirely from its inner face, from the interiority provided by the pure and absolutely musical movement of Tristan and Isolde's love. The opera is about inner motives and a drive of nature so deep that it resists mere psychological description. "Life and death," he explained, "the whole import and existence of the outer world, here hang on nothing but the inner movement of the soul. The whole affecting action comes about only because the soul demands it, and brings to light the very shape foretokened by this inner shine."[14] Accordingly, *Tristan's* inner springs of action admit of no outer explanation, yet from the inner depths of the soul the outer form is "fearlessly" and "perfectly built." From the outer form all extraneous detail is removed. The historical story is reduced to the pure (musical) expression of the universal myth contained therein and the libretto is reduced to essence: there are no unnecessary repetitions and no artificial words. "The myth, in whatever age or nation it occurs, has the merit of seizing nothing but the purely human content of that age and nation, and of bringing forth that content in a form that is peculiar to itself, in sharpest outline and immediately understandable."[15]

Like Kierkegaard's *Don Giovanni*, Wagner's *Tristan* is not reducible to a specifically musical or purely instrumental expression formalistically conceived. Although metaphorically symphonic in expression, the symphony conceived merely as an empirical musical genre would be insufficient for the interpretative task at hand. Although *Tristan*'s words and verses are said to articulate only what is already in the music, it is the melody that is brought in this act of articulation beyond itself to ultimate dramatic expression. This expression thus has a dual character: it is empirically purely musical insofar as the opera ends with the final resolution of the so-called *Tristan* chord. But it is also, in Wagner's view, the consummating metaphysical moment of a cry or a lament that spans the entire opera. As in Kierkegaard's *Don Giovanni*, the temporal movement of *Tristan* is transfigured into an absolute and infinitely extended metaphysical moment.

In this dual or transfiguring character Wagner claimed to find the solution to the insuperable contradiction he saw in the operatic genre, the contradiction between music and words, given their interminable battle for control. Wagner's solution did not depend upon his giving to the words and music a shared control. That would offer only a bourgeois marriage (I shall return to this). Instead his solution depended upon his making the words and music work together to produce some sort of transcendent merger aimed toward a single expressive end. He called that end the drama. The relation between music and word is bidirectional: the poet's (outer) idea is inspired by, but gives shape and determinacy to, the composer's (inner) vision. This bidirectionality serves as the means for which the performance, drama, and expression is the end. Through this *refiguring* of means and ends Wagner claimed to *transfigure* opera into music drama.

To bring home just how internally complete (*gesamt*) his new dramatic *Kunstwerk* would be, Wagner rejected (on rather dubious grounds) the idea that a composer's music be set to another man's libretto. Were it to be so set, he surmised, the relationship would be external and artificial. The poet and composer must originate in a single person, and I use the word *person* here deliberately to suggest the possible androgyny or at least the transcendent or internalizing union upon which Wagner wanted to rely (as Kierkegaard relied), not only to generate his solution for opera but also to bring out a core theme of *Tristan and Isolde*. "If I wish to demonstrate that music (as a woman) must necessarily be impregnated by a poet (as a man)," Wagner wrote to Liszt on November 25th, 1850, "then I must ensure that this glorious woman is not abandoned to the first passing libertine, but that she is made pregnant only by the man who yearns for womankind with true, irresistible love."[16] In Mozart's opera the Don was punished for being an extreme libertine. Wagner comparably punished Mozart for not composing his own libretto, although he did praise Mozart for at least having had genius enough to transcend the libretto he did use, a libretto Wagner thought impoverished. In Wagner's *Tristan* no such punishment apparently needs be administered, for Wagner composed his own libretto in union with the music and, through that union, transfigured the erotic drive of the absolutely musical into a drive also of true or perfect love. Conceptually, Wagner insisted that for a drama to be absolutely musical, its content and form do not have to be purely musical in empirical terms, but its expression must be so in metaphysical terms. This happens paradigmatically in *Tristan* where there is a perfect match, so Wagner claimed, between man and woman, poet and composer, subject matter and sensuous content.

Now we know why *Tristan* qualifies, given Wagner's conception, as a Kierkegaardian classic par excellence: it is absolutely musical in subject matter, form, and expression. By synthesizing the *two* lovers—the word and the tone, the man and the woman—into a *single* love, Wagner was able to identify this movement, as Kierkegaard identified Don Giovanni's movement, with the singular but absolute drive of the work itself. Given the purely aesthetic terms of the argument, the fact that one drive mirrors a heartfelt love and the other a heartless seduction makes absolutely no difference, which is why eventually the moral voice must return.

Like *Don Giovanni*, *Tristan* offers a tight analogy between the erotic experience of love and the aesthetic experience of ecstatic listening. Wagner demanded: "The audience should he held throughout." His wife, Cosima, comparably observed of *Tristan* that "everyone who has ever been in love, even if it was a false or foolish love, must have felt the tragedy of love and of life, and will respond to the magic." Cosima continued: the listeners "will feel increasingly liberated from [their] burdens" and will be "transformed by inner impressions which, slumbering inside [them], now awake to enlighten [them]."[17]

Recall Wagner's instruction to Nietzsche that we close our eyes. This instruction was a demand for a change in the way we look, a demand that we turn our *out-sight* into an *in-sight*, our eye of seeing into an ear of seeing, or our eye of seeing into an eye of listening. Such a transfiguration in consciousness is exactly what happens, so Wagner claimed, to Tristan and Isolde in the realization of their love. Hence, just as they are erotically involved, just as they experience sublime ecstasy (and Wagner had no problem in regarding the highest form of love as erotically embodied), so, in comparable mental and physical condition, are we as listeners supposed to engage with the work as lovers. "It is a question, you see," Wagner now wrote to his lover Mathilde Wesendonck, "of pointing out the path of salvation, which has not been recognized by any philosopher, and especially not by Sch[openhauer], but which involves a total pacification of the will through love, and not through any abstract human love, but a love engendered on the basis of sexual love."[18] Wagner, as Kierkegaard, was making no mere ontological point when he said, as Kierkegaard said, that the musical work exists only in the moment of performance or when the music assumes so total visible or dramatic form that the music comes fully to the senses.

As our experience as listeners begins, we are supposed like lovers to be drawn in sympathy into a sensorial or synesthetic confusion of our eyes and ears. Following or perhaps surpassing Schopenhauer, we are meant to be drawn away from day into night. Like Tristan and Isolde, we are not supposed to know any longer whether we see what we are seeing with our eyes or with our ears: "Wie, hör' ich das Licht?" Tristan asks in his last sublime moments of life. The world we see from the perspective of the everyday is transfigured into the perspective of night. For night is a place, or better an experience, without time or space. At night one enters the world of dreams, the secrets, the silence, and the selflessness that marks one's suspension of individuation and absorption into the world as Will. "The inward face of consciousness attains the power of sight only when our waking daylight consciousness feels nothing but a vague impression of the midnight background of our will's emotion, so that from out of this night a tone bursts upon the world of waking, a direct utterance of the will."[19] In act 2 the lovers comparably sing:

> Oh, sink around us / night of loving / let me now / forget I'm living, / bear me softly / unto thee, / from the world / oh set me free / . . . Heart on heart / and mouth on mouth; / one the breath that now we breathe; / bright desire of joy / will blind me, / and all the world / I leave behind me: / all that the day / lit with its lie, / and all of its madness / I can defy, / I, myself. / am the world.[20]

Absorbed in endless love, in endless aesthetic experience, we are also meant like the lovers to suspend our questions, in Schopenhauer's terms, the principle of sufficient reason and, in Wagner's, all the "whys, whences, and wherefores." Drama, Wagner wrote,

> at the moment of its actual scenic representation, arouses in the beholder such an intimate and instant interest in an action borrowed faithfully from life itself, at least from its possibilities, that our sympathetic Feeling already passes into that ecstatic state where it clean forgets the fateful question "Why?" and willingly yields itself, in utmost excitation, to the guidance of those new laws whereby Music makes herself so wondrously intelligible and—in a profounder sense—supplies withal the only fitting answer to that question "Why"?[21]

We are not supposed rationally to clarify our experience, as Tristan does not and cannot clarify Isolde's erotic confusion over her identity: "*Du (ich) Isolde, Tristan ich (du)*." Of course the drama is notable for just how many questions Tristan and Isolde do ask. Yet these questions are posed not to make worldly sense of them, to give answers, but rather to mark the process of transfiguration, the fact their consciousness is entering into a different state. The questioning releases the lovers, as it is intended to release us, from the illusory understanding (*Wahn*) and suffering that comes with daylight reflection, and takes them, as it is intended to take us, to a heightened consciousness that comes with nighttime insight. This transfigured consciousness is, in Wagner's terms (but actually quoting Feuerbach), "a purely-human power of discernment" that moves us beyond our selves and our reason. Following Schopenhauer again, Wagner aims to reveal the limits of a (Cartesian) clarity to show a purportedly higher clarity, a clarity that comes less from our becoming literally insensible or unconscious, as one Wagner scholar describes it[22] (and as Wagner sometimes described it himself), than from our senses and consciousness becoming epistemologically enhanced. The potion the lovers drink at the beginning of the work serves as a channel toward not merely love but also truth. Tristan sings: "From the vision of my inmost heart did enshrine, gone was the daylight's false shrine; and night-sighted, before me I saw truth in glory."[23]

For Wagner, aesthetic experience stands to everyday experience as love stands to arranged marriage. In both the world is seen from two different attitudes: that determined by bourgeois codes of honor and duty, from one perspective, and by freedom from such codes, from the other. "When for death's dark night," Tristan sings:

> loving, have yearned; / when all her holy / secrets have learned: / then daylight's falsehood, / fame and might, / praise and renown, / that shine so bright,

/ like motes in sunbeams scattered / are turned to dust and shattered! / And of daylight's idle burning / all that remains is yearning, / that yearning deep / for holy night, / where endless and / always true, / Love brings laughing delight![24]

Consider again the drama's end, the death of Tristan and Isolde, and the end of the aesthetic experience. Wagner wrote:

> [*Tristan* is about the] endless yearning, longing, the bliss and misery of love; world, power, fame, honor, chivalry, loyalty and friendship, all scattered like an insubstantial dream; one thing alone left living—longing, longing unquench-able, a yearning, a hunger, a languishing forever renewing itself; one sole re-demption—death, surcease, a sleep without awakening. . . . [But] shall we call it death? Or is it not the wonder-world of Night, whence, as the story tells, an ivy and vine sprang of old in locked embrace over Tristan and Isolde's grave?[25]

Does this ending suggest that we ought now to challenge the analogy between the lovers' and the listener's experience? Only if we accept the utterly banal contrast that the lovers die (or at least lose consciousness) and listeners do not. But perhaps the analogy still holds if we think of Wagner as having helped preserve a universal myth about love to which listeners can return every time they enter aesthetically into his drama. Or, to put the option differently, if we regard Tristan and Isolde's death to be the sort of permanent transfiguration into heightened consciousness that we take to be the aspiration of our own aesthetic experience. That this is the aspiration of aesthetic experience needs support. For this, I turn to Gadamer's *Truth and Method*, although just to the section that allows us to see just how much is involved in Wagner's concept of an action (*Handlung*). For Gadamer ties the concept of a work of art closely to that of an *Erlebnis*, with the consequence that the aesthetic state or the im-pact of art is located just where we now want it to be located (at least for the purposes of the present argument), namely, in a life that strives to be lived, as Don Giovanni strives to live, at the fullest, or in a life that strives to be lived, as Tristan and Isolde strive to live, in truth.

Gadamer describes the history of the concept of an *Erlebnis* from Hegel to Simmel via Dilthey, Schleiermacher, Husserl, and Bergson. It originated, he says, along with a particular kind of biographical (Rousseauan) writing. Cap-turing the immediacy of inner experience, the experience of totality and infin-ity, a living freedom, or an aesthetic spirit, the concept began quickly to sub-vert the claims of cold reason and the restraints of a positivistic or mechanistic society. An *Erlebnis* increasingly suggested an act or element of life that succeeds in remaining connected to the infinity of life, something like a complete picture of the universe removed from all explanatory contexts. In this view an *Erlebnis* comes to be conceived of as a self-contained, significant whole. Its meaning cannot be spelled out conceptually; it remains condensed and intensified. Its teleological and temporal direction or directionlessness is such as to set it apart from the usual flow of life's experiences. Once put into the past, the total experience remains in memory to be reconstituted at will in an intentional act of consciousness. In memory it is retained as irreplaceable and inexhaustible in significance.

Over the course of its history the *Erlebnis* assumed the character of a lived adventure, an adventure that always interrupts the customary course of events. However, as an interruption it remains related to the whole it interrupts. Remaining so, it changes the way we feel about the whole; it allows us to feel the whole as an entire life in which all obligation, restraint, and habit has been removed. However, though the adventure allows us to change our perspective on the everyday, it remains for us a distinct experience that exists outside of our lives. As such it retains its exemplary or exceptional character. An *Erlebnis*, Gadamer concludes, is like a test from which one emerges enriched and more mature. The life-affirming point of the *Erlebnis* now emerges: the living self is transfigured by the experience it has the courage to undergo. It takes courage to be released from one's self or to stand ecstatically beside one's self.

The essence or paradigm of an *Erlebnis* is, then, an aesthetic experience, where the aesthetic experience is to be understood, if we are to use more of Gadamer's terms, as *the work of the work of art*. The work that a work of art does results in a symbolic representation of life. The use of the term *symbolic* conveys the sense in which a pure work of art becomes something abstracted from context in the process of play and aesthetic differentiation. A work of art takes place in and as a performance in which listeners or observers abstract the artwork out of the context of the empirical or real world to render it purely aesthetic, an abstractive and active deed that requires them to achieve a state of self- or world-forgetfulness as they enter into the new world of the work of art. In an *Erlebnis* the aesthetic state to which we aspire through the movement of aesthetic differentiation is not only an ecstatic emotion of the moment; as I have already suggested, it may well be experienced as a movement toward a heightened, absolute, or consummating moment. But even more, the experience makes a claim to permanence in its aspiration to transfigure the living self.

As I have already argued, *Tristan*, according to Wagner's own conception, is not well conceived formalistically, as a work of pure music. It is far better conceived as a dramatic action or as a performance of the absolutely musical.

But more, to draw on Gadamer's description, it is also well conceived of as an *Erlebnis*, almost a self-reflective one, that both expresses and articulates within the work itself the very conditions of an *Erlebnis*. This is not entirely surprising; the theorists of the *Erlebnis* increasingly came to have Wagner's works in mind when determining the condition of the experience. In these terms, *Tristan* is not just an example of, but it is also self-reflectively *about,* the aspiration to transfigure consciousness or free subjectivity (the freeing of subjects from the world's constraints) through the immediacy of musical-erotic performance.

And yet, in the absolutely musical or erotic drive, in the construction it promotes of a self-enclosed aesthetic experience, all the dangers lie. Wagner once remarked that *Tristan* might lead his listeners to madness. "This *Tristan*," he wrote to Mathilde in April 1859, "is turning into something terrible! This final Act!!!—I fear the opera will be banned–unless the whole thing is parodied in a bad performance—: only mediocre performances can save me! Perfectly good ones will be bound to drive people mad,—I cannot imagine it otherwise. This is how far I have gone!! Oh dear!"[26]

What might Wagner have meant by this? Perhaps he was genuinely expressing a fear that his music would drive people mad. Or perhaps that his drama would arouse listeners to so ecstatic a frenzy that they would undertake not just unseemly behavior in the boxes (as, apparently, an early critic once feared) but also acts of violence in the world. Or, more metaphysically, perhaps Wagner was worrying that *Tristan* would put his listeners into an eternal state of transfigured consciousness without hope of return to the everyday. Would this actually be so bad? Or would this not just be an overly anxious expression of the Romantic aspiration to live life as aesthetically as possible, in nighttime vision? Or following Gadamer, was not the point of the experience to bring the learning it yields back into our everyday lives precisely to make our ordinary lives feel less ordinary?

For all the optimism associated with improving our lives by aesthetic means, this improvement cannot function, as both *Don Giovanni* and *Tristan* demonstrate, without consideration also of the moral or social character of the aesthetic *Erlebnis* we construct. Although Kierkegaard tells us that, as lovers, we should suspend our judgment of the drive that is Don Giovanni as *Idea*, we are never really allowed to forget the moral failings that belong to Don Giovanni as *individual.* If we do forget, the entrance of the stone guest returns ruthlessly to remind us. Because of this, it seems to be a consequence of Mozart's opera that its aesthetic drive is never brought to completion and is rather interrupted where it should be, with the entrance of the moral voice. What occurs after Don Giovanni's fall is not a continuation of his drive but the new beginning of a balanced and harmonious song, a song that brings the work to an apparently ordered and happy end. Where, for the entire opera, all the characters are drawn into the seductive space that Don Giovanni creates, they return after his fall to live with more wisdom in worlds again of their own making. They return to what Bernard Williams describes as the "real conditions of a human life."

Comparably in *Tristan*, the aesthetic or musical drive of the lovers is interrupted by the return of daylight and the hunting party. Judgment is issued. Tristan's punishment is administered and accepted. However, the return is a double-edged sword, as Tristan realizes when his too faithful or too faithless friend pierces his body. For the sword is either a death blow to, or a sober reminder of, the truth that a life that fully escapes life is not a life at all: at best it is a life lived in an opera. As in *Don Giovanni*, even if aesthetic experience improves or brings eventual wisdom to the "real conditions of human life," life itself cannot and should not be transfigured entirely into a purely aesthetic mode.

And yet in *Tristan* this is arguably exactly what is allowed to happen, because even though King Marke enters as the Commendatore enters to describe the moral crime, he ultimately forgives the lovers their transgression. Probably the assumed fact that they acted out of true love rather than out of seductive desire made all the difference to his moral assessment. In *Don Giovanni* the moral moment disturbs the construction of the aesthetic space of seduction; in *Tristan* moral forgiveness keeps the aesthetic drive in movement, so that when, finally, we hear Isolde's *Liebestod* we hear that drive brought to completion. If there is a danger in *Tristan*, it lies here, in the fact that the aesthetic remains supreme over the moral, i.e., that the aesthetic drive of the opera absorbs the moral interruption. However, that one sees danger in the supremacy of the aesthetic drive does not mean that one should rather endorse the supremacy of the moral. For to allow the moral moment to reign supreme might run the risk of letting the opera end, as arguably it ends in *Don Giovanni*, in no more than a didactic, moralizing gesture. Surely it is better because it is most truthful, despite its being the most difficult thing to achieve, to have an ending that keeps the moral moment and aesthetic drive in suspended tension.

With this thought, one may further capture the import of Wagner's worry about driving his listeners mad. For now we may ask about the control Wagner wanted to impose over the redemptive possibilities of his drama. As it has often been said, Wagner left the endings of his works often frustratingly but fascinatingly inconclusive. *Tristan* was no exception, and this despite its dramatic appearance of utter finality. Indeed Wagner's endings can be read, and have been read, as suggesting almost the entire range of aesthetic, religious, and political visions of redemption and utopia. Surveying the range, critics often try to determine whether the endings express an optimism or pessimism about the redemptive possibilities of art in an era where religion has purportedly declined. Partially, it is thus said, the inconclusiveness of Wagner's works resulted from his own uncertainty as to how to complete his philosophical thoughts, his uncertainty as to the coherence of his proposed *Kunstreligion*. More relevantly for the present argument, critics also try to assess the extent to which Wagner's music dramas end up aestheticizing their moral or political content.

Recall Wagner's claim that music offers a way for us to escape or transfigure the ordinary sense of our words or utterances. Moving, as we said, from out-sight to in-sight, the assumption is that we like the lovers move closer to the truth. But, as we know from the work's beginning, the love potion is always also a death potion: a poison. We are just made by the musical drive to forget that fact. Perhaps then, like the lovers and King Marke, we are led through their transfiguration to anything but the truth.

Wagner once commented to Cosima that "music has the power to transfigure everything." It "never permits the hideousness of the bare word, however terrible the subject."[27] Is this a good or a bad thing? We do not know. When critics say that Wagner's dramas are left essentially open or that they fail to complete their lesson, it is in part because they are, as *Tristan* is, aesthetic performances whose effects on audiences cannot be fully controlled. *Tristan* ends, one might say, not as a conclusion to a metaphysical treatise would end, with a definite statement about what is true, but rather as the culminating point of an absolutely musical movement that, through the entire work, has worked through the bodies as much as the minds of its listeners perhaps altogether for the bad. We hope this is not so but we are given no guarantee by the work that this will not be the case.

In tandem with this, it is because Wagner's dramas refuse conclusively to articulate their messages that they also lay themselves open to ideological appropriation (even by Wagner—as a writer on his own works—himself). Herein lies the *curse* of the openness of works of art, the easy appropriation of purely musical expression by the sometimes hideous bare word, an appropriation that succeeds because it is believed that the purely musical expression will disguise the hideousness. However in the same place, in the indeterminacy or openness, lies also the *promise* of a freedom from ideological control and the *possibility* also to expose the latter for what it is. The distinction between the purely and absolutely musical proves pertinent once more to sustain the idea I am proposing of a double or suspended ending. Wagner held the view that whenever the absolutely musical is brought under our control it ceases to be absolutely musical; instead it becomes pure or absolute music in a negative sense—music that is "meaningless" or "lacks expressive import." The point was a clever one even if Wagner's articulation of it was profoundly unfortunate. For when he spoke negatively of music's being "pure" or "absolute" he spoke of it as "French," "foreign," and "Jewish." In this articulation he submitted to the curse he was arguably trying to resist.

Consider finally the thought that Wagner's *Tristan* transfigures opera into music drama not only because it solves its problem but also because it renders that solution fully conscious by using both the terms and means of art. Many have claimed that *Tristan* is the first work of Modernism or the last work of Romanticism. One critic declared it to be "a milestone in the history of music"; another said it marked "the moment when modern music began" or when "romanticism came to an end." Another declared the opera "a primary source in the history of modern music." One simply insisted it was "the beginning and end of all music."

The obvious claim is this: to the extent that *Tristan* brought opera to its end it did so by initiating (alongside Wagner's other dramas) the modern movement of the music drama. However, the more subtle claim is that when or if *Tristan* brought opera to its end, it brought music to its end as well, but when *Tristan* initiated the modern movement of the music drama it initiated also the Modernist movement of the absolutely musical. Many critics of the twentieth century have claimed that music died around 1900 and that after that composers no longer composed music. An early critic of *Tristan* seemed to have had the foresight: "50 years of this music," he said, "and music [will be] dead, for melody will have been slain and melody is the soul of music."[28]

The only point in taking this claim seriously (although not too seriously) is to allow the thought that even if composers did not strictly speaking compose melodies after 1900, some of them at least continued to express the absolutely musical in another way: perhaps as an eloquent expression of suffering or as an eloquent escape from suffering through the erotic expression of bodily delight. In a century of radically new and horrifying experience, such forms of aesthetic expression—desperate and decadent—were arguably the least nostalgic ways to sustain music's utopian moment. "Is it only I," Isolde asks in her final lines, "who hears these . . . wondrous strains?" The question here is whether it matters that the strains we hear after her song has been sung are no longer the wondrous strains of traditional melody. Isolde seems to offer an answer and arguably a progressive one. It has been claimed of Isolde's transfiguration that it brought tonality to the brink of extinction.

But in the song she sings she seems to express no regret for the world or for the music she leaves behind. Lament, to reuse Wagner's term, is not always accompanied by regret.

At the same time, however, one may hear Isolde's song as a song sung by and for those who have been disempowered in the world. Were Tristan to have sung the final lines, we might have spoken of this disempowerment in terms of a Modernist impotence. No one articulated the thought here better than Adorno, the thinker who, with his own comparisons of Kierkegaard and Wagner, finally enters the account. Adorno described an *aesthetic vision* —in this case the vision of the absolutely musical—in order to unmask it also as *social delusion*. In the lovers' escape he saw only a fatal recognition of the truth that the world (as it had emerged through Enlightenment) was false. Thus, with the deepest deliberation, he concluded his own book on Wagner with something very like a *Liebestod*, in which he tried to capture the dialectical relationship between the curse and promise of the absolutely musical. Music, he would argue, has the ability both to create and to break its own spell.

> Music, the most magical of all the arts, learns to break the spell it casts over the characters. When Tristan curses love, this is more than the impotent sacrifice offered up by rapture to asceticism. It is the rebellion—futile though it may be—of the music against the iron laws that rule it, and only in its total determination by those laws can it regain the power of self-determination. It is not for nothing that those phrases in the *Tristan* score which follow the words "*Der furchtbare Trank*" stand on the threshold of modern music in whose first canonic work, Schoenberg's F# minor quartet, we find the words, "Nimm mir die Liebe, gib mir dein Glück!" They mean that love and happiness are false in the world in which we live and that the whole power of love has passed over into its antithesis. Anyone able to snatch such gold from the deafening surge of the Wagnerian orchestra would be rewarded by its altered sound, for it would grant him that solace which, for all its rapture and phantasmagoria, it consistently refuses.

In this refusal Adorno found a moment of hope, the possibility of an old protest of music to promise a life without fear.[29] But the promise was not pure since it was offered only against the background of works that had already capitulated to the demands of a world that was false. Thus, with Horkheimer, Adorno brought *Tristan* into close relation to the products of the culture industry. He used Wagner's dream of the *Gesamtkunstwerk* to signify the totalitarian tendency toward the sort of uniformity and sameness he took to characterize the modern production of cars and films. Though such products were advertised as offering something different or unique, they collapsed each and every time into a cold repetition of the "everywhere the same." Relevant here is less Adorno's critique of "sameness" and "conformity" and more how he used *Tristan* to establish a direct line or a social form of the seductive drive from Bayreuth to Hollywood. For here was a line, according to Adorno, that ended in a terrifying celebration of "invested capital." "The accord between word, image, and music," he wrote accordingly (with Horkheimer),

> is achieved so much more perfectly [even] than in Tristan because the sensuous elements, which compliantly document only the surface of social reality, are produced in principle within the same technical work process, the unity of which they express as their true content. This work process integrates all the elements of production, from the original concept of the novel, shaped by its side-long glance at film, to the last sound effect. . . . To impress the omnipotence of capital on the hearts of expropriated job candidates as the power of their true master is the purpose of all films, regardless of the plot selected by the production directors.[30]

I have argued that in the construction of the endings of *Don Giovanni*, first, and *Tristan*, second, there is a shared assumption at work, namely, that through the means of art transfigurative experience is possible for its spectators. It is tempting to assume that transfigurative experience always has a positive effect or outcome. This is a false assumption. We have seen how the drive of the absolutely musical, be it a drive of pure seduction or of pure love, constructs an aesthetic space into which an audience enters. The drive is constructed as a drive toward freedom or liberation. Yet, at the same time, the drive fails to fully control the audience it claims to liberate. Accordingly, we are forced to ask: what freedom does music unleash? Freedom in what form? Freedom at what cost? Does not the drive toward freedom too easily transform itself into one toward absolute control precisely to keep the "madness" of its audience in check?

Adorno described a historical dialectic between desirable and undesirable freedom. What he feared in music, and in Wagner especially, was a freedom transformed into an authority, the absolutely musical drive in *Tristan* transfigured through the dialectical movement of history into a politics of absolute mastery (*Allmacht*). Behind Wagner's desire to construct an aesthetic space that would transfigure experience was the presumption of an authority to control the future of music and society. Adorno described this "politics" of aesthetic transfiguration precisely, with Walter Benjamin, to warn against what he saw to be a dangerous political use made of the aesthetic as part of a totalitarian drive to aestheticize the ordinary conditions of everyday life. Yet he did not intend thereby to remove from the absolutely musical the residual moment of hope and desirable freedom. To do so would have been to allow artworks to capitulate entirely to a politics they had the power also to survive. Correctly, in my view, Adorno sought to articulate the terms by which to keep endings suspended such that one could hold onto the promise of the drive of the absolutely musical in full acknowledgment simultaneously of its curse. One way to keep the endings suspended is through the technique of interruption, the interruption of the aesthetic by the moral, but also of the moral by the aesthetic. For such a suspension leaves the audience neither mad, nor morally superior, but rather more conscious of the deep contradictions manifested in these dramatic masterpieces.

In other terms, if the survival of a promise is inherent to *Tristan*'s absolutely musical drive, then it is so, or should be so, also in *Don Giovanni*. Both resist having and becoming the final word. This I think was exactly not shown in a recent, and otherwise excellent, Peter Konwitschny production of *Don Giovanni* at Berlin's Komische Oper (2003). Underplaying the Don Giovanni moment—the interrupting entrance of the Commendatore—the production concluded instead with the hero-sinner's castration by the community of people he had both hurt and pleasured. The punishment was little different from being sent to hell: there was no difference in the extremity of the punishment. Even so, the moral import of the moment was altered. Dressed in a suit, Don Giovanni was transformed into an impotent businessman in whom neither women nor men any longer took an interest. The hero was doubly divested, both of his *vitality* and his *freedom,* to use Bernard Williams's terms once again. No longer able to put "the conditions of real life" into question, he was made to capitulate to present conditions. He was denied the possibility of difference and was reduced to the always and everywhere "the same": the gray suit of modern times. If this was Adorno's fear for music and society, it was Williams's fear too insofar as he took the opera's moral import to turn not just on the actual conditions of real life but also on the possibilities of living life to the fullest in a world that is through and through real. What it means to live life to the fullest in a world that is real but false puts an Adornian dent into Williams's sanguinity. Be that as it may: in both accounts, as in my own account, there is still a shared thought, namely, that to castrate Don Giovanni, to transfigure him into a Modernist figure only of impotence, is to deny the possibility of an interruption of art in life or life in art, a denial that marks an end no less puritanical or censorious as denying in Isolde's song the possibility of a future for music.

NOTES

An earlier version of this essay appeared in 1999 under the title "Wagnerian Endings: The Curse and Promise of Purely Musical Listening, a Metaphysical Reading of *Tristan und Isolde*," for the yearbook of the Amsterdam School of Cultural Analysis, Netherlands. The present version is completely revised.

1. "Doch, was das Schicksal für das Leben trennte, lebt nun verklärt im Tode auf; die Pforte der Vereinigung ist geöffnet. Über Tristans Leiche gewahrt die sterbende Isolde die seligste Erfüllung des glühenden Sehnens, ewige Vereinigung in ungemessenen Räumen, ohne Schranken, ohne Banden, unzertrennbar!" Richard Wagner, *Sämtliche Schriften und Dichtungen (SSD)* (Leipzig, 1911), 12:345; *The Wagner Operas*, trans. Ernest Newman (New York, 1949), 205.

2. Richard Wagner, letter to Franz Liszt, December 1854, *Sämtliche Briefe, SSD* 6:298; ed. and trans. Stewart Spencer and Barry Millington, no 177, in *Selected Letters of Richard Wagner* (New York, 1987), 323.

3. "Mild und leise / wie er lächelt, / wie das Auge / hold er öffnet: / seht ihr, Freunde, / seht ihr's nicht? / Immer lichter / wie er leuchtet, / sternumstrahlet / hoch sich hebt: / seht ihr's nicht? / Wie das Herz ihm / mutig schwillt, / voll und hehr / im Busen quillt; / wie den Lippen / wonnig mild / süsser Atem / sanft entweht:— / Freunde! Seht!— / Fühlt und seht ihr's nicht?— / Hör ich nur / diese Weise, / die so wunder— / voll und leise, / . . . / soll ich atmen, / soll ich lauschen?/ Soll ich schlürfen, / untertauchen? / süß in Düften / mich verhauchen? / In dem wogenden Schwall, / . . . / ertrinken— / versinken— / unbewußt— / höchste Lust!" *SSD* 7:81; *Tristan and Isolde*, trans. Andrew Porter, English National Opera (London, 1981). All quotations from this libretto are from these sources.

4. Dieter Borchmeyer and Jörg Salaquarda, eds., *Nietzsche und Wagner. Stationen einer epochalen Begegnung* (Frankfurt, 1994), 1:191; trans. no. 409 of *Selected Letters*, 810.

5. "Es scheint sich da in früher Zeit das Selbe oftmals ereignet zu haben, was jetzt vor unseren Augen und Ohren in der Entwickelung der Musik, namentlich der dramatischen Musik, vor sich geht: während zuerst die Musik, ohne erklärenden Tanz und Mimus (Gebärdensprache), leeres Geräusch ist, wird durch lange Gewöhnung an jenes Nebeneinander von Musik und Bewegung das Ohr zur sofortigen Ausdeutung der Tonfiguren eingeschult und kommt endlich auf eine Höhe des schnellen Verständnisses, wo es der sichtbaren Bewegung gar nicht mehr bedarf und den Tondichter ohne dieselbe *versteht*. Man redet dann von absoluter Musik, das heisst von Musik, in der Alles ohne weitere Beihülfe sofort symbolisch verstanden wird." Giorgio Colli and Mazzino Montinari, eds., *Menschliches, Allzumenschliches, Kritische Studienausgabe*, vol. 2 (Munich, 1999), no. 216, 176–177; *Human, All Too Human: A Book for Free Spirits*, trans. Marion Faber and Stephen Lehmann (Lincoln, NE, 1986), 129.

6. Wagner, *"Zukunftsmusik,"* *SSD*, 123; *Richard Wagner's Prose Works*, trans. William Ashton Ellis (Lincoln Nebraska, 1995), 3:331.

7. Carl Dahlhaus, *Richard Wagner's Music Dramas*, trans. Mary Whittall (Cambridge, 1979), 5–6.

8. Joseph Kerman, *Opera as Drama* (California, 1988), 171.

9. Patrick Carnegy, "The Staging of *Tristan and Isolde*: Landmarks Along the Appian Way," Opera Guide, 29.

10. John Deathridge, "Post-Mortem on Isolde," in David J. Levin, ed., *Richard Wagner, New German Critique* 69 (1996): 103.

11. Hans-Georg Gadamer, *Truth and Method* (London, 1975), 55–90. Many theorists, including Gadamer and often following Benjamin and Adorno, argued not only for preserving the distinction between two concepts of "experience," *Erlebnis* and *Erfahrung*, but also for the preferability of employing the latter concept in various contexts of aesthetic and philosophical theory.

12. Søren Kierkegaard, *Either/Or*, trans. David F. and Lillian Marvin Swenson, vol. 1 (New York, 1959), 1:45–134. All passages on Kierkegaard are drawn from these pages.

13. In this section, unless specified otherwise, Wagner's remarks are all drawn from his *Zukunftsmusik*, 118ff; trans. 320–329.

14. "Leben und Tod, die ganze Bedeutung und Existenz der äußeren Welt, hängt hier allein von der inneren Seelenbewegung ab. Die ganze ergreifende Handlung kommt nur dadurch zum Vorschein, daß die innerste Seele sie fordert, und sie tritt so an das Licht, wie sie von innen aus vorgebildet ist"; Wagner, *Zukunftsmusik*, 123; trans. 331.

15. "Die Sage, in welche Zeit und welche Nation sie auch fällt, hat den Vorzug, von dieser Zeit und dieser Nation nur den rein menschlichen Inhalt aufzufassen und diesen Inhalt in einer nur ihr eigenthümlichen, äußerst prägnanten und desshalb schnell verständlichen Form zu geben"; Wagner, *Zukunftsmusik*, 120–121; trans. 328 (modified).

16. "Wenn ich der musik, als weib, die nothwendige befruchtung durch den dichter, als manne, nachweisen will, so muß ich sorgen, daß dieses herrliche weib nicht an den ersten besten wüstling preisgegeben werde, sondern daß nur der mann sie befruchtet, der aus wahrer, unwiderstehlicher liebe nach dem weibe sich sehnt"; Richard Wagner, *Sämtliche Briefe*, ed. G. Strobel and W. Wolf (Leipzig, 1983), 3:467; trans. no. 118 of *Selected Letters*, 220–221.

17. "Ich behaupte, daß jeder, der geliebt und selbst in einer falschen oder törichten Liebe befangen war, eben die Tragik der Liebe und des Lebens empfunden haben wird und sich dem Zauber hingeben wird"; Cosima Wagner, *Die Tagebücher*, ed. M. Gregor-Dellin and D. Mack (Munich, 1976–1977), 2:255–256; trans. *Cosima Wagner's Diaries*, G. Skelton (New Haven, 1997), 337.

18. "Es handelt sich nämlich darum, den von keinem Philosophen, namentlich auch von Sch. nicht, erkannten Heilsweg zur vollkommenen Beruhigung des Willens durch die Liebe, und zwar nicht einer abstracten Menschenliebe, sondern der wirklich, aus dem Grunde der Geschlechtsliebe, d.h. der Neigung zwischen Mann und Weib keimenden Liebe, nachzuweisen"; *Richard Wagner an Mathilde Wesendonck. Tagebuchblätter und Briefe* 1853–1871 (Leipzig, 1913 [1908]), 79; trans. no 227 of *Selected Letters*, 432.

19. Wagner, "Beethoven," *SSD*, 9:68; trans. *Prose Works*, 67.

20. "O sink' hernieder, / Nacht der Liebe, / gieb Vergessen, / daß ich lebe; / nimm mich auf / in deinen Schoß, / löse von / der Welt mich los! . . . Herz an Herz, dir, / Mund an Mund, / Eines Atems / ein'ger Bund; / bricht mein Blick sich / wonneblindet, / erbleicht die Welt / mit ihrem Blenden: / die uns der Tag / trügend erhellt, / zu täuschendem Wahn / entgegengestellt, / selbst dann / bin ich die Welt."

21. "Den Weg hierzu wird die Poesie leicht finden und ihr letztes Aufgehen in die Musik als ihr eigenes, innigstes Verlangen erkennen, sobald sie an der Musik selbst ein Bedürfniß inne wird, welches wiederum nur die Dichtkunst stillen kann. Um dieses

Bedürfniß zu erklären, bestätigen wir zunächst die unvertilgbare Eigenthümlichkeit des menschlichen Wahrnehmungsprozesses, welche ihn zum Auffinden der Gesetze der Kausalität drängte, und vermöge welcher vor jeder eindrucksvollen Erscheinung er sich unwillkürlich fragt: Warum? Auch die Anhörung eines symphonischen Tonstückes bringt diese Frage nicht gänzlich zum Schweigen"; Wagner, *Zukunftsmusik*, III–112; trans. 320.

22. Cf. Peter Wapnewski, "The Operas as Literary Works," *Wagner Handbook*, ed. Ulrich Müller and Peter Wapnewski, trans. J. Deathridge (Cambridge, Mass., 1992), 71.

23. "Von dem Bild in des Herzens / bergendem Schrein/ scheucht' er des Tages / täuschenden Schein, / daß nachtsichtig mein Auge / wahr es zu sehen tauge."

24. "Wer des Todes Nacht / liebend erschaut, / wem sie ihr tief / Geheimnis vertraut: / des Tages Lügen, / Ruhm und Ehr, / Macht und Gewinn, / so schimmernd hehr, / wie eitler Staub der Sonnen / sind sie vor dem zersponnen. / In des Tages eitlem Wähnen / bleibt ihm ein einzig Sehnen, / das Sehnen hin / zur heil'gen Nacht, / wo urewig,/ einzig wahr / Liebeswonne ihm lacht."

25. "Nun war des Sehnens, des Verlangens, der Wonne und des Elendes der Liebe kein Ende; Welt, Macht, Ruhm, Ehre, Ritterlichkeit, Treue, Freundschaft—Alles wie wesenloser Traum zerstoben; nur Eines noch lebend: Sehnsucht, Sehnsucht, unstillbares, ewig neu sich gebärendes Verlangen, Dürsten und Schmachten; einzige Erlösung: Tod, Sterben, Untergehen, Nichtmehrerwachen! . . . Nennen wir es Tod? Oder ist es die nächtige Wunderwelt, aus der, wie die Sage uns meldet, ein Epheu und eine Rebe in inniger Umschlingung einst auf Tristans und Isoldes Grabe emporwuchsen?" Wagner, *SSD*, 12:345; "Prelude to *Tristan and Isolde*," *Prose Works*, 8:387 (trans. modified).

26. "Dieser Tristan wird was furchtbares! Dieser letzte Akt!!!————Ich fürchte die Oper wird verboten—falls durch schlechte Aufführung nicht das Ganze parodirt wird—: nur mittelmässige Aufführungen können mich retten! Vollständig gute müssen die Leute verrückt machen,—ich kann mir's nicht anders denken. So weit hat's noch mit mir kommen müssen!! O weh!—" *Richard Wagner an Mathilde Wesendonck*, 58; trans. no 238 of *Selected Letters*, 451–452.

27. "Die Musik verkläre alles; bis zum Gräßlichen des Wortes lasse sie es nie kommen, selbst beim furchtbarsten Gegenstand." Wagner, March 12, 1869, *Die Tagebücher*, 1:71; *Cosima Wagner's Diaries*, 16.

28. Quoted by Ernest Newman in Robert Bailey, ed., *Prelude and Transfiguration from Tristan and Isolde* (New York, 1985), 29.

29. "Musik, die zauberischste aller Künste, lernt den Zauber brechen, den sie selber um alle ihre Gestalten legt. Die Verfluchung der Minne durch Tristan ist mehr als das ohnmächtige Opfer des Rausches an die Askese: sie ist die sei's auch ganz vergebliche Auflehnung der Musik gegen den eigenen Schicksalszwang, und erst im Angesicht ihrer totalen Determination durch jenen gewinnt sie die Selbstbesinnung wieder. Mit Grund stehen jene Figuren der Tristanpartitur nach den Worten *der furchtbare Trank* an der Schwelle der Neuen Musik, in deren erstem kanonischen Werk, Schönbergs fis- moll Quartett, die Worte erscheinen: *Nimm mir die Liebe, gib mir dein Glück!* Sie sagen, daß Liebe und Glück falsch sind in der Welt, in der wir leben, und daß alle Gewalt der Liebe übergegangen ist an ihr Gegenteil. Wer es aber vermöchte, den übertäubenden Wogen des Wagnerschen Orchesters solches Metall zu entreißen, dem vermöchte sein veränderter Klang zu dem Trost zu verhelfen, den

es trotz Rausch und Phantasmagorie beharrlich verweigert. Indem es die Angst des hilflosen Menschen ausspricht, könnte es den Hilflosen, wie immer schwach und verstellt, Hilfe bedeuten, und aufs neue versprechen, was der uralte Einspruch der Musik versprach: Ohne Angst Leben"; Theodor W. Adorno, *Versuch über Wagner, Gesammelte Schriften* (Frankfurt, 1997), 13:145; *In Search of Wagner*, trans. Rodney Livingstone (London and New York, 1991), 156 (trans. modified).

30. "Die Übereinstimmung von Wort, Bild und Musik gelingt um so viel perfekter als im Tristan, weil die sinnlichen Elemente, die einspruchslos allesamt die Oberfläche der gesellschaftlichen Realität protokollieren, dem Prinzip nach im gleichen technischen Arbeitsgang produziert werden und dessen Einheit als ihren eigentlichen Gehalt ausdrücken. Dieser Arbeitsgang integriert alle Elemente der Produktion, von der auf den Film schielenden Konzeption des Romans bis zum letzten Geräuscheffekt. Er ist der Triumph des investierten Kapitals. Seine Allmacht den enteigneten Anwärtern auf jobs als die ihres Herrn ins Herz zu brennen, macht den Sinn aller Filme aus, gleichviel welches plot die Produktionsleitung jeweils aussersieht"; Theodor W. Adorno and Max Horkheimer, *Dialektik der Aufklärung, Gesammelte Schriften* (Frankfurt am Main, 1997), 3:145; *Dialectic of Enlightenment: Philosophical Fragments*, ed. G. S. Noerr, trans. Edmund Jephcott (Stanford, 2002), 97–98.

Ten

Authority and Judgment in Mozart's *Don Giovanni* and Wagner's *Ring*

PHILIP KITCHER AND RICHARD SCHACHT

LEAR: Dost thou know me fellow?
KENT: No sir; but you have that in your countenance
    which I would fain call master.
LEAR: What's that?
KENT: Authority.

From the moment the curtain goes up after the overture to *Don Giovanni*, Leporello seems to be trying to leave his master. His opening ruminations express a wish to at least change places (eventually granted in act 2, but with unfortunate consequences). Later, after coping with the arrival of Zerlina and Donna Elvira, he announces his resolve to go his own way. Nevertheless, even after serving as scapegoat in the assault on Zerlina, he is still dragged off (not unwillingly) by his master in the wonderful confusion that ends act 1.

Leporello is no more successful in act 2. Once more he declares his intent to leave, but, a few minutes later, having been bought off, he falls in again with the latest skirt-chasing scheme and pursues his role of diverting Elvira with some gusto. Even the terrifying encounter with the Statue is not enough to make him quit; he is still in place at the start of the finale, sneaking pheasant and serving as his master's foil. His last solo declaration, made after the forcible removal of the Don, is to find a new and better master. Did he ever really *want* to leave? Probably not, and, even if he did, he couldn't. For until the very end the Don has in his confident music as well as in his countenance that which Leporello can only serve: authority.

More strictly, the Don has a *certain type* of authority, and one that Leporello plainly lacks: namely, the ability to *make things happen*—the power (of one sort or another) to impose his vision of things and his designs upon others, and indeed to enlist them in the service of realizing his ends, even when their inclinations and interests are more or less strongly to the contrary. This efficacious and often charismatic type of authority might be called "directive authority." To recognize authority of this type, as Leporello does, is not necessarily to express approval or suppose that the authority is legitimate. Rather, it is simply to acknowledge the sway someone may have over others (oneself perhaps included), their own (possibly divergent) predilections notwithstanding. Directive authority can derive from mere power or even sheer brute strength; although, in the case of the Don, charisma and charm plainly play important roles, along with evident vitality and forcefulness.

Leporello is hardly alone in lacking directive authority. His deficiency in this respect is shared by almost all of the rest of the cast. Throughout the entire opera Don Giovanni is judged; and the judgment—whenever made by someone not under his spell—is always negative (even if many of those who deliver it are hard put to be resolute when he undertakes to beguile them): he is a moral monster, a murderer, a betrayer, a man with a heart of bronze. And yet, although the castigations rain down on him, they have no impact upon him. He goes right on doing the sorts of things for which he is condemned, often enlisting those who judge him (most obviously Leporello) in his ventures. Nor is this because he is either subhuman or inhuman, for he clearly is neither (even if he is also no conventional hero). It is rather because his critics lack what it takes to make their judgments stick. Because those who render the judgments have no directive authority, their condemnations amount to little more than poignant, sometimes dramatic and even moving musical phrases, remarkable chiefly for their ineffectuality.

There is another type of authority that the Don's detractors claim, and at least seem to have, and that he himself lacks. They speak with the authority of those who *know* what the moral order allows and what it forbids. Even if they are not effective in getting results, Donna Anna and her supporters purport (and may even seem) to make the *right* judgments. They may lack *directive* authority, but they suppose themselves to have a form of "epistemic" or *cognitive* authority. They claim the sort of authority that is associated with having *knowledge* that entitles one to pass judgments, even if it is only knowledge of what prevailing conventional norms prescribe and proscribe. They all take themselves and each other to have a clear vision of the moral order. Moreover, it is easy to see this group of characters as embedded in a broader society within which their moral authority would be almost universally conceded. We, the audience, are invited to identify with this broader society, join the consensus, and take the Don's judges to have cognitive authority with respect to the moral qualities of his conduct. To accept that invitation is to suppose that cognitive authority is not only ceded to them by almost everyone on stage, but that it is ceded *rightly*—that the judges are not merely *taken* to know that the actions they denounce are morally wrong but do actually have reliable insights about genuine moral turpitude as well.

So, one might suppose, the cognitive authority of the Don's accusers is finally vindicated, and their triumph is celebrated on stage in the closing sextet. Yet that sextet not only sounds but surely is meant to be heard as feeble. This is not only because there is little point in listening to the ratification of an assessment that these characters have been trying to make stick since the beginning of the opera and that has now been enforced for them. It is also because the very idea that these people have the right to the last word on the Don is suspect—indeed, almost a joke. In this concluding scene Mozart seems to want to give us qualms about accepting the invitation to acquiesce in the conventional moral consensus even as it appears to prevail. The pallid jubilation, set in the context of the celebrants' lack of directive authority, in fact raises questions about their cognitive authority, calling into question the simple interpretation that Moral Rectitude has ultimately triumphed. What is it that these people actually know, and what is their knowledge really worth?

The closing sextet undermines the simple idea that the drama has been moved by a clash between directive authority and cognitive authority, and that this disharmony has finally been resolved. The Don's directive authority proves to be a spell that has now been broken; yet the cognitive authority of his rejoicing detractors is little more substantial. If any resolution has come, that is because there is one character who does have the directive authority to judge the Don with real effect: the Commendatore, in his statuesque reincarnation. Mozart provides him with dramatic lines, full of confident fifths and octaves, lines that match the Don's own authoritative music. The combat of the first scene is balanced by the vocal duet of the final one, in a double confrontation of authoritative figures. In the second and decisive episode, in a struggle over keys, the Stone Guest eventually forces capitulation into D minor, defining the musical space in which the Don sings his last lines.

Why (or how) does the lapidary Commendatore succeed where others who share his moral perspective fail? A simple interpretation (based on the invitation to the audience to join the moral consensus on stage) would view him as an especially privileged cognitive authority: the Commendatore knows the moral order, and his station in society gives him the right to pass judgment in accordance with it that his posthumous supernatural powers enable him to enforce. He is (or was), after all, an injured father (his daughter has been abused, and the claims of patriarchy must be satisfied). Moreover, he is a soldier whose military prowess has probably contributed to the security of the state. Society and tradition are concentrated in him. Anna, Elvira, and Zerlina are mere females, Masetto and Leporello are too low-class to count, and Ottavio is a lightweight. The Commendatore, by contrast, is a heavyweight even in life, and is all the more so—literally, to underscore the figurative point—in the form in which he reappears upon and beyond the grave, as that form makes unmistakably clear. Yet he only prevails when he has been transformed into a superhuman figure—a preposterous phantasm who can redirect the action with his stentorian summons and frigid clasp. Why should this marmoreal monstrosity even count as a cognitive (much less directive) authority?

Consider the final sextet. It is easy to construct convincing explanations why these celebrants of the Don's downfall advance the moral judgments they do, for reasons as unflattering to them as they are deflating to their cognitive authority. They issue their verdicts because they have been conditioned in particular ways by the surrounding society; and if they are taken to have cognitive authority, it is not because of their daring in probing matters for themselves, but because they have acceded to convention, and the conventional wisdom has turned out to have the upper hand. The concurrence of their judgments is no touchstone of truth; it is an expression of their shared conventionality, reinforced by timidity.

Are matters so very different with the Commendatore? Or are the things he stands for and "knows" also simply reflections of his time, place, and biography? He is not timid, to be sure, even in life; yet he returns, as a frozen monument, to reinforce conformity to the rules of his world. Is his triumph indicative of a cognitive authority deserving of acceptance and obedience, or does it mark only the fate of one who has the temerity to pay it no heed, thereby challenging whether what is commonly taken to be authoritative with respect to moral matters really is? In any event, if the very possibility of a viable alternative to the Don, on the one hand, and to the likes of those by whom he is surrounded, on the other, hinges upon the plausibility of taking literally and seriously the figure of the postmortem Commendatore and the mythology he evokes, that would be a slender reed indeed upon which to stake everything—as Mozart quite clearly knows and means to convey.

Don Giovanni thus presents and illuminates two kinds of authority: one epistemic or *cognitive* (knowledge-based, deriving from or relating to significant knowledge of some sort, but by itself impotent), and the other *directive* (power-based and action-related, having to do with the ability to get things done oneself or by others). They can and often do diverge—and even conflict. The opera's secondary characters make judgments, claiming authority of the first sort; and their judgments have both a *focus* and a *content*. The focus of their judgment is the Don; and the content of the judgment corresponds to conventional moral appraisals—various specific ways of expressing the thought that the Don's actions are reprehensible. On a simple interpretation of the work, most of those who make such judgments not only take themselves to have epistemic authority but actually do have it, in that they are *right* to think that the Don is morally awful; their problem is that they lack directive authority (their judgments are ineffectual). The Stone Guest, however, is an exception to the rule. He has what they lack. He combines epistemic *and* directive authority; and so he is able to see to it that the Don receives his comeuppance.

The final sextet subverts this interpretation. Indeed, the opera as a whole is actually subversive of it, even though it superficially supports it. Throughout the opera Mozart makes it clear that, even if the Don's judges are right, they do not take his measure. Their judgments are as often conventional pieties and frozen relics of cultural correctness as they are expressions of real moral insights—between which they are incapable of distinguishing. The Don is no revolutionary epistemic authority; and Mozart clearly does not offer him as a moral visionary and reformer, whose insights with respect to the moral order and its contingency are tragically rejected and defeated. Yet he does present the Don as drawing attention—in an admittedly problematic way—to the equally if differently problematic character of unquestioning acquiescence in traditional morals by his cavalier disregard of them. *Of course* he is a cheat, bully, scoundrel, seducer, and (as the opening scene would appear to indicate) when seduction fails, a rapist, capable of killing without much more than a shrug. Yet to stop at that does not do justice to what is at once appealing and appalling about him.

More is at stake here than mere morals. In *Don Giovanni* Mozart powerfully poses a larger question of the greatest seriousness and importance, with which he deals in a manner that has no equal in opera before him and none after until Wagner: the question of how life might best be lived. Yet the conventional answer that question is given at its conclusion is no real answer at all; and the question is made all the more vivid and disturbing by the radical unsatisfactoriness of all of the alternatives that have been explored in it. None of the forms of authority and judgment we are shown come even close to resolving it, the conventional ones claimed and expressed in the final chorus least of all. Those associated with the Don and the Commendatore, while vastly more interesting, are no less problematic, even if differently so. Wonderful as the Don and the Commendatore are dramatically (and as their parts are vocally), they only serve to raise the ante, framing the challenge with which Mozart leaves us with their contrastingly vivid demarcations of humanity's outer limits. Are there humanly possible forms of authority and judgment that can serve us any better than those that Mozart here considers, and finds wanting, as we attempt to come to grips with the very question with which he confronts us? That is a challenge indeed. And it is a challenge Wagner in effect (if not in actual intent) undertakes to meet—nowhere more impressively than in his *Der Ring des Niebelungen*.

In Wagner's tetralogy, and at all stages of this complex drama, different characters offer judgments relating to the moral structure of a world. The world of the *Ring* is more remote than that of *Don Giovanni*; but similar questions loom larger in it and are posed with greater complexity. The mythical cast given to that world adds to the heightened challenge of identifying and addressing these sorts of questions in it; and the answers to them suggested are far from obvious. But their interest amply rewards the effort of attempting to discern them. For in the *Ring* Wagner rises to Mozart's challenge as few others have—even if his pursuit of them takes him to places Mozart would never have dreamed of going.

The most obviously judgmental characters in the *Ring* are Alberich and Fricka. Alberich's judgments, while essential to the unfolding of the action, are of such a pathological nature that they have no possible claim to authority and validity, however all-too-humanly understandable they may be. But he shows how radically lacking in authority and yet consequential such judgments can be, as well as how a wrathful judgment of such power can develop out of next to nothing in a soul that is more pitiful than diabolical to begin with.

Fricka is a different matter. Her conventional moral judgments, while understandable enough, quite evidently lack authority. Yet her judgments do not stop there. She appreciates something that Wotan, for all his intelligence, misses. She brings him to see that the realization of his godly objective (to make the world a better place in which law and order prevail) has turned out to require an action (namely, regaining the Ring of Power from the Giant-turned-Dragon Fafner—to whom Wotan gave it in fulfillment of a contractual obligation—to keep it from falling into the wrong hands) that he himself cannot perform without subverting its very foundations. Wotan's attempt to resolve his predicament by engendering a supposedly independent agent (Siegmund), able to do what he can neither do himself nor command, must fail because (as Fricka makes clear to him) any success that Siegmund might have would be thoroughly dependent upon his actions. However, because Fricka is oblivious to the larger picture, her judgment with respect to his plan (driven by her preoccupation with her moral agenda) has only negative significance and plays no further role. She is a foil and an accessory who helps force Wotan to a new judgment. Her perspective is myopic, narrowly circumscribing the significance of her own judgments and the scope of her authority. She is only able to trump Wotan because he has dealt the hand.

That Wotan has a different and larger authority is clear. The status of his judgments, however, is another matter; and they are not easily discerned and disentangled. Judging initially that the world as he found it leaves much to be desired, he conceives of an admirable new order and undertakes to establish and secure it. The nobility of his aspiration, more than the sheer power he contrived to obtain, is the basis of his authority. Supposing order to be a precondition of meaning, Wotan seeks the power to achieve and safeguard it out of a deep appreciation of the savagery of disorder, the force of the dark instincts that motivate his fellows, and the need for a comprehensive solution to the problems they present if things are ever to go any differently. His aim is not merely to rule the world but to render it one in which baseness is banished and savagery superseded, with the rule of law supplanting primordial nature, bringing its impulses under rational control, and giving its formlessness intelligent and admirable form—the susceptibility of both (old and new) orders to corruption and disruption notwithstanding, and indeed with that susceptibility very much in mind. Wotan uses the spear he fashioned from the World Ash long before the first curtain rises to found an institution of *contracts*. The rule of law, by way of his system of contracts, is to make possible a new sort of dignity and worth, superseding the merely natural order of things, and so to transform the character of existence in this world, endowing it with a new interest and significance.

With the building of Valhalla, Wotan aims to consolidate this outcome. His contract with the giants Fasolt and Fafner puts him in a bind, however, for it seems to require him to relinquish one or another of a number of things, the loss of any of which would be disastrous to things that matter to him: Freia (upon whom the gods' immortality depends), the Ring (the power of which is greater than his own, and so in the wrong hands can defeat him), or his own commitment to the rule of law that is the basis of his authority and power. By the time Fricka is through with him, he is defeated and deeply shaken; for she forces him to recognize that his solution (Siegmund retrieving the Ring in his stead, thereby enabling him to remain law-abiding, and so to retain his authority and power) is incoherent and must be abandoned. Indeed, his despairing overreaction to this defeat at her hands may reflect the dawning of a realization that his larger project itself is fatally flawed, not merely the particular strategy of pursuing it. The soundness of his judgments is henceforth in doubt, his authority is no longer sure—and he knows it.

There is something further that we take Wotan more fundamentally (and only eventually wittingly) to be yearning to achieve, which comes to be of increasing importance to him—all the more so as his difficulties increase. It is crystallized in a moment that is at the center of the *Ring*, in a line that he sings at the nadir of his despondency at the climax of his long scene with Brünnhilde in *Walküre's* second act. Just before we hear a fragment of the motif we associate with the sword, he declaims with great vehemence: "nur Eines will ich noch: das Ende—das Ende!" (one thing alone do I still want: the end—the end!) The most natural way to understand this, and true enough as far as it goes, is to suppose that it involves a change of attitude; that, prior to the disturbing exchange with Fricka, Wotan was after something different but now wants only an end to it all, in one way or another.

But this oversimplifies his problem (and also its eventual resolution) in an impoverishing way. There is indeed a change here; but Wotan's predicament is defined by a large problem within an even larger one, to which Siegmund was to provide a particular solution and to which Wotan now (at least initially) responds by conceiving the general form of solution in this despairing fashion. His overt goal is to impose a new and better order upon the world. Yet we suggest that Wotan also is (and indeed may long have been) grappling with the ultimate human problem of *finding an ending*—an ending that would be no mere final defeat, making a mockery of all he has stood and striven for. As he eventually begins to understand, there are endings—and there are, or at any rate might be, other sorts of endings, less devastating, and more meaningful. And so, while tempted repeatedly to nihilistic despair, he gropes toward what would be the positive achievement of a *tragic* ending. That is an achievement, however, that eludes and surpasses him. Indeed, its very possibility remains uncertain when we see the last of him as he leaves the stage defeated following his encounter with Siegfried.

In short: Wotan is a god dedicated to the creation of a world of law who finds himself confronted with powers he cannot completely subdue, and with which he therefore is obliged to compromise—in ways leaving, and indeed even creating, room for further challenges. The *Ring* shows him twisting and turning in an attempt to find a way of resisting and overcoming the sort of disorder that has arisen in the world with the rupture and loss (perhaps for the better, perhaps for the worse, but in any event irretrievably) of its primordial order. His inability to do so leads him to conclude, in his despairing exchange with Brünnhilde, that there can be no solution (so that the world must be left to the untender mercies of the likes of Alberich). But the problem continues to exercise him, even in his failures. So, from the mid-point of *Walküre* on, the focus of his judgment is how to prepare for something that goes beyond his own doomed strategy of solution—how to end the system he has created without simply negating it, thereby acceding to the return of the denatured chaos and degradation that preceded it. He can save neither himself nor his order. The best he can realistically hope for, he finally grasps, is an ending for both himself and his world-order that preserves some version of the meaning that order was to have and so gives meaning to what he has done. But he does not know how to do this. And as he comes to learn, to his chagrin, it is no task for someone like Siegfried either.

For a time, after having to give up on Siegmund (and indeed to consent to his doom), Wotan has high hopes for Siegfried, whom Siegmund had sired (and who thus is his grandson), and Wotan judges to have the true independence of his will that is required for his purposes to be served. Envisioning the fearless hero Siegfried is to become, he dares to hope yet again for a solution to the problem of order, in the belief that a counterpoise to the vengeful and destructive egoism of Alberich and Hagen may be possible after all, in the form of a contrasting set of (heroic) dispositions and qualities—even though its realization spells his own end and indeed requires it. His own previous efforts to institute and secure an admirable sort of order may thus be seen as but a preliminary advance beyond both the blandness of the primordial natural order and the viciousness of its degeneration into greed and need toward something that is to transcend them all. Siegfried is to be its avatar and the agent of its advent.

This is Wotan's new hope and judgment, in which his daughter the Valkyrie Brünnhilde rapturously joins him in the last act of *Walküre*, and with which she no less rapturously greets Siegfried in the last act of the sequel that bears his name. And their enthusiasm makes perfect sense, for it answers to something fundamental in both their natures. Indeed, Brünnhilde would be a fine exemplar of it herself, were she not a god and also bound to a kind of absolute obedience that is at odds with one of its crucial features: profound independence of spirit. She comes closest to it, prior to *Götterdämmerung*'s last act, precisely when she casts off that bond and so provokes (and earns) Wotan's wrath and de-deification of her—while at the same time gaining markedly in authority in her own right rather than merely derivatively from him.

Yet when Brünnhilde is awakened by Siegfried's kiss from the trance in which Wotan had left her and Siegfried finds her, it is not to a new life as coexemplar of human heroism with him, even though her own ending an opera later certainly has something of the heroic about it. For Wagner has her almost immediately vault over and beyond the adulation of Siegfried's sort of heroism and into another possibility that is only fully realized when transposed from the realm of the divine into that of the human. It is, of course, *love*—human love, which not only is not free of the shadow of death but lives and burns all the more brightly in that very shadow. Brünnhilde's great significance in the *Ring* is her evolution into one of Wagner's several supreme embodiments of his vision of the ultimate in human love. Her eye-opening and will-liberating discovery of it, in her encounter with Siegmund, begins her transformation. She at first is led, both by her own warriorlike predilections and by Wotan's new preoccupation, to lionize the heroic qualities Siegmund also displays and Siegfried is literally conceived to epitomize. But she eventually arrives at the judgment that the reign of heroic virtue as well as the order of laws and contracts must yield to the rule of love.

The new but differing cases of Siegfried and Brünnhilde raise the interesting question of what becomes of the theme and problem of order when heroism prevails over commitment to legality—or when love rules instead. It is already clear that, however much may be said for their effects upon human affairs and relations, *stability* is not to be expected from either one. Something akin to stability in principle, but differing greatly from it in form and practice, may be the most that can be expected. But that, the *Ring* suggests, may be enough—enough, that is, to live and die for, and to live and die by, even if not enough to establish and secure a stable social order. The gain in meaning may be greater than the loss in mundane viability. One or the other (and it turns out to be love) may be the best we can humanly do, even if both tend to self-destruct. (This is, after all, tragedy on the grandest of scales.)

Thus Wotan might well take the rule of love too to be unstable—as it will indeed turn out to be—and thus to offer no solution to his original problem, of the secure establishment of a new and better sort of order in the world. It is only if he (or we) can accept a crucial modification in the conception of that problem, substituting something for the "stability" requirement that does not entail long-term mundane viability but nonetheless satisfies our desire for enduring significance, that the possibility of a solution may be discerned. But Wotan cannot accept this modification and so is doomed to remain disconsolate to the end.

Wotan, in the guise of the ironist Wanderer of *Siegfried,* clings to the hope for a heroic accomplishment of a divine-civic order of laws and contracts after all, in a world thereby made safe for love and the flourishing of the just, with vileness vanquished and baseness banished, under Siegfried's banner. However, after his encounter with the bearer of this last desperate hope, he realizes that it is in vain. And although we might still harbor this hope ourselves, it is a major part of the work of *Götterdämmerung* to dash it and direct our attention to the rule of love itself, although in an altered guise and with equally poor practical prospects. This redirection in turn requires a fundamental transformation of one's capacity for affirmation, if the upshot is to be seen as anything other than bleak. But Wotan does not achieve it. He returns disconsolate to Valhalla, at a complete loss. All that remains for him is to arrange the conditions for his own passing and to play out the game according to the rules he has instituted. Wotan's final judgment thus appears to be a despairing one—to which the new authority deriving from the defeat of his every hope and best efforts amply entitles him.

Brünnhilde does not think as Wotan does at any point along the way. Her reactions are intuitive, sympathetic, and in tune with the emotions that she and others feel—love most of all, whether Wotan's for Siegmund, Siegmund's for Sieglinde, or her own for them. Having discovered love's reality and power, and convinced of its primacy, she illustrates something important about it, that is at once a part of its glory and its Achilles' heel: its single-mindedness. Brünnhilde too (like her father) sees with a kind of single-eyed sight. Love is not blind; it is tunnel-visioned and myopic. That is why there can be no viable love-based order; for this kind of love is as heedless as is Siegfried's brand of heroism—and, as Wotan knows full well, order and heedlessness do not combine. It is not for nothing that "love that knows no bounds" figures so prominently in tragedy; for where such love rules, tragedy reigns. This is by no means to condemn it (particularly for Wagner); but the alternatives this indicates are not happy ones for those who share Wotan's sensibility, even if those in whom it burns and glows couldn't care less.

Brünnhilde is in love at first not with Siegfried himself but rather with The Hero as an ideal human type, for which his father Siegmund's free-spirited, fearless heroism serves as her prototype. Present her with such a hero and her love will have its proper object. Siegfried is to be the former and therefore the latter. But Siegfried in the flesh will not settle for that sort of love. Once he gets past his initial awkwardness upon awakening her, he begins to burn with a sexual passion that soon sweeps all before it; and Brünnhilde finally responds in kind. Her last words (and his) in the final scene of *Siegfried* are the startling refrain "lachender Tod!" (laughing death!), recalling the direct association of intense sexual love and death that is familiar to us from *Tristan*. But that surely is not their thought here. This joyously (indeed, deliriously) sung refrain is expressive of the enraptured conviction that, though living means dying, it may also mean loving, and that this miracle is what makes life worth while. If Brünnhilde had any regrets about losing her divinity, she has none now; for her foretaste of this kind of love persuades her that nothing could matter more, and she is prepared to give it (and Siegfried) her all. Death would not matter as it does without love; but love would not matter as it does without death—and life would not matter as it does without both. Brünnhilde does not have this worked out with any clarity; but she does grasp it intuitively. (And in this she greatly surpasses Siegfried, who, while equally impassioned, is constitutionally incapable of comprehending very much at all.)

This may be the beginning of Brünnhilde's wisdom in the *Ring*; but it presents her with a problem. She judges both that love should be intense and exclusive, divorced from the world and consummated in the denial of the world, with life purified of anything other than its essentials of love and death—*and also* that love should do its work *in* the world, encouraging and sustaining what is noble and worthy of it (as exemplified by her caring for Wotan, Siegmund, Sieglinde, and the unborn Siegfried). The oscillation between these two judgments cannot end by simply affirming one and rejecting the other. Brünnhilde must find a way to satisfy both. That is her dilemma.

The ultimate task of *Götterdämmerung* (and multiple judgment of the work itself) is to reveal how a solution to Wotan's apparently impossible problem is achieved in Brünnhilde's escape from her own dilemma after eliminating Siegfried and the rule of the heroic as competition. Along the way she is led to reconsider both Siegfried and love. Siegfried betrays her, unwittingly but undeniably in her eyes; and her disillusionment with him is profound. Hero *nonpareil* though he may be, such heroism turns out to leave a good deal to be desired; and instead of calling or even yearning for yet another even greater and truer hero, she abandons her hero worship along with her hero. But she also despairs of the worth of love without justice, and perhaps even of the supremacy of love itself as she has come to know it with Siegfried. If love is indeed the best answer to be found, her love will have to be transfigured yet again.

In the end, it is. Brünnhilde is further transformed herself and attains a new authority. She has this authority because she has attained a wisdom transcending Wotan's. She poses a crucial question to the gods and answers it herself: "Do I now know what you need?—All things, all things, all things I know, all is clear to me now!" In her new state she is able to love Siegfried differently, and to love more wide-rangingly and compassionately, rising to a new sort of heroism, and accomplishing a higher justice. In the spectacular ending she effects following Siegfried's death—in which she joins him in a way that also sweeps away the corrupt world of the Gibichungs below and gives the coup de grace to the moribund realm of the gods above—she manages at once to fulfill Wotan's longing for a fitting ending and, at the same time, to vindicate his basic values of order, valor, and love, which are conjoined and transfigured into the new nobility she attains and reveals at the end.

Brünnhilde now understands that, while love trumps all, the dominion of love constitutes no solution to Wotan's problem of order. She knows that the dark side of things is too powerful and that love cannot remake the world in its own image. Thus the problem of order, as Wotan has conceived it, remains insoluble. Brünnhilde affirms and consummates his strivings in the only manner possible, achieving the closest thing attainable to the order he tries to establish: a sublime justice crowned by a love that death can end but not destroy. So she at once resolves her own dilemma and ends Wotan's world in a doubly meaningful expression of her new and more complex love. And she does so in a way that provides a kind of resolution to Wotan's problem after all, despite the inevitable failure of any and all attempts to establish stable order in the world.

Brünnhilde goes beyond Wotan. He doesn't see how to end meaningfully; she does—and does it. She succeeds where he fails, establishing something more important than the existence of the kind of order he envisioned: the truth of the *order of value* that accords highest significance to this love and to valor, power, and justice when animated by it beyond all consequences. So she validates the world that makes possible the realization as well as the subversion of these values—and thereby Wotan, Siegfried, and herself along with it—even as she ends it as it has been, and the vestiges of a contrasting divinity along with it. The glorious theme that soars in the orchestra at this point, in the traditional nomenclature, is referred to as "Redemption through Love," but this is a misdescription, for nothing is "redeemed" in any standard sense of this term at either point. The Christian term is out of place here. This is something else, with a resonance that is Greek rather than Christian, tragic rather than salvific yet more profoundly affirmative precisely on that account. It is "vindication."

Siegfried pales in comparison. There is nothing vindicating—or even particularly admirable—about him. An entire opera bears his name; and the whole *Ring* grew out of Wagner's original intention to write a music drama entitled *Siegfrieds Tod* (Siegfried's Death). Yet his ultimate significance is to make it palpable that his sort of heroism is no panacea and indeed carries within it the seeds of its own destruction (as well as a good deal of collateral damage), particularly owing to the way the world is. It is a part of the burden of *Götterdämmerung* to deliver this judgment and make the case for it painfully clear. Hero though he may be, Siegfried comes across from the outset of the opera bearing his name as a shallow, silly, hot-blooded, and impulsive lout; and he remains remarkably little changed throughout most of its sequel—except, perhaps, to become capable of blithe and appalling caddishness as well. It is only when felled with a mortal wound that he begins to show glimpses of a more truly human countenance.

Siegfried's death is not only entirely fitting but also very important. It signals the end of the heroism he epitomizes as a viable solution either to

Wotan's problem or to ours, as we attempt to find our way into a future beyond the *Dämmerung* of all gods. When he ceases to be the embodiment of
heroism and is transformed into a human being capable of the kind of love
that is worth living and dying for, he has already ceased to exist as the Siegfried he was born to be. We can and should welcome the transformation and
the meaning of it. But the dream of The Hero as The Answer is a dream that
dies hard. And its death is hard to take. Yet die it must, along with the gods.
The fourth opera is more than *Götterdämmerung*; it is also *Heldendämmerung*.
And the death of Siegfried is also the death of that dream and hope—except
as part of love, in the service of love, and deriving its meaning from love. The
overwhelming Funeral March pays shattering tribute to its passing, doing
justice to the loss it represents even as it leaves no doubt about the finality of
that loss. To be sure, Brünnhilde makes good on the promise she and Siegfried share at the conclusion of *Siegfried* of joyful death. But ultimately it is
Siegfried as her heroic true love rather than as her beloved hero whom she
joyfully joins in death.

At the end of the *Ring* Wotan's struggle has failed, his order is gone, he and
the rest of the gods are gone as well. Siegfried is dead, Brünnhilde rides into
the flames and is consumed, and the petty world of the Gibichungs is swept
away, leaving only the Rhine flowing on, the Rhine maidens back at mindless
play in a world purged of all that had made it both troubled and interesting—and Alberich, whom we may be sure is up to no good. Yet Brünnhilde's
action stands as testament to something at once evanescent and of great and
enduring significance. The love it expresses endows the world and humanity
she leaves behind with vindicating grace and worth. Her way alone holds the
promise of an answer to the problem of how to endow life and death with a
meaning that can survive and transcend the inevitable failure of all worldly
quests. Neither the best of strategy nor the greatest of heroism will suffice.
Love does not and cannot not conquer all, any more than can the best laid
plans of gods and men, or the greatest feats of the best of heroes—at least as
victory is commonly reckoned. But its possibility and reality change everything in a way that heroism does not, even in the face of death and the ending
of the world as we know it. We have this on the highest authority we encounter here, which is that of none of the *Ring*'s characters alone. It is rather that
of the *Gesamtkunstwerk* itself at its close, which in its final incredible minutes
gives the most powerful expression imaginable to its Last Judgment.

Oddly, perhaps, Wagner does not give the last line to Brünnhilde. He gives
it instead to the malevolent Hagen, of all people—and it is an expression of
utter futility as Hagen makes a last desperate and doomed lunge for the Ring.
But that is fitting as well, as a final judgment concerning those who cannot

or will not learn Brünnhilde's lesson. And the real last lines are neither his nor hers but rather the incredible last pages of Wagner's orchestral score, which speak with unsurpassable eloquence. They bespeak affirmation as well as ending. They do not mourn and salute the devastating conclusion of a long day's journey into night in a majestic and overpowering lament, as does Siegfried's Funeral March, with which they stand in marked contrast. Rather, they celebrate the wonder of what we witness thereafter, its truth beyond all mere mundane reality, and the prospect of its perpetual possibility.

All of the *Ring*'s great figures, in the classic manner of tragedy, are doomed by the very qualities that elevate them above the rest. The order of nature can indeed be disrupted, but its disruption tends more readily toward its corruption than toward its reordering perfection, even by the greatest of powers and lofty intentions that detach themselves from it and aspire to transcend and transfigure it. Even a divinity that makes bold to improve upon the basic character of life and the world is hubristic and must fail and fall. If the wisdom and power of Wotan cannot succeed in imposing and securing a new and more glorious order upon the world, it should come as no surprise when it turns out that neither the heroism of Siegfried nor the love of Brünnhilde fare any better in this respect. Indeed, neither proves to be much of a match for the unruly world that Wotan seemingly was able to master in his prime, superficial and self-subverting as that mastery turned out to be. But of the two alternatives, Brünnhilde's receives a final musical judgment that stands in the most radical of contrasts to Siegfried's.

And though this world ends, the earth remains, still capable of renewal, and still charged with this promise that we have come to know. We also know that everything that comes to be in it must end, including all order, and the very best of lives and loves. But in their mere appearance, however ephemeral, they have the power to illumine the world in a manner that vindicates all. Life may be tragic at best, but that does not preclude its vindication and affirmation, despite everything. The *Ring*'s greatest gift is to make this inestimable truth and invaluable human possibility palpable.

Don Giovanni may seem to be—and in many respects is—light-years away from all of this. It poses a profoundly important and difficult problem—at once deeply philosophical and compellingly human—to which the *Ring* proposes a solution. It is nothing less than the problem of what can render life most meaningful. But the solution proposed in the *Ring* is a radical one, involving a kind of "revaluation of values" (in Nietzsche's phrase) that requires us to change the way in which we think about life quite fundamentally if we are to be able to affirm it on the *Ring*'s terms.

Don Giovanni is not a tragedy; for the Don is not a tragic figure. His character, the manner of his life, the relation between his life and his doom, and the nature of that doom are striking, to say the least; but they are far from the stuff of tragedy. Yet *Don Giovanni* is no mere morality play either. There is a real sense in which the Don is utterly immoral, and in some obvious sense the morality he flouts prevails in the end; but that does not begin to convey the interest and upshot of what unfolds before us, both dramatically and musically. One might think of it as a "problem opera," which raises *our* consciousness without really raising that of any of its characters, and leaves the problem it poses in search of a resolution that none of them can truly be taken to represent—in contrast to the *Ring*, at the conclusion of which there can be no doubt that a resolution is being presented or about who represents it (even if one may be far from clear about just what that resolution amounts to).

In both cases conventional morality is shown to have the power to bring down those who are heedless of it, but in both it also is shown to be problematic as a true locus or measure of worth and meaning. The same is even suggested to be the case with respect to the more impressive variants exemplified by the system of laws and contracts Wotan seeks to establish and by the code for which the Commendatore—in death as in life—speaks. This is made evident not only dramatically but also musically in both cases, but in very different ways. All of the forms of obligation we encounter in the *Ring*—those associated with hallowed custom (Fricka), legality, deference owed, oath given, and even troth pledged—are given powerful dramatic and musical expression. Yet they pale when confronted with the even more powerful expressions given to desires and emotions that overwhelm them—in some cases for the worse by any way of reckoning, but in others for the better despite their heedlessness of the obligation in question and even despite the calamitousness of the consequences. Should we have doubts, the music banishes them.

In *Don Giovanni*, while the Don is overwhelmed in the end both musically and dramatically, and richly deserves the negative judgments he receives not only by conventionally moral lights but by genuinely human ones as well, the right of those who so judge him to have the last word with respect to him—and with respect to human worth—is subverted rather than supported by the very manner of its delivery. Neither the lilliputian contingent that celebrates his demise nor the brobdingnagian figure who effects it can be taken seriously as ultimately authoritative with respect to matters of human worth. Mozart's dramatic and musical devices make it impossible for us to identify with either of them, notwithstanding the ability of the various celebrants to amuse, charm, and occasionally even move us, and despite the power of the Statue—who really is no character at all but rather a kind of *deus ex lapide*—to stun and amaze us.

In *Don Giovanni* as well as in the *Ring* drama and music work powerfully and masterfully together to cultivate a sensibility that is both transformative of our sense of human reality and possibility and profoundly affirmative with respect to what this life in this world has to offer. This endows them with authority and is the basis of the fundamental judgments they pass, the expression of which is achieved above all through their musical guidance. But it is a different sensibility in each case. In the *Ring* it is a sensibility that revolves around the kind of extraordinary higher humanity that Brünnhilde finally attains and represents; while that toward which *Don Giovanni* moves us has to do with what it means or might mean to live a human life in the most genuinely human way. In both cases love looms large. But Wagner asks more of it than Mozart does, for whom we do well enough to love and be loved on more modestly human terms.

Brünnhilde's ultimate kind of love, with seventeen hours of development behind it, spectacular staging around it, and incredible orchestration beneath it, is one of the most awesome things in the annals of opera or indeed of Western culture. It was intended to be so. Her love is the real flame that consumes gods and Gibichungs alike, giving both the kinds of endings they differently deserve. The Commendatore's hellfires cannot hold a candle to that flame; for they can no longer be taken seriously, literally or even figuratively. They merely give vivid dramatic expression to a negative judgment, and—in contrast to the conflagration at the end of the *Ring*—no longer represent anything that can truly awe us. But Brünnhilde's kind of love does do just that; for it does at least point to a real human possibility. And it awes us in a way that Siegfried's heroic deeds and even Wotan's Valhalla and grand designs for the world (not to mention the wealth and power represented by the Rhinegold and Ring) do not.

Awe, in the world of the *Ring*, is the key to directive authority. The limits of Wotan's authority are the limits of his ability to inspire awe. When he encounters Siegfried, who not only is not awed by him but does not even respect him, his authority is ended. Siegfried famously does not know the meaning of fear. More important, he does not know the meaning of awe—at least until he meets Brünnhilde, who temporarily remedies that situation. He himself has no real authority because the awe he is capable of inspiring is only superficial. Brünnhilde initially accepts Wotan's authority because she reveres him, holding him in adoring and admiring awe, yet she transfers her allegiance to love, which inspires greater awe in her heart and becomes her highest authority. She attains unsurpassed authority by the *Ring*'s end owing to the awe that is inspired in us by her embodiment of love—which is all that we have left now that the gods are no more—raised to the limits of human possibility.

Awe, for Wagner, is the key to meaning and authority; and it is the key to authority precisely *because* it is the key to meaning. The limits of awe, he seems to be convinced, are meaning's limits. When awe fades, meaning fades—and, by the same token, if awe can be inspired anew, meaning can be engendered along with it. The problem, therefore, is to come up with something that can be made awe inspiring in our time and world. And that, for Wagner, is neither wealth nor power; nor is it the best of social systems or even the greatest of heroes and heroic deeds. It is Brünnhilde's kind of love.

Mozart, on the other hand, would appear to be deeply suspicious of awe, providing us only with caricatures of it that almost seem designed to inoculate us against it. He seems far from sure that there is anything at all, other than the Almighty, perhaps, that is truly deserving of it. It is not even clear how seriously he takes the idea of that religious exception. The traditional view of the matter is that God alone is deserving of awe. *Don Giovanni* might be regarded as a kind of testing of the waters of a secular future, as the idea of the sort of God who would warrant our awe becomes less vivid and compelling. Can we conceive of any entirely human possibilities that are contenders for anything like awe, or even for admiration?

Most of the characters we meet in *Don Giovanni* do not come close—not even the Commendatore, at least in life. And in death, while his reappearance in marmoreal form is awesome enough in its way, it is a caricature of awesomeness and therefore represents no real human possibility at all. Leporello is awed, to be sure, but the comical nature of his reaction and lines (which threaten to steal the scene) ensures that we will not be similarly affected. The Don, on the other hand, while amazed, is not awed in the least and refuses to grant his Stone Guest any real authority, notwithstanding his recognition that he is overmatched and doomed. And he is right. The Statue may have been given the dramatic ability to overpower the Don and drag him down into the inferno below, but a device in the service of a judgment deserves no more respect than the judgment itself, however extraordinary it may be.

That leaves only the Don himself in *Don Giovanni* as a candidate for our awe—but, remarkable and interesting though he is, he neither gets it nor deserves it. We are invited to be in awe of the number of his conquests, and of his willingness to do anything in his quest for more; but that invitation is not a serious one, even though the human possibility of such a person is very interesting indeed. If we think in terms of esteem rather than awe, the Don is an even less compelling figure, even if, as we observed at the outset, he certainly has a kind of authority, owing to his ability to charm, fascinate, dazzle, appeal, deceive, and dominate. We cannot esteem what we cannot affirm. The Don illuminates what it means to turn out well as a genuinely human being more by indirection than directly, accentuating the inadequacies of the others but also vividly displaying his own, even while providing tantalizing glimpses of a human possibility that, differently developed and configured, might well be admirable.

Finding our way to this sort of enhanced human flourishing is what Mozart would have us aspire to—and that, for him, is aspiration enough. For Wagner it is not, perhaps because he did not share Mozart's confidence in the sufficiency of what is humanly attainable along these lines. For him life without awe is insipid at best, if not simply untenable. In the absence of the sort of inspiration it alone can engender in the human heart, life is devoid of worth, all sound and fury signifying nothing. For Mozart, on the other hand, awe is something we are going to have to learn to live without. Our desire for it is an addiction of which we must somehow cure ourselves if we are to come to terms with life in a healthy human way. *Don Giovanni* may be thought of as a contribution to that cure.

Don Giovanni does not simply herald the *Ring*'s basic problem, thereby setting the stage for it. It is in rivalry with the *Ring*. Both raise our consciousness in importantly similar ways, making a compelling case for the necessity of moving "beyond good and evil" (as these notions are commonly understood) in thinking about what it takes to render life more meaningful than it is in its merely natural and all-too-human forms, while at the same time showing how problematic it may be to do so. But they cultivate sensibilities that are differently attuned to the question of how we might best come to terms with this issue. The sensibility of the *Ring* revolves around and culminates in the emergence of the Brünnhilde of its final act. One can hardly imagine a sensibility more alien to those of the entire cast of *Don Giovanni*—or to Mozart himself.

Mozart was ahead of his time. In this most profound of his operas he might be seen as firing a preliminary salvo in the contest of reinterpretation and revaluation that was to become a preoccupation in the following century and with which the names of Wagner and Nietzsche are vividly associated. His fundamentally optimistic secular humanism could not satisfy someone like the Wagner of the *Ring*, for whom it would have seemed hopelessly naive and utterly inadequate. Mozart, by contrast, appears to have been animated by a Shakespearean conviction that, the death of the gods notwithstanding, a tragic sensibility—grand as it is—is not enough, that humanity requires its supersession, and that its supersession is humanly possible. Mozart was not oblivious to tragedy; but for the Mozart of *Don Giovanni* human life at its best begins on the far side of it. His optimism is hard won and without illusions. It is oblivious neither to the pervasiveness of the all-too-human nor to the precariousness of the humane. But it is resolute in its affirmation of the possibility and value of the truly human. For Wagner that is not enough. For Mozart it had better be—and is.

NOTE

For a considerably expanded discussion of ideas advanced here with respect to the *Ring*, see our *Finding an Ending: Reflections on Wagner's Ring* (New York: Oxford, 2004), which had its origin in an earlier version of this essay.

Eleven

Mozart's *Don Giovanni* in Shaw's Comedy

AGNES HELLER

efore Mozart composed his opera *Don Giovanni* (first performed in Prague in 1787), the character Don Juan always
had a touch of the comic about him. In Tirso de Molina's *El burlador de Sevilla*
(1630), and even more in Molière's *Don Juan ou le festin de pierre* (1665), Don
Juan is depicted in situations where he appears in a comic light. Many of those
situations are repeated in Mozart, but Don Giovanni himself is never presented as comic. Mozart's music endows him with a kind of grandeur, which, as
Aristotle knew, is incompatible with a comic element. George Bernard Shaw
notes this in the dedicatory epistle of his *Man and Superman: A Comedy and a
Philosophy* (1903) addressed to Arthur Bingham Walkley: "after Molière comes
the artist-enchanter, the master beloved by masters, Mozart, revealing the
hero's spirit in magical harmonies, elfin tones, and elate darting rhythms as
of summer lightning made audible."[1] Shaw believed that one could not retell
Don Giovanni in the twentieth century except by recontextualizing it. At first
look he simply retranslates the old story into the language of prose drama.
This alone would return it to a comedy, yet Shaw writes a comedy unlike that
of Molière's—he pays tribute to Mozart's *Don Giovanni* while writing a play
that is also a paraphrasis of Mozart's opera. In Shaw it is Mozart/Da Ponte's
story of Don Giovanni—not just the legend of Don Juan—that becomes

comic. In reversing almost all the traditional roles, Shaw follows the rules of the comic genre, yet all his role reversals contribute to the deconstruction of the Don Juan myth. Thus Shaw deconstructs *Don Giovanni*. He writes a comedy and an essay on Don Giovannism in the times of nihilism, socialism, and feminism, and he writes it through the lenses of Wagner and Nietzsche. In Shaw's analysis "Don Juanism is no longer misunderstood as mere Casanovism"; the essential or "developed Don Juan" is "a true Promethean foe of the gods" with an instinctive suspicion of women that no longer has to be masked as Shakespeare masked Hamlet (243). Shaw's modern Englishman, psychically ascetic and determinedly antimatrimonial, embodies the essential Don Juan even though he "is superficially unlike the hero of Mozart" (243): Don Juan resists and subverts the institutional and, in particular, the matrimonial.

Shaw's play *Man and Superman*, with the subtitle *A Comedy and a Philosophy*, is a witty social comedy, a parody, as well as a paraphrasis of Mozart's opera *Don Giovanni*. John Tanner, a modern Englishman, is none other than the parodied reversal of Don Juan Tenorio, the name José Zorrilla gave Don Juan in his 1844 play. The comedy contains a play within the play. Tanner and the sentimentalist brigand Mendoza are both falling asleep one night on the Sierra while listening to the tunes of Mozart. Both dream that they are in Hell, where the Don meets a strange trio: an old lady, a statue, and the Devil. Both sleepers are present in each other's dream, yet only John Tanner remembers the dream.

If one forgets for a moment the nested play, that is, the dream, Shaw's main play possesses many elements in common with a classic Shakespearean comedy such as *Much Ado about Nothing* (1600).[2] Wit and puns play a significant role; there is also the usual side story that develops in the plebeian regions as well as at the crossing point between the two when the "low" happily interferes with the "high." There is likewise a series of errors and misunderstandings and finally the happy ending in marriage. That this happy ending is perhaps not so happy is not a unique feature in Shaw; one can also interpret a few of Shakespearean comedies in Shaw's skeptical spirit, as frequently happens with *The Taming of the Shrew*. Since Shaw is perhaps the most conscious and self-conscious playwright, he reflects upon his own project. In Shakespeare, Shaw notes, women are always the ones who take the initiative in love (245). Since this aptly describes Shaw's lady, Ann Whitefield, we see that Shaw intends her character to be essentially Shakespearean. Thus is the spirit of Shakespeare reborn in the twentieth century. It is a spirit both like and unlike its previous incarnation. People's morals become neither better nor worse, yet the beauty that lingers in all Shakespearean comedies, the renaissance beauty, is no longer present in the times of the "automobile."

It would be a misunderstanding to believe that only the play *within* the play references Mozart's *Don Giovanni,* and not the social comedy as well. As is frequently the case in Shakespeare, the play within the play is a reflection of the play itself, expressed in the genre of parody, joke, or statement. I take this to be true of Shaw's comedy notwithstanding Shaw's disclaimer that he inserted "the Mozartian dissoluto punito and his antagonist the statue" into his version of the Don Juan story as "a simple device" or as a "trick of the strolling theatrical manager who advertises the pantomime of Sinbad the Sailor with a stock of second-hand picture posters designed for Ali Baba" (243).

Only five of the major characters in Shaw's comedy are borrowed from Mozart's *Don Giovanni.* One of them, Roebuck Ramsden, a middle-aged gentleman and follower of Herbert Spencer, only represents the Commendatore by appearing as a statue in the play within the play. The relation between Leporello and Enry Straker, "the Motor Engineer and New Man," is so vague that without Shaw's explicit assurance we would hardly detect it (254). What remains is the trio—John Tanner, Octavius Robinson, and Ann Whitefield. This trio, or triangle, if you will, personifies the comedy of sexual or erotic subversion, adjustment and political sham/subversion, and the tensions between social expectations and desires, the artificial and the natural, poetry and lived actuality. Not such a far cry from Mozart, even though the trio there maneuvers in the world of prose, pettiness, and prejudices. The counterpoint will come in the dream/play where Ann Whitefield/Doña Ana hears about Nietzsche's Overman and cries out: "I believe in the life to come. . . . A father—a father for the Superman!"(374) It is this funny, untimely cry that brings us back to the world where Mozart's *Don Giovanni* is indeed no longer possible.

The most thoroughgoing Mozartian character of the trio is Octavius Robinson, alias Don Ottavio. Shaw writes: "Octavius I take over unaltered from Mozart; and I hereby authorize any actor who impersonates him, to sing (if he can) *dalla sua pace* at any convenient moment during the representation"(254). In Shaw's version, as we all know, Ann seduces John Tanner into marrying her, thus the love of Octavius ("*dalla sua pace!*") will be ironically refused. Shaw offers here an unorthodox interpretation of Mozart's Don Ottavio, one entirely different from the famous interpretation offered by Søren Kierkegaard, which Shaw did not know and so many interpreters have since repeated. In Shaw's comedy Don Ottavio is no weakling, nor is he bourgeois or a man of convention. On the contrary. This Ottavio/Octavius is, throughout the entire play, the only man who does not give in to bourgeois reality, which being so relentlessly pervasive has become life. Even John Tanner, the subversive bourgeois, remains a bourgeois just as Don Giovanni, the subversive nobleman, remains a nobleman. John Tanner, at least, concedes defeat—there are, in any case, no avenging statues in modern

London. In contrast, Octavius is a poet. He needs to love absolutely, love only his Beatrice, for the sake of his poetry. However, the love of Octavius is pure poetry; he would never have accepted Ann as she was and so would have made the worst possible husband. As Ann tells him in their final showdown: "Perhaps it's because you're a poet. You are like the bird that presses its breast against the sharp thorn to make itself sing. . . . Oh Tavy, Tavy, Ricky Ticky Tavy, heaven help the woman who marries you!"(393–394). Nietzsche's insistence that man should say "yes" to life is here echoed by Ann as much as by the play. The poet can further the work of the Nietzschean life force only insofar as he stays apart from everyday life. In fact Nietzsche said something very similar about philosophers: it would be absurd for them to marry. Surely Nietzsche is also just a prop in Shaw's comedy and is thus treated ironically. The Great Life Force is here unmasked as the erotic energy that appears in the sexual fantasies and plays of bourgeois children and is finally consummated in bourgeois marriage, the pleasure in intercourse for the sake of propagation. This is exactly what the quasi-anarchist John Tanner believes to be true. He writes in the "Revolutionist's Handbook" that is attached to the play: "Marriage is popular because it combines the maximum of temptation with the maximum of opportunity"(439). On the other hand, this is not what Octavius/Ottavio means when he says "I love you"—Ricky Ticky Tavy desires only what he does not possess.

In his letter to Walkley, Shaw attempts to clarify his palimpsest. Why is John Tanner the Don Giovanni of the early twentieth century? This Don Juan inhabits a world where "Man is no longer, like {the prototypic} Don Juan, victor in the duel of sex," although Shaw doubts whether Man has ever been (242). Michel Foucault would have pointed out that the "duel of sex" is in itself a modern perception of gender relations. In fact, the theme of gender combat first appeared in Mozart's times in the two famous novels by Samuel Richardson, especially in his *Clarissa* (1747–1748). While it is easy to interpret Mozart's opera *The Marriage of Figaro* (first performed in Vienna in 1786) as a "duel of sex," it is difficult to read his *Don Giovanni* in that way. But Shaw insists that *Don Giovanni* be presented as a duel of sex won by Woman in an early twentieth-century replay. The modern Don Juan must be different however because "instead of pretending to read Ovid he does actually read Schopenhauer and Nietzsche, studies Westermarck, and is concerned for the future of the race instead of for the freedom of his own instincts"(242). In the play within the play where John Tanner appears as Don Juan, he will become, by the end, the mouthpiece of Nietzsche. Without having read Kierkegaard, Shaw translates the Don Juan of "non-reflected, immediate" sensuality into a Don Juan of reflected sensuality. Who is Don Juan after all but the representation of the subversive man? Sensuality, as a principle, is the creation of

Christianity, or so Kierkegaard says. Yet when no one any longer believes in damnation, sensuality cannot be a subversive principle, even if translated into the language of sexual discourse. But reflection on sensuality is outside sexual discourse. It is again Nietzsche who becomes subversive, according to Shaw, although he turns to him frequently and ironically. In the play everyone talks about sex, everyone is obsessed with sex in an utterly hypocritical manner. This is indeed, and as Foucault would have echoed, real "Victorianism." Only the poet is not obsessed with sex, adds Shaw, and this brings us again back to Octavius Robinson, Ottavio as Shaw interprets him.

Let us now turn to the play within the play, where the Mozartian ancestors appear. The music is played: in the book the score is presented. Shaw employs the music of Mozart in a quasi-descriptive sense as signals of expectation, remembrance, and identity, using a kind of *Leitmotivtechnik*. Thus the flute, the horn, and the bassoon sound and then Don Juan appears. The whispers of "a ghostly clarinet" accompany an aged lady's appearance on the stage. The two characters enter into conversation. We learn that they are in Hell. It turns out that the lady is Doña Ana, now seventy-seven and mother of twelve children whose husband died a long time ago. While the witty dialogue unfolds, the reinterpretation of Mozart's opera begins. Don Juan cannot be called a murderer for he killed the statue in a duel. This is what the Commendatore, who is now younger than his daughter, never ceases to repeat: "He maintains that he was a much better swordsman than I, and that if his foot had not slipped he would have killed me. No doubt he is right: I was not a good fencer. I never dispute the point; so we are excellent friends" (339). Doña Ana is shocked by the thought that her father is in Hell, yet Don Juan reassures her that her father is in fact in Heaven, but bored there, and so comes to him frequently in Hell. At this point music again takes the place of words.

DON JUAN: Ha! Mozart's statue music. It is your father . . .
The Statue enters.
DON JUAN: Ah, here you are, my friend. Why don't you learn to sing the splendid music Mozart has written for you?
THE STATUE: Unluckily he has written it for a bass voice. Mine is a counter tenor. Well, have you repented yet?
DON JUAN: I have too much consideration for you to repent, Don Gonzalo. If I did, you would have no excuse for coming from Heaven to argue with me.
THE STATUE: True. Remain obdurate, my boy (340).
At that point Doña Ana reappears and is shocked to see her father as a statue.
THE STATUE: My dear: I am so much more admired in marble than I ever was in my own person that I have retained the shape the sculptor gave me (341).

Surely, who would remember Doña Ana's father if not in the marbled form of a statue? Mozart's genius treated avenging as a function, for "the Avenger" is a character fit only for comic portrayal. Later in the dialogue the statue continues his sardonic boasting: "as a young man I was admired by women; and as a statue I am praised by art critics" (363).

Let us follow the dialogue with the entrance of the Devil. This breaks with Mozart's opera since there is no Devil in that work. Shaw writes: "this time Mozart's music gets grotesquely adulterated with Gounod's. A scarlet halo begins to glow; and into it the Devil rises, very Mephistophelean, and not at all unlike Mendoza, though not so interesting" (342). The device of the scarlet halo mocks the music of French composer Charles-François Gounod, treating it as kitsch. The Devil, it will turn out, has a strong attraction to kitsch. In Shaw's portrayal Hell is the domain of kitsch, a world of sham existence. Furthermore, life as kitsch is indistinguishable from Hell. For this reason the poet Ottavio is not in Hell, nor does he visit Hell; this is also why Don Giovanni chooses Heaven.

The dialogue turns immediately to the merits and demerits of Heaven and Hell respectively. The statue then decides to move from Heaven to Hell. Here we enter the complex network of role divisions and also of role reversals. The Devil begins to speak Nietzsche's language. He speaks with only one of Nietzsche's voices; his is the language of the popular Nietzsche. In the following exchange of thoughts, and ever increasingly, Don Juan will speak like the other Nietzsche. As the dialogue develops, the exchange between Don Juan and the Devil becomes a duel between two Nietzsches, a vulgar one and a subtle one. This is Shaw's replay of the duel of swords in Mozart's opera between Don Giovanni and the Commendatore. The Devil is the better fencer, yet he slips. Here in Shaw's duel of words, which is also a dream of John Tanner and Mendoza, the slip is not of the foot but of the tongue. Just as it seems the duel is about to be again won by Don Giovanni, it is terminated by the cry of Doña Ana, wanting a father for the Superman.

In the following conversation the Devil begins to generate propaganda for Hell; he succeeds with the statue but not with the Don.

THE DEVIL: I call on it [the world] to sympathize with joy, with love, with happiness, with beauty—

DON JUAN (*nauseated*): Excuse me, I am going. You know I cannot stand this . . .

THE DEVIL: Oh, by what irony of fate was this cold selfish egoist sent to my Kingdom . . . we had the greatest hopes of him. . . . You remember how he sang? (*He begins to sing in a nasal operatic baritone, tremulous from an eternity of misuse, in the French manner.*)

Vivan le femmine!
Viva il buon vino!
THE STATUE (*taking up the tune an octave higher in his counter tenor*):
Sostegno e Gloria
D'umanita.
THE DEVIL: Precisely. Well, he never sings for us now.
DON JUAN: Do you complain of that? Hell is full of musical amateurs: music
    is the brandy of the damned (393–394).[3]

Here Shaw does several things simultaneously: he introduces us to Hell
as the homeland of sentimental kitsch, he reverses the roles of the Mozartian
characters, he writes a parody of French music and opera performances,
and he makes sport of regressive listening. The Devil is a very enthusiastic
creature. He has only good words for everyone; he regrets it deeply if someone—irrationally!—chooses to go to Heaven. ("Mozart would be delighted if
he were still here; but he moped and went to Heaven" [344].) Heaven is, so
the Devil assures everyone, a dull place, and the statue agrees: "Nobody could
stand an eternity of Heaven" (345).

Here we learn together with Doña Ana that everyone is free to go to either
place. No high tribunal directs you: you choose according to your taste. The
Devil explains that there is a gulf between Heaven and Hell; this is the gulf
between the angelic and the diabolic temperament. Just as there is a gulf
between the philosopher's classroom and the bullring. Those who love the
bullring would be bored to death by the philosopher's classroom, although
they are free to go there. And those who enjoy the philosopher's classroom
would be bored stiff if they had to spend their whole life in the bullring. The
lovers of racing could go to concerts, they just do not like to go there. Heaven,
says Shaw's Don Juan, is the home of the masters of reality: there you live and
work instead of play and pretend (347).

This is the focal point of the most decisive twist. As Don Juan interprets
him, Nietzsche is from this point onward contrasted to the Nietzsche of the
Devil's presentation. This Nietzsche makes the decisive distinction between
high and low, noble and base, between the real, the hard, and the difficult,
between *suffering* on the one hand and the *mediocre*, between the banal and
the easy. Shaw's Hell has a master, the clown Mephisto, yet Heaven has none.
There you are your own master. With this twist, Shaw's Don Juan, who
decides to go to Heaven, again matches Mozart's Don Juan who ends up in
Hell. Both are, as the Devil points out, "asocial" creatures. However, each is
asocial in a different manner. The situation in the nether world differs from
the situation on earth, just as the eighteenth century differs from the twenti-

eth century. As Don Juan in Hell explains to his interlocutors: on earth one is embodied, "there one has only one prayer, make me a healthy animal" (347). Yet in the nether world humans are bodiless. The happiness of Hell is therefore unreal: "There are no hard facts to contradict you, no ironic contrasts of your needs with your pretensions, no human comedy, nothing but a perpetual romance, a universal melodrama" (347). Since the dead are now bodiless, their only possible reality lies in contemplation. And Heaven is about contemplation: "So would I enjoy the contemplation of that which interests me above all things: namely, Life: the force that ever strives to attain greater power of contemplating itself" (348). And when the statue bursts out in laughter, the rules are again reversed, albeit ironically.

> DON JUAN: Audacious ribald: your laughter will finish in hideous boredom before morning.
> THE STATUE: Ha ha! Do you remember how I frightened you when I said something like that to you from my pedestal in Seville? (348)

In the following duel the Devil plays the part of a cultural critic and Don Juan that of the Nietzschean defender of the human race.

> THE DEVIL: . . . Man is a bungler. . . . [This] marvelous force of Life of which you boast is a force of Death.
> DON JUAN: . . . You can make any of these cowards brave by simply putting an idea into his head . . . [and] it is not killing and dying that degrades us, but base living, and accepting the wages and profits of degradation" (352–353).
> DON JUAN (*continuing with his rhetoric after Anna's interruptions*): Men should be more than the mere means for Women in the process of propagation— . . . The Life Force is stupid; but it is not so stupid as the Forces of Death and Degeneration. . . . Life is a force, which has made innumerable experiments . . . attempts to build up that raw force into higher and higher individuals, the ideal individual being omnipotent, omniscient, infallible, and withal completely, unilludedly self-conscious: in short, a god? (354–355).

Shaw's genius puts sentences in Don Juan's mouth that express the most extreme transgressions of the twentieth century, in comparison to which the transgression of a Don Giovanni in the seventeenth and eighteenth century seems to be no more than a minor faux pas. Every transgression of the twentieth century is grounded in the idea of the deification of man. And this idea was brewed in the sorcerer's kitchen of philosophy: "I sing, not arms and the hero, but the philosophic man," declares Don Juan passionately, "he who seeks in contemplation to discover the inner will of the world, in invention to discover the means of fulfilling that will, and in action to do that will by the so-discovered means" (356–357).

At this point Shaw switches suddenly back to the ironic interpretation (self-interpretation) of Mozart's *Don Giovanni*. This Don Giovanni is more John Tanner than Nietzsche or, more precisely, the John Tanner who read but did not understand his Nietzsche. We are back in London at the beginning of the twentieth century; remember this is all happening in John Tanner's dream. Thus Don Juan/John Tanner explains that he had to run away from women for they regarded him as their property and prey. But he never shared in romantic lies: "I was not duped: I took her without chloroform" (359). And, "when I stood face to face with Woman . . . my morals said No. My conscience said No. My chivalry and pity for her said No. My prudent regard for myself said No. . . . And whilst I was in the act of framing my excuse to the lady, Life seized me and threw me into her arms as a sailor throws a scrap of fish into the mouth of a seabird. . . . I saw then how useless it is to attempt to impose conditions on the irresistible force of Life" (359–360). And later he adds (it is close to a quotation from John Tanner's "Revolutionist's Handbook"): "Marriage is the most licentious human institution" and "Nature, my dear lady, is what you call immoral" (366). And then he adds: "I tell you that in the pursuit of my own pleasure, my own health, my own fortune, I have never known happiness. . . . That is what has made this place of eternal pleasures [Hell] so deadly to me" (368).

While Don Juan keeps talking as a metaphysician of life, the Devil continues with his philosophy of history. In a deep sense this Don Juan remains close to his original role in the opera of Mozart: he represents something ahistorical, something that is thought to be below or above the historical, either as the Life Force or as the Contemplation of the Life Force, whereas the Devil remains close to Mephisto (Goethe's version rather than Gounod's). Thus the Devil says: "[I] confess to you that men get tired of everything, of heaven no less than of hell; and that all history is nothing but a record of the oscillations of the world between these two extremes. An epoch is but a swing of the pendulum; and each generation thinks the world is progressing because it is always moving. . . . You think, because you have a purpose, Nature must have one" (370–371). To which Don Juan answers (among other things): "But I should not have them if they served no purpose. . . . The philosopher is in the grip of the Life Force. . . . The Philosopher is Nature's pilot. And there you have our difference: to be in hell is to drift: to be in heaven is to steer"

(370–371). The Devil continues with a few sharp comments: "Beware of the pursuit of the Superhuman: it leads to the indiscriminate contempt for the Human" (373). The Superman is, so the Devil goes on, the latest fashion among the Life Force fanatics, among them a madman called Nietzsche who decided to move to Heaven. Don Juan wants to follow him, and asks for directions. But then, with another switch, it is the statue who will explain elementary Nietzsche to him: "Oh, the frontier is only the difference between two ways of looking at things" (373).

Shaw cannot resist introducing Wagner into the conversation. The statue declares that he would like to see "this Nietzsche," but the Devil informs him that "he met Wagner here, and had a quarrel with him," though not about music (374). He explains: "Wagner once drifted into Life Force worship, and invented a Superman called Siegfried. But he came to his senses afterwards. So when they met here, Nietzsche denounced him as a renegade; and Wagner wrote a pamphlet to prove that Nietzsche was a Jew; and it ended in Nietzsche's going to heaven in a huff. And a good riddance too" (374). To which the statue remarks: "All the same, the Superman is a fine conception. There is something statuesque about it" (374).

With this ironic tone the conversation ends. The rest is the last appearance of Doña Ana. She wants to find the Superman for herself, but she is enlightened: "He is not yet created, Señora"(374). The last sentence of the play within the play is the cry of Doña Ana: "A father! A father for the Superman!" (374) Yet the father of the Superman, as Shaw knew, was Nietzsche, the man who would never have begotten a man with a woman.

In Mozart's *Don Giovanni* Don Juan goes to Hell. Hell is made of fire and smoke, a space of damnation. In Shaw's play John Tanner marries Ann, instantiating the comedic form with an apparently happy ending. Don Giovanni three times says "No" to repentance, and he does not repent. John Tanner three times says "No!" to marriage, yet he marries. In the play within the play, Don Juan in Hell says "Yes" to the Life Force and thereby vindicates both Don Giovanni and John Tanner. There is no moral of the play, there are just conflicting political, historical, and metaphysical positions—different perspectives. Yet there are aesthetic judgments. Shaw plays his enthusiastic tribute to the miracle of the masterpiece, to Mozart's *Don Giovanni*, and he also, albeit only on the sideline, plays aesthetic tribute to Nietzsche and to Wagner. In this comedy of manners, of ideas and of interpretations, there is only one thing that remains strictly serious: artistic taste. There is no one single aesthetic judgment among the witty paradoxes of John Tanner's "Revolutionist's Handbook." The characters of Mozart dispute, but Mozart's opera is beyond all disputes.

NOTES

1. George Bernard Shaw, *Man and Superman: A Comedy and a Philosophy* (New York, 1960), 240. First published in London in 1903. All page references to Shaw's comedy are to this text.
2. Interestingly, this comedy has its own Don John, who is involved, as ever, with the disruption and delay of matrimonial union.

Twelve

Giovanni auf Naxos

BRIAN SOUCEK

*I*t did not take long, not even two months after the premiere of *Der Rosenkavalier*, for Richard Strauss and Hugo von Hofmannsthal to begin planning its successor. They said their next opera would be "related to *Zauberflöte* as *Rosenkavalier* was to *Figaro*." The relationship to Mozart's work was not to be one of mere imitation, but rather, as Hofmannsthal wrote to Strauss in March 1911, that of "a certain analogy" (*eine gewisse Analogie*).[1]

The resulting opera was *Die Frau ohne Schatten*, and its commentators, critics, and program annotators still speculate on just what "certain analogy" Hofmannsthal might have intended. What, indeed, does it mean to speak of one opera standing in analogy to another? In this essay I want to pursue this question by looking at a certain analogy that Strauss and Hofmannsthal did *not* speak of. In discussing *Figaro* and *Zauberflöte*, these two lifelong admirers of Mozart's work conspicuously left out what some have called the "opera of all operas," *Don Giovanni*. *Giovanni* remains nearly unmentioned in their entire correspondence, its influence unclear and seldom considered. And yet, so I shall argue, *Don Giovanni* found among their works an analogue of its own: *Ariadne auf Naxos*.

This is not to say that Strauss or Hofmannsthal ever set out to make their own *Giovanni*. Even if Strauss had never heard Mozart's opera, the connections I want to trace between it and *Ariadne* might still remain. To say that Mozart's opera found an analogue in Strauss's work is not to say that *Giovanni* had any direct historical influence on *Ariadne*.[2] It means instead that the kinds of interpretive questions that have long plagued *Giovanni* can be asked of *Ariadne auf Naxos* as well. The reception history of *Don Giovanni*—and, I am saying, of *Ariadne* too—is one divided over how to classify the work, over what meaning should be sought there, even over which of the work's scenes should be included in its performance.

Of course, *Giovanni* and *Ariadne* are not alone in having problematic performance histories. What I would like to suggest is that their parallel interpretive challenges stem from a "certain analogy" between the works themselves. (Though, once again, this connection need not have been intended. Nothing turns on there being an explicit or conscious link between the two works.) Both works exist in two distinct versions, each having undergone important revisions; both blur the line between high and low, comic and serious; and both do so in part by incorporating the same diverse array of source materials.

Importantly, however, *Ariadne* does not just recapitulate *Don Giovanni*'s ambiguities; it addresses them. Strauss and Hofmannsthal's opera shows an awareness of the interpretive problems it shares with Mozart's work. In a word, *Ariadne auf Naxos* has a *self-consciousness* that *Don Giovanni* (not to mention Giovanni himself) lacks. If *Ariadne* is an analogue to Mozart's opera, it is a decidedly Modernist one, an opera concerned with its own status as a "serious, important work." As we will see, *Ariadne*, like *Giovanni*, is centrally concerned with issues of fidelity. Fidelity is also the key theme of the present essay. Constancy and betrayal play an important role in both operas, but, unlike *Giovanni*, *Ariadne* is concerned also with interpretive fidelity—the fidelity (or often infidelity) shown to works of art. Questions of fidelity *within* Strauss's opera are thus mirrored by questions of interpretive fidelity *to* it. *Ariadne* attempts to make explicit the sorts of commitments that often lie hidden behind interpretations of works like itself. And insofar as *Don Giovanni is* one of those works, *Ariadne* exposes the interpretive commitments behind it as well. I might, in what follows, have more to say about *Ariadne* than *Giovanni*, but that is only because *Ariadne* has something to say about both. Learning to interpret Strauss's opera is to learn, by analogy, something about Mozart's work.

Ultimately, then, the main reason for drawing analogies between these operas is because they underscore a philosophical difference between them: namely, *Ariadne*'s increased self-consciousness. In the following pages I will compare the works' parallel histories of revision and performance. I will discuss changes that their composers felt compelled to make as well as those that later

interpreters felt free to make on their own. I will try to find in the works themselves certain structural parallels that might have led to their similar subsequent
treatment. But, in the end, I argue for a "certain analogy" between *Giovanni*
and *Ariadne* largely in order to differentiate between them. It is the later work's
unique self-consciousness about its own faithful interpretation that allows *Ariadne* to become a commentary—on itself and *Don Giovanni* both.

The most striking analogy between *Ariadne auf Naxos* and *Don Giovanni* is
one that Strauss and Hofmannsthal could not have foreseen when they began
writing what was to be a "slight interim work."[3] They could not have known as
they prepared *Ariadne* for its 1912 premiere that the version they were producing would not be the one generally performed in the century that followed:
that their work's original ending would be cut and its overall mood transformed. Had they known what was to come, however, both would certainly
have recognized that much the same thing had happened to *Don Giovanni* in
the first century or so of its performance.

The circumstances surrounding *Giovanni*'s composition have often been
described.[4] The long-held story that Mozart completed the work in just
three weeks (writing the Overture the night before its premiere in Prague on
October 29, 1787) might be a legend, but the real story is no less impressive.
Mozart and Da Ponte's commission to follow up their hugely popular *Figaro*
with a new opera came only ten months before the latter's first performance.
If the orchestra did not really perform the Overture with its ink still wet at
the premiere, they almost certainly did so the day before at the final dress
rehearsal. Equally hasty were the additions made for the work's second, Viennese version of May 1788. Its three additional pieces—including Elvira's
second act scena ("In quali eccessi . . . Mi tradì") and Ottavio's aria "Dalla sua
pace"—were all entered into Mozart's catalogue within a single week.

The music *deleted* in the revision was no less significant. Scholars are just
not sure how much of that there was. Mozart, we do know, omitted two arias,
one for Ottavio and one for Leporello. What is unclear is how the Vienna
Giovanni ended. Hypotheses and evidence vary: some believe that Mozart
considered a cut to the final scene but decided against it; others observe that
the final scene (the section following Giovanni's descent into Hell) is missing
from the 1788 Vienna libretto—and that Da Ponte himself was responsible
for printing libretti in Vienna at the time.[5] The autograph score suggests two
possible cuts: in one (written but then crossed out by Mozart) the women and
Ottavio enter at Giovanni's death and join Leporello in a D-major scream,
ending the opera there; in the other, only the sixty bars of the final scene's *lar-
getto* middle section are omitted, so the opera still ends with its *fugato*—and

its "moral."[6] It is unknown which of these suggestions were tried in performance and which Mozart or Da Ponte might have preferred.

Far better known is the widespread aversion to the final scene in the century that followed. Attempts to "improve" upon it were common. Audiences in Germany and Austria saw *Don Giovanni* around sixty-five hundred times in its first hundred years, but—unlike Mozart—they often saw a Don Giovanni who called himself Schwänkenreich, avoided a creditor, and killed Ottavio (himself sometimes called Fischblut).[7] As Julian Rushton has pointed out, versions in which Giovanni kills Ottavio certainly could not end with Mozart's sextet.[8] Instead, nineteenth-century productions invariably concluded with an unscripted host of devils filling the stage upon Giovanni's death. Or sometimes worse: some brought in the spirits of Giovanni's mistresses; others showed Giovanni stabbing himself; some had the Commendatore bless Anna and Ottavio; others still ended with Anna's suicide and funeral, accompanied by the "Dies Irae" of Mozart's Requiem![9] Even without such additions, merely omitting the final scene—as, again, Mozart and Da Ponte might themselves have done in Vienna—placed enough emphasis on the story's supernatural and tragic sides to attract the attention of the Romantics. It has often been observed that as a character Don Giovanni is surprisingly characterless, that, lacking traits of his own, other characters can freely attribute to him any traits they choose.[10] Much the same, it seems, could be said about *Don Giovanni* the opera. Lacking its original ending, the Romantic era could read into *Giovanni* the fulfillment of any of its own desires. It was not until the end of the nineteenth century and then, increasingly, in the twentieth, that Mozart's final scene would again be performed. Among the first to do so, in fact, was Richard Strauss, in a well-known Munich production of 1896.

Similar revisions, if not similar gaps in evidence, characterize Strauss's *Ariadne auf Naxos*. There too, important additions *and* cuts were made to the original score. An entire act, the Prologue, was added for the 1916 revision (written, like the revised *Giovanni*, for Vienna). In the original, 1912 *Ariadne*, the opera had been preceded by a play: Hofmannsthal's update of Molière's *Le Bourgeois Gentilhomme*, punctuated with incidental music by Strauss. A *Zwischenspiel*, on which the Prologue was later based, linked the two halves. For the 1916 *Ariadne* Strauss and Hofmannsthal omitted the play as well as sections of a solo (the comedienne Zerbinetta's) and a duet between her and Ariadne later in the opera. (Interestingly, unlike Mozart's cuts from the middle of *Giovanni*—Ottavio's aria, say—Strauss's cuts are not reinstated in contemporary performance, despite their musical interest.)

It is the cuts, however, made to the end of the Vienna *Ariadne* that mostly closely recall those of the Vienna *Giovanni*. Strauss's original ending was classical, distancing—a balance to the Romantic effusions immediately preceding it. Like Mozart (possibly) before him, Strauss's cut—of a scene in which Zerbinetta reappeared to deliver her ironic "moral"—gave his opera's Romantic side, its otherworldy element, the final word. The difference is that Strauss's decision, unlike Mozart's, is indubitable. The historical record is complete.

We assume that this difference matters, that contemporary performances generally employ Strauss's revised ending but not Mozart's precisely because Strauss's intentions on the matter are better known than Mozart's. Why otherwise would scholars be so interested in finding out what Mozart might have conducted in Vienna? Yet it is unclear how much our current performance practices would change even if there were a scholarly success story—the discovery, for example, of a detailed diary entry about the 1788 performances. After all, we know with confidence that Mozart never intended Ottavio's "Il mio tesoro" and Elvira's "Mi tradì" to follow each other—adding one for Vienna meant deleting the other—and yet most performers today find the music of both too good to forgo. Both are now generally included in a "mixed version" unlike any Mozart himself ever might have heard. In our current interpretation of *Don Giovanni* authorial intentions might not be the driving concern. But then, what is? What, in other words, makes a given performance a faithful one, and is the answer always the same? The parallel revisions of *Giovanni* and *Ariadne*, with their disputed claims to authenticity, clearly raise these questions. Yet for *Ariadne auf Naxos* questions of interpretive fidelity are raised not only by its performance history but also within its very plot.

In its revised, currently canonical version, that plot unfolds within a wealthy eighteenth-century Viennese household where a feast is to be followed by two commissioned performances. First to be performed is a new opera by a new Composer—a character Strauss suggested modeling on "a young Mozart."[11] As the Composer himself likes to emphasize, the opera is a serious, heroic piece, telling the story of Ariadne, who has been abandoned by her former lover, Theseus, but who remains faithful to him as she waits for his return on the desert island of Naxos. Following the opera is to be a commedia dell'arte performance by "the inconstant Zerbinetta" and her troupe of buffo companions. Plans change, however, when the owner of the house demands that the two works be performed simultaneously to save time. Chaos ensues, as do cuts in the opera's score, while the Composer sinks into despair: not only must he mutilate his work, he must also expose it to the vulgarity of Zerbinetta's. With the Composer wishing rather to starve in his own ideal realm than submit to *this*, the curtain falls on the Prologue.

The Composer's wish that his work be burned rather than altered goes unfulfilled, for the second act is nothing other than that work, altered. On her desert island Ariadne laments her fate while Zerbinetta and her troupe keep appearing from the wings to cheer her up. Zerbinetta's philosophy on men takes eleven minutes of coloratura and several high e's to deliver, but can be summarized by the thought that each man who enters her life comes "like a god"; to each she "surrenders without a word."[12] None of this has the slightest effect on Ariadne, who remains oblivious, even if, unintentionally, she will later confirm Zerbinetta's message. Roused by the sudden news that a young god is about to appear, and thinking he must be Hermes arriving finally to carry her to her death, Ariadne rushes to meet the new arrival. The god is actually Bacchus, but Ariadne uncomprehendingly gives herself to him anyway. Yielding to a new love, Ariadne and Bacchus are transformed, spiritually reborn.[13] And in the midst of this "miracle" (Hofmannsthal's term and fervent belief) Zerbinetta reappears to sing her refrain, tenderly this time: "When the new god comes along, / We surrender, without a word."

There is a clear sense in which *Ariadne*'s concern for fidelity recalls that of *Giovanni*. Giovanni's aversion to fidelity is as central to his character as his addiction to women, and the trait is not his alone. It is shared by Donna Anna, as she leads Ottavio constantly on, always delaying the marriage he so desires; by Zerlina, who proves capable of infidelity at her own wedding; and by Leporello, whose devotion to Giovanni is (perhaps justifiably) intermittent: he tries to quit his employment no less than three times in the course of the opera. In *Ariadne* Zerbinetta's inconstancy threatens to become the one constant of her character. Her list of former lovers ("Dann war es Cavicchio, / Dann Buratin, / Dann Pasquariello . . . ") is not as long as Don Giovanni's, but it is backed by rather more evidence. Ariadne, on the other hand, is as forlorn as Zerbinetta is successful. And yet, like Donna Elvira, betrayal and despair do not shake her faith. As the Composer says of his character: "She is one of those women who belong to only one man in life and after that to none more." After being abandoned by that "one man," Theseus, Ariadne waits only for death, just as Elvira plans to do in her convent. Nothing else remains for either once their loves have disappeared. Our—and Zerbinetta's—observation that in fact someone else, namely, Bacchus, *does* remain for Ariadne does not fully alter that fact. Ariadne never clearly understands that Bacchus is not just the death she has awaited; their dialogue is built almost entirely on misunderstandings. To her claim that he is "captain of a dark ship," he answers characteristically and uncomprehendingly: "I am the captain—of a ship." Bacchus may transform her and take her away, but not in the way or to the place she expects. If Zerbinetta proves no more true than Giovanni, Ariadne is no less deceived than Elvira.

In *Ariadne*, however—unlike in *Giovanni*—the more interesting issues of fidelity focus less on either of these characters than around the nameless Composer. In his case the fidelity he desires—and mourns—is not to a woman but to a work. His desire is for *Werktreue*, the sort of fidelity he both shows and expects others to show his opera. Early in the Prologue the Composer's teacher worries that his student "will kill himself" if he learns his opera must be abridged. In fact, having made the "mutilations" required, the Composer regrets having ever associated with the real world, instead wishing he had been allowed to "freeze, starve, and petrify" in his own ideal realm. To him, the suffering of Ariadne, a victim of infidelity, is no different than that of *Ariadne*, a piece which is similarly victimized in its performance.

The Prologue's backstage squabbles over what to do with the Composer's opera thus turn on the same theme of fidelity that prompts Ariadne's lament and eventual transformation in the opera itself. That theme is the same one driving the quests for revenge and repentance that comprise Mozart's opera. The difference between the two operas is that *Ariadne* treats their shared theme twice over. In *Ariadne* the question of fidelity is discussed within the work and also in regard *to* the work. Ariadne's abandonment is a concern; so too is the fidelity owed a work of art, the respect due to authorial intentions in a work's interpretation and performance. Such questions have often been asked *of* Mozart's opera, but in Strauss and Hofmannsthal's the questions are asked *within* it—the work is self-conscious of its own interpretive problems.

Of course the problems made conscious in *Ariadne* are not uniquely those of it or *Giovanni*. All operas, indeed all works of art, raise questions for us about autonomy, interpretation, and the status of generative intentions. But, as we have already seen, the performance histories of *Don Giovanni* and *Ariadne auf Naxos* are more than merely problematic; they are analogously problematic. This analogy is more than a coincidence. I would like to suggest that their parallel histories stem from similar ambiguities lying at the heart of these works. First among these is a question that has plagued them both since their composition: just what kind of operas are *Don Giovanni* and *Ariadne auf Naxos*?

In the case of *Don Giovanni* the official answer, that it is a *dramma giocoso* (or "jocular drama"), merely restates the ambiguity. The term *dramma giocoso* was sometimes used synonymously with opera buffa in Mozart's time (perhaps even by Mozart himself), but it also represents an operatic tradition that goes beyond the merely comic. By the mid-eighteenth century it was used by librettists such as Carlo Goldoni to refer to works that combined elements of opera seria and opera buffa.[14] Works like Goldoni's came to include three classes of characters. In Michael Robinson's description:

> There were first of all the so-called "serious" characters (*parti serie*), who displayed qualities like earnestness, courage, steadfastness, sensitive and passionate

feelings concerning love and honour—such qualities were more likely to be assigned, though they were not in every case, to the higher classes than to the lower. There were then the "comic" characters (*parti buffe*), usually from the lower classes, who displayed the opposite tendencies: inconstancy, cowardice, coarse feelings, deviousness and/or servility. Finally, for the reason that it was undesirable to split the cast into two completely contrasted serious and comic groups, librettists often included one or more *mezzi caratteri*, "middle characters," who had either no facets of personality that identified them as serious or comic or else facets of both.[15]

Goldoni's innovation could not have been lost on Mozart. Mozart set one of Goldoni's *drammi giocosi* to music (*La Finta Semplice* of 1768); years later he employed Goldoni's distinctions when describing to his father his instructions for a prospective librettist. "The most necessary thing," Mozart wrote in 1783, "is that the story, on the whole, be truly *comic*, and, if then it were possible, he ought to introduce *two equally good female roles*; one must be seria, the other *mezzo carattere*, but both roles must be absolutely equal *in quality*. But the third female character may be entirely buffa, and so may all four male characters, if necessary."[16]

Whether this wish was still in Mozart's mind when he turned to *Don Giovanni* in 1787, the division of parts he described fits *Giovanni* as well as any of his operas. Intentionally or not, Da Ponte's libretto provided Mozart with the exact female roles he had requested: Donna Anna as the indisputable seria character, Donna Elvira as her *mezzo carattere* equal, Zerlina as the buffa third part.[17] The men's parts are divided just as nicely with Don Ottavio and the Commendatore in the *parti serie*, and Leporello and Masetto in the *parti buffe*. That leaves Giovanni himself as the paradigmatic *mezzo carattere*, moving easily between the low-born and the high-born, trying always to seduce both.

If interpreters have long struggled to determine what genre *Don Giovanni* falls within, it perhaps is because Mozart's opera originated in a tradition distinctive for its *mixing* of operatic genres. This is no less true of Strauss and Hofmannsthal's work. *Ariadne auf Naxos* contains much the same mix of elements as *Don Giovanni* and with largely the same results. It is hard to imagine another twentieth century opera that so clearly retains the categories of the *dramma giocoso*. All are there, from steadfast, upper-class characters concerned with love and honor (Ariadne, the daughter of a king, and Bacchus, the son of a god), to servile, coarse, and inconstant buffo characters, amply represented in *Ariadne* by Zerbinetta and her commedia dell'arte troupe. (As with Zerlina and Donna Anna, the distance between Zerbinetta's and Ariadne's characters is reflected alphabetically in their very names.) *Ariadne* even includes its own mezzo carattere. In Hofmannsthal's description, he is "a figure half tragic, half comic"; Hofmannsthal adds: "the whole antithesis of the action (Ariadne, Zerbinetta, Harlekin's world) is . . . firmly focused on him."[18] The middle character he has in mind is the Composer, written to be "tragic and comic at the same time, like the musician's lot in the world."[19]

Mixing the tragic and the comic in the role of the Composer keeps the Composer, just as it keeps Don Giovanni, from ever becoming one or the other. Much the same could be said for *Ariadne auf Naxos* as a whole. Like *Don Giovanni*, *Ariadne* is able to balance a mix of contrasting musical and literary styles side by side. Strauss once described *Ariadne* as "beginning in the most sober of comic prose and proceeding via ballet and *commedia dell'arte* to the heights of purest, wordless music."[20] His description is notable for touching upon two of *Ariadne*'s most important sources. "Comic prose" refers to that of Molière; his play *Le Bourgeois Gentilhomme*, condensed and translated by Hofmannsthal, formed the first act of the original 1912 version. The second source, related to the first, is the commedia dell'arte. Hofmannsthal once identified "the *maschere*, the dancing and singing comedians" as one of "two theatrical elements of Molière's age."[21] Three of Hofmannsthal's commedia characters—Zerbinetta, Harlekin, and Truffaldin—were even used by Molière in various of his intermezzi.

The relevant point here is that these two sources lie behind *Don Giovanni* as well. As the most notable of Mozart's *Giovanni* predecessors, Molière's *Dom Juan ou Le Festin de pierre* was an undeniable influence on Da Ponte.[22] So too, if less obviously, was commedia dell'arte. Without the popularization it received there, the story of Don Juan might never have reached Molière, or Da Ponte and Mozart, in the first place.[23] In its presentations of the Don Juan story the commedia added and emphasized the buffoonery of characters like Giovanni's servant—originally played by none other than Arlecchino (Strauss and Hofmannsthal's Harlekin). The commedia's legacy can be seen also in the immediate (if unacknowledged) precursor to Da Ponte and Mozart's version, that of Bertati and Gazzaniga, in which "after formally condemning Don Giovanni, [the surviving characters] join in a '*commedia dell'arte*' *buffo* finale imitating musical instruments."[24]

Giovanni and *Ariadne* thus mix diverse musical and literary traditions with similarly incongruous results. Here, again, the important difference is that *Ariadne* does so self-consciously. Strauss and Hofmannsthal's opera does not just mix comedy and drama, opera seria and opera buffa—as *Don Giovanni* undoubtedly does. It announces that it will do so. It makes their conjunction a problem, the problem that drives the Prologue. In its 1916 version the whole work opens with the Music Master's complaint that something "in the Italian *buffo* style" is to follow his student's opera seria. As he insists to the *Haushofmeister*: "That cannot be allowed to take place!"

For whatever reason, the Music Master's judgment has been shared by an untold number of interpreters of both operas. His fear that "a serious, important work" should be connected to buffoonery—or conversely, Zerbinetta's worry that her comedy would be spoiled by the tedium of the heroic opera—suggests why such fusions have so often been hindered. *Ariadne auf Naxos* and *Don Giovanni* get pushed toward pure comedy or drama perhaps because in both, the balance between the two seems too precarious to maintain. If *Ariadne* and *Giovanni* attempt an analogous balance—if their shared sources and themes are acted out by a parallel division of characters—it should come as less of a surprise that these operas' histories of revision and reception should also prove alike. The real question is how these analogies between *Ariadne* and *Giovanni* might be used to illuminate either opera. It is here that *Ariadne*'s self-conscious concern with interpretive fidelity becomes useful. Concerned with the challenges of being true to a hybrid work, *Ariadne* makes a statement not only about its own interpretation but about the interpretation of works like it—*Don Giovanni* among them.

As we have seen, questions of fidelity arise for both *Don Giovanni* and *Ariadne auf Naxos* in part because it is not entirely clear what interpreters are meant to be faithful *to*. Both operas exist in two importantly distinct versions, though in the case of *Don Giovanni* Mozart might not have personally endorsed the second. Whether or not Mozart himself ever omitted the final scene in performance, his nineteenth-century successors almost unanimously did.

Strauss and Hofmannsthal's intentions are better known. In its original 1912 version *Ariadne* ended with the reappearance of Zerbinetta (and the music of her earlier aria), a restatement of her theory on men—"When the new god comes along" we are "transformed over and over!"—and a reprise of her list of former lovers. It is always amazing, she concluded with characteristic coloratura, "that a heart so utterly, / So utterly does not understand itself." Then, as she and her companions danced off stage, the evening's host, Monsieur Jordain (redubbed "the richest man in Vienna" in the 1916 version), appeared one last time to repeat his wish that he'd been born a count or marquis. As with the final scene of *Giovanni*, the original *Ariadne* ending returned the proceedings to the mundane. It offered glimpses of the various characters' futures, reasserted their class distinctions, reintroduced the comic element missing from the previous scene, and admitted something like the tutti ending standard in opera buffa.

None of this survives in the revision of 1916, where Strauss and Hofmannsthal themselves did what history, if not Mozart and Da Ponte, had done to *Don Giovanni*. Gone is the irony, the comic framing, the distancing effect of the earlier ending. Gone too is the reassertion of the social, worldly realm against the Romantic individuality of the opera's heroes. Instead the work ends with transfiguration—with the Heldentenor Bacchus wishing that his Ariadne would outlast even the "eternal stars." Formerly given the last word, Zerbinetta now drifts in during Bacchus and Ariadne's love duet. Singing dreamily over chords that in 1912 had accompanied the lovers' transformation, Zerbinetta's old refrain suddenly assumes a new meaning. "When the new god comes, we surrender silently," she still sings. But now the god is real, and it is Zerbinetta who surrenders to the true transfiguring love to which, in the Prologue, she had admitted an occasional temptation. The concluding mix of death, love, transformation, and blessing suggests why Strauss's revised ending has so often been accused of "Wagnerizing"; we might as well be watching *Tristan*.

This is the point, however, where the histories of *Ariadne* and *Don Giovanni* seem to diverge. Opera houses today invariably reinstate the entire final scene of *Don Giovanni*, but they keep Strauss and Hofmannsthal's cuts in *Ariadne*. For various reasons (not least of which is the difficulty of staging a play and opera together in one evening, as the 1912 version requires) it is the 1916 version of *Ariadne auf Naxos* that has entered the canon. In Strauss's case, but not in Mozart's, it is the shorter ending that seems to have won.

Yet the victory may not be so decisive. Though the 1916 version of *Ariadne* is inarguably the more frequently performed, many of the same interpreters who perform Strauss and Hofmannsthal's shortened score—with its turn away from the 1912 version's irony—try to reinstate that irony in their writing *about* the score. Program notes and critical commentaries are littered with the claim that, near the end of the opera, Zerbinetta "sneaks out to say that she was right" or that, "warbling derisively," she proves "totally superficial . . . incapable of deep feelings, and consequently cut off from achieving transformation to another level of existence."[25]

No evidence of this irony can be found in the 1916 score. There the character of Zerbinetta's final line is in keeping with Ariadne and Bacchus's transformation and the libretto's instruction that Zerbinetta "repeat her Rondo with mocking triumph" is conspicuously missing. Why, then, do so many writers insist upon the ironic interpretation? One reason is that Hofmannsthal himself did so. In a letter to Strauss outlining his original conception of the role (a letter later printed publicly as the "Ariadne-Brief" and reprinted in program notes ever since), Hofmannsthal claimed that Zerbinetta "sees in

Ariadne's experience the only thing she *can* see: the exchange of an old lover for a new one. And so these two spiritual worlds are in the end ironically brought together in the only way in which they can be brought together: in non-comprehension."[26] Even as the 1916 version was being completed, Hofmannsthal insisted that Zerbinetta should seem at the end to have "some last word," to appear as a "counter-voice" who lends a "symbolic, mocking presence." Strauss agreed, promising Zerbinetta would "sing mockingly."[27] The fact, however, that Strauss and Hofmannsthal both stated these intentions explicitly does not mean that their intentions were fulfilled. As interpreters, we need some additional motive for reading Zerbinetta's final line this way. With nothing in the music to suggest irony, our reason for hearing it there can only come from somewhere beyond the score.

One plausible reason for reinstating the first version's irony is that doing so makes *Ariadne* a better opera. Criticisms of the revised ending are certainly widespread. As Romain Rolland wrote of an early performance: "Instead of ending, as they should have done, with an ironic septet of the five comic and two tragic characters, the comic characters are eliminated and we are offered nothing but a pompous and frigid tragedy involving two bombastic persons." Later commentators have called it "a lengthy failure" or "a Romanticism which doesn't quite succeed in parodying itself."[28] The latter, I believe, *is* the problem of the ending: its expectation that we take its sentiments seriously. No one winks in the revised ending; the commedia characters have disappeared and their parody is missed. Audience members who do not take the "miracle" of transformation as piously as Hofmannsthal did are left largely unmoved. Why not, then, pretend that Zerbinetta's final appearance is meant to lighten things up, to provide the needed wink at the end? Why not make Zerbinetta a kindred spirit, even if doing so ignores a bit of the score?

Doing this is no different from what the nineteenth century revisionists did when they saw in *Don Giovanni* what they wanted to see there—or more precisely, when they left out whatever they did not want to see. With *Giovanni* as with *Ariadne*, making the opera more aesthetically, emotionally, or intellectually rewarding provides some justification for such willful reinterpretations.

This, however, raises the question of what reasons might lurk behind the twentieth century's own reinterpretation of *Don Giovanni*. If nineteenth century interpreters cut the score to make it a better opera (which for them meant a more Romantic one), what prompted the widespread reintroduction of Mozart's final scene in the century that followed? The answer cannot be that there was suddenly a heightened concern for authenticity. Several reasons suggest why not. First, if authenticity were truly the driving concern, performances that incorporated pieces—like Ottavio's two arias—which Mozart never intended or heard together would be far less common. Second, as has already been pointed out, the question of what ending can rightly be called authentic is itself contentious. The historical record is not complete enough to settle the question. Finally, as Stefan Kunze has argued, talk of "authentic versions" might be entirely misplaced in discussions of this time period. "From the viewpoint of the operatic conventions of the eighteenth century," he writes, "emphasizing the 'original version' of an opera seems to be as little justified as the concept of a 'last-touched version.'" In a context wherein it was expected that revisions would be made to accommodate new singers and new locales, no one performance of a work could take precedence over another. In Kunze's words, barring a sign from Mozart to the contrary, "Every note that Mozart composed in connection with that ideal whole that bears the name *Don Giovanni* is in principle . . . 'authentic' to the same extent."[29]

Beyond questions of authenticity, what remains is an aesthetic preference, what the philosopher Ronald Dworkin, writing about the relation of law and literature, has called the "aesthetic hypothesis": that interpretation attempts to show which way of reading (or performing) a work reveals it as the best, most internally coherent, work of art it can be.[30] In the present case this means that we should include and combine those elements of Mozart's composition (for *Don Giovanni* at least) that together produce the most satisfying whole. As such, contemporary performances predominantly include Donna Elvira's "Mi tradì" scena because its music is too good to forgo, or perhaps because it gives her already conflicted character yet more complexity. Often performances include the final sextet for similar reasons: because, in the opinion of the performers, Mozart's longer ending is just more rewarding. As Bernard Williams wrote, in his article on "Mozart's Comedies and the Sense of an Ending": "The sextet is in truth, as all modern productions acknowledge, absolutely essential, as defining—in a sense—a 'return to normal,' something which itself helps to define the meaning of previous events and of Giovanni himself."[31] Williams argued for the inclusion of the final scene because it draws a line between Giovanni's extraordinary freedom and the conventional morality of the others, showing how elements of each are necessary for life. In other words, he argued for the final scene because of the satisfaction it affords, the way it ties together the work as a whole. He argued for the final scene because it best meets something like Dworkin's aesthetic hypothesis.

Aesthetic impact is surely a valid criterion for deciding what to include in a performance of a work or a production of an opera. We might just remember that this criterion is no different than that invoked by nineteenth-century interpreters. They too were trying to interpret works like *Giovanni* in a way that made them the best works possible. Interpreters of the last century differed only with respect to what they considered "best"—that is, what they chose to look for in a work of art. Where one century wants the emotional terror of a fiery damnation, another seeks an intellectually or ethically rich ambiguity. As Dworkin puts it, giving an interpretation cannot be separated from an idea of what a good interpretation should achieve.

What I am suggesting is that interpreting Zerbinetta's final statement ironically in *Ariadne* and celebrating the ambiguous "return to normal" in the final sextet of *Giovanni* are *both* examples of attempts to make those works the best they can be. Those two particular interpretations even share a notion of what it means to be "the best." Both share a contemporary taste for complexity; both link ambiguity with depth. Still, a difference between them remains. Unlike disagreements over whether or not Zerbinetta is sincere at the end of the 1916 *Ariadne*, the difference between, say, Bernard Williams's interpretation of *Giovanni* and that of the Romantics is more than a disagreement over how to read the same score. In the *Giovanni* case interpretative differences entail disagreements over what notes—what entire scenes—should be performed. For interpreters trying to make *Don Giovanni* the best work it can be, the limits of what constitutes that work's score remain rather flexible.

The question has to be asked whether the same is true of *Ariadne*. If contemporary audiences prefer their works to be ironic, and if aesthetic impact can permissibly serve (as it does in *Giovanni*) as a means to determine which parts of a work to perform, might not opera houses of today reincorporate Strauss and Hofmannsthal's original, distanced—and generally preferred—ending into their productions of *Ariadne*? Might there legitimately be, in other words, a production of *Ariadne* that mixed its 1912 and 1916 versions in just the way most contemporary productions mix the Prague and Vienna versions of *Don Giovanni*?

If the answer is no, then the reason must have to do with the sort of musical conventions Kunze was quoted as describing above. Mozart may not have ever intended the particular hybrid performances now common with *Giovanni*. But nor, on the other hand, did he ever intend to produce formal, autonomous, or fixed works, the integrity of which he expected to be observed. Strauss did. The line between making his work the best *it* can be and making it another work altogether is more sharply drawn.[32]

The question cannot be settled that easily, however, because in *Ariadne auf Naxos*, Strauss did not just produce an autonomous work. He produced an autonomous work that is itself significantly about the autonomy of musical works. *Ariadne*, as we have already seen, is concerned with the fidelity owed to works of art; because of that it might be expected to offer insight into what kinds of performances—of it—could be called legitimate. As an opera in which a hybrid work is put on stage, *Ariadne* likely expresses an opinion about its own potential hybridization. In short, for an opera like *Ariadne*, deciding whether Strauss's two versions could legitimately be mixed together need not be settled on the basis of any outside conventions or pregiven philosophical principles, such as the principle of *Werktreue* (the ideal of fidelity to the work that the Composer anachronistically espouses). It can perhaps be settled by listening to the work itself. Depending on what one found there, it might be the case that respecting that particular work's autonomy would actually allow for performances ordinarily seen as an infringement of the *Werktreue* ideal: performances, in this case, in which elements from the work's different versions were mixed. The work might allow—even argue for—such a mix. There is more than one way to be true to a work.

The same cannot be said for *Don Giovanni*. Yet again the difference is that *Giovanni* lacks *Ariadne*'s heightened consciousness of itself, of its status as a work. *Don Giovanni* juxtaposes comedy and tragedy, but it is not explicitly about that juxtaposition—as *Ariadne* is. Performers might mix material from *Giovanni*'s different versions, but they do not do so at that work's own urging. They might hybridize *Giovanni* in their performances, but what they cannot rightly do is claim that *Giovanni* is a work about its own hybridization. In the case of *Giovanni*, but not *Ariadne*, making the work the best it can be requires an outside notion of what constitutes it as that work rather than another. Interpretation thus comes with its own ontological commitments in addition to its aesthetic ones.

In the end *Ariadne*'s self-consciousness turns out to be a consciousness of those commitments. It makes explicit the questions that lie behind interpretation—questions about what an opera should aim to be (the interpreter's aesthetic commitment) and about how much freedom interpreters should be given in helping make it so (their ontological commitment—the flexibility of their work concept). Interpreting *Ariadne* does not simply require those commitments, as all interpretation does, according to Dworkin; it actually reveals an argument as to what those commitments should be.

This is what lies behind the success of the 1912 ending to *Ariadne*. While it and the original ending of *Don Giovanni* share a similar ambiguity, the 1912 *Ariadne* clearly presents its ambiguity knowingly. It builds up to it; it makes it purposive. Finding complexity in the ending of the 1912 *Ariadne* does not simply result from some interpreter's particular pregiven commitments. It is not a case in which a modern critic might value one thing (as in *Giovanni*) while the Romantics value another. Instead the complexity of the 1912 version is a value put forward by the work itself. Interpreting *Ariadne* is not just making it the best work it can be. It is, at least in part, recognizing what that work thinks being the best means.

With its self-asserted aesthetic preferences—for open-ended complexity, ironic distance from Romantic striving, the social over the individual—*Ariadne* in its first version avoids a criticism made against *Giovanni's* original ending: namely, that it is naively conventional rather than richly or knowingly ambiguous. As Julian Rushton has complained of the Prague *Giovanni*: "What gives rise to doubt in the case of *Don Giovanni* is not ambiguity in itself, but the authors' unawareness of it, their apparent belief that everything has been resolved."[33]

Strauss and Hofmannsthal's own awareness of and preference for ambiguity is never in doubt in their 1912 version. No wonder, then, their revised ending seems like such a step backward. Not only does it lose the open-endedness of the earlier version, it also loses much of its self-awareness. Of this ending that "doesn't quite succeed in parodying itself" we might adapt Rushton's complaint against *Giovanni*: "what gives rise to doubt" is the authors' "apparent belief that everything has been resolved." Transfiguring Ariadne through her love for a god, a literal deus ex machina, can sound to modern audiences as blindly conventional as a major-key tutti finale. Strauss reinstated the latter in his famous Munich performances of *Don Giovanni* in 1896, and the popularity of Mozart's original ending has grown ever since. Perhaps the same needs to be done to *Ariadne*. Perhaps the original version of *Ariadne* needs an interpreter like Strauss, just as *Giovanni* once did. Regardless, the point here is that Strauss's most important interpretation of *Giovanni* might not have been in performance at all. It might have been his own *Ariadne of Naxos*, which at least in its first version made explicit the sort of interpretive commitments so often unacknowledged in *Don Giovanni*.

The ultimate irony, of course, is that insofar as the 1916 *Ariadne* lacks some of the self-awareness so characteristic of the 1912 *Ariadne*, it actually becomes *more* like *Giovanni*. Even as it loses some of its significance as commentary, it begins to bear in yet one more respect "a certain analogy" to Mozart's work. For once we might just wish that it did not.

NOTES

1. Letter from Hofmannsthal to Strauss, March 20, 1911, in *A Working Friendship: The Correspondence between Richard Strauss and Hugo von Hofmannsthal*, trans. Hanns Hammelmann and Ewald Osers (New York, 1961), 76 (trans. modified).
2. Other studies have explored the specifically musical links between *Ariadne* and

Mozart's operas—though generally not *Giovanni*. The most recent of these points to a number of instances within *Ariadne* in which Strauss seems to quote *Die Zauberflöte*. See Walter Frisch, *German Modernism: Music and the Arts* (Berkeley, 2005), chapter 6.

3. Letter from Hofmannsthal to Strauss, March 20, 1911, in *A Working Friendship*, 76.

4. See, for example, Julian Rushton, *W. A. Mozart: Don Giovanni* (Cambridge, 1981), 1–4.

5. The former view comes from Daniel Heartz, *Mozart's Operas*, ed. Thomas Bauman (Berkeley, 1990), 174. The latter is from Michael F. Robinson, "The Alternative Endings of Mozart's *Don Giovanni*," in *Opera Buffa in Mozart's Vienna*, ed. Mary Hunter and James Webster (Cambridge, 1997), 261.

6. Ruston, *W. A. Mozart*, 141, note 4.

7. Ibid., 68–69. For the number of performances, see Gernot Gruber, *Mozart and Posterity*, trans. R. S. Furness (London, 1991), 170.

8. Rushton, *W. A. Mozart*, 69.

9. Gruber, *Mozart and Posterity*, 171. Katharine Ellis, "Rewriting 'Don Giovanni,' or 'The Thieving Magpies,'" *Journal of the Royal Musical Association* 119 (1994): 212–250, 214.

10. Cf. Rushton, *W. A. Mozart*, 109; Joseph Kerman, *Opera as Drama* (New York, 1956), 121; See also Søren Kierkegaard, *Either/Or*, trans. Howard V. Hong and Edna H. Hong (Princeton, 1987), part 1, "The Immediate Erotic Stages or the Musical-Erotic."

11. Letter from Strauss to Hofmannsthal, March 16, 1916, in *A Working Friendship*, 243.

12. Throughout, translations of the *Ariadne* libretto are mine, based on that of Peggie Cochrane (Decca Record Company, 1979) and those that appear in Karen Forsyth, *Ariadne auf Naxos by Hugo von Hofmannsthal and Richard Strauss: Its Genesis and Meaning* (Oxford, 1982).

13. On the notion of transfiguration (*Verwandlung*), see Donald G. Daviau and George J. Buelow, *The* Ariadne auf Naxos *of Hugo von Hofmannsthal and Richard Strauss* (Chapel Hill, 1975), 127 and 155.

14. Cf. Heartz, *Mozart's Operas*, 195–196.

15. Michael F. Robinson, "The 'Comic' Element in 'Don Giovanni,'" in Nicholas John, ed., *Don Giovanni* (New York, 1991), 9.

16. Letter from Mozart to his father, May 7, 1783, in *The Letters of Mozart and His Family*, ed. and trans. Emily Anderson (London, 1938), 3:1264. Also quoted in Heartz, *Mozart's Operas*, 199–200.

17. The addition of Donna Elvira's scena in the Viennese revision of the score does push Elvira's role toward *seria* (cf. Ruston, *W. A. Mozart*, 53). But this move away from the comic is in keeping with Mozart's other possible revisions to the end of the opera, as I have described them above.

18. Letter from Hofmannsthal to Strauss, June 3, 1913, in *A Working Friendship*, 169.

19. Letter from Hofmannsthal to Strauss, June 12, 1913, ibid., 170.

20. Richard Strauss, *Recollections and Reflections*, ed. Willi Schuh, trans. L. J. Lawrence (London, 1953), 161 (trans. modified).

21. Letter from Hofmannsthal to Strauss, July 26, 1911, in *A Working Friendship*, 101. For a superb account of the genesis of Hofmannsthal's original libretto, see Forsyth, *Ariadne auf Naxos*, chapter 1.

22. See Edward Forman, "Don Juan Before Da Ponte," in Rushton, *W. A. Mozart*, 30–31.

23. Ibid., 29.

24. Christopher Raeburn, "Lorenzo da Ponte," in John, *Don Giovanni*, 36.

25. The quotations come, respectively, from the Metropolitan Opera Guild, "*Ariadne auf Naxos* Study Guide," online at http://archive.operainfo.org/; Ernst Krause, Synopsis, trans. Robert Jordan, in *Ariadne auf Naxos*, conducted by Kurt Mazur (Philips); and Daviau and Buelow, *The* Ariadne auf Naxos, 154.

26. Letter from Hofmannsthal to Strauss, mid-July 1911, in *A Working Friendship*, 94–95.

27. Letter from Hofmannsthal to Strauss, May 15, 1916, ibid., 246–247; letter from Strauss to Hofmannsthal, May 18, 1916, ibid., 247.

28. Richard Strauss and Romain Rolland, *Correspondence*, ed. Rollo Myers (Berkeley, 1968), 163; William Mann, *Richard Strauss: A Critical Study of the Operas* (London, 1964), 116; Forsyth, *Ariadne auf Naxos,* 180.

29. Stefan Kunze, "Werkbestand und Aufführungsgestalt," in "*Don Giovanni*: Prag 1787–Wien 1788–1987," *Mozart-Jahrbuch* (1987/1988), 206–207 and 211. My thanks to Ryan Bremner for discussions about this article.

30. Ronald Dworkin, "Law as Interpretation," in W. J. T. Mitchell, ed., *The Politics of Interpretation* (Chicago, 1983). The definition here is a paraphrase of Dworkin's that is specifically concerned with literature.

31. Bernard Williams, "Mozart's Comedies and the Sense of an Ending," *Musical Times* 122 (July 1981): 453.

32. Like Kunze, I am here accepting the thesis that the work concept was not as firmly in place in Mozart's musical practice as it was in Strauss's. On this, see Lydia Goehr, *The Imaginary Museum of Musical Works* (Oxford, 1992).

33. Rushton, *W. A. Mozart,* 65.

Thirteen

Homage to Adorno's "Homage to Zerlina"

BERTHOLD HOECKNER

"HOMAGE TO ZERLINA" BY THEODOR W. ADORNO[1]

Amid the high-stilted gentlemen and tragic ladies she succeeds only in being
an episodic figure. Indeed, an irresistible glance has been cast toward her—over
the abyss of the classes the dissolute grandee offers his hand to her, and she is
perhaps too shy not to come with him at once to his castle. It is not far from
here. But because the opera buffa does not allow the seduction of the innocent,
whom Masetto surely could not revenge as elegantly as the correct Ottavio his
Donna Anna, Da Ponte thwarts the planned promiscuity where there is no exchange of equal parts. He restores the moral and social hierarchies and through
the Stygian night he shines the lantern light of blissful nearness on her reconciliation with the one who lends his name to the blundering and the clumsy. In
Mozart's orchestral postlude divided mankind seems to be reconciled.

Such reconciliation takes place in the name of freedom. Zerlina's music
sounds as if it would enter into the white and golden hall of the eighteenth
century through the open casement window. She still sings arias, but their melodies are already songs: nature, her breeze breaking the spell of the ceremonial
manner, remains surrounded by form, sheltered by a fading style. In Zerlina's
image, the rhythm of rococo and revolution halts. She is no longer a shepherd-

ess, but not yet a *citoyenne*. She belongs to the historical moment in between, and, in passing, she reflects a humanity, which would not be mutilated by feudal force but protected from bourgeois barbarity. Some poems of the young Goethe are of this kind. "And thus she steps before the mirror in all her cheerfulness"[2] is a miniature portrait of Zerlina, and like Friederike she stands "on the boundary between country and city woman. Slender and light, she tripped along as she had nothing to carry and her neck seemed almost too delicate for the large fair braids on her dainty little head. Through cheerful blue eyes she looked very plainly around and her turned-up nose peered as freely into the air as if there could be no harm in the world; her straw hat hung on her arm and thus at the first glance, I had the delight of seeing her and acknowledging her at once in all her grace and loveliness."[3] Suspecting nothing she compensates her lover for her infidelity by encouraging him to beat her, thus transfiguring rustic rudeness into refinement and anticipates the utopian state in which the difference between city and country is effaced.

Does not her radiance, however, also shed light on her seducer who, finally, has been cheated out of all sweetness? For where would her grace and loveliness have been had not the half-powerless noble on his flight through the opera only just awakened them. Since he no longer possesses the power for the *ius primae noctis,* he becomes the messenger of desire—already a little comical for the bourgeois who all too quickly forbid it for themselves. They have learned the ideal of freedom from the fearless one. But by becoming common that ideal turns against him for whom freedom had been a privilege. Soon they will introduce licence to freedom, thus perverting it to absurdity. Don Juan, however, was free from the lie that his despotism would be the freedom of others; thus he honored what he took away. Zerlina was right to have liked him.

Forever she will be the allegory of history at a standstill. He who falls in love with her expresses the ineffable that sounds with a silvery voice from the no-man's land between battling epochs.

Amid his high-flying and severe writings, Adorno's "Homage to Zerlina" succeeds only in being an episodic moment. Of all the pieces Adorno published under the title *Moments musicaux* (including "Schubert" and "Beethoven's Late Style," some of his most imaginative and provocative writing on music), this one comes closest to being a veritable *moment musical* itself. It is a kind of bagatelle, possessing that refined reciprocity between miniature and maxim typical of late works. "Homage to Zerlina" echoes the aphoristic philosophy of Adorno's *Minima Moralia*, which places the blend of Nietzschean style and Benjaminian thought in the service of critical theory. Its form, condensed to the utmost into a vignette, is the essay. The late Adorno championed that form because it would "rebel" against the notion that the "ephemeral is unworthy of philosophy" while causing "totality to be illuminated in a partial feature . . . without asserting the presence of the totality."[4] Adorno's "Homage" may be no more than sketch, but it claims for itself no less than the transcendent quality of a master painting. Such is precisely the paradox of a materialist metaphysics. Analogously, as an episodic figure, Zerlina is merely a moment, but a moment whose music rings "forever" in our ears.

Today, to be sure, we tend to protest the modernist radicality of such contradictory claims, even though they were themselves once born out of protest. Of course, taking Adorno's "Homage" as the occasion for an homage to Adorno conflates, with deliberate risk, his declaration of love for Zerlina with my own fondness for the philosopher (or rather his philosophy). It concedes that Zerlina's seductiveness is transmuted into that of Adorno's text (which is not unlike the structural parallel that Shoshana Felman draws between the seduction of Don Juan and Austin's speech act theory).[5] What matters is that love functions not as a suspension of critical theory, but as its instrument. This contradiction is the premise of what is well called Adorno's aesthetics of the moment: it rescues Eden as the glimmer that flashes up against the darkness of a terrible totality. Hence in Zerlina's image, as the most musical phrase of Adorno's *moment musical* has it, "the rhythm of rococo and revolution halts" to become an instance of reconciliation. Adorno grasps that image through a hermeneutics of the moment, which is not a substitute for critical theory but rather its most compelling practice in the interpretation of artworks. It is the hermeneutics of the physiognomic gaze that he learned from Benjamin, and which endows the particular with redemptive power. This hermeneutics assumes the radical historical perspective that the late Benjamin condensed into his "Theses on the Philosophy of History," where a materialist historiography explodes the false continuity of historicism to lend a voice to the oppressed, the marginal, and the neglected.

Adorno's Zerlina embodies that rupture, and this despite the fact that her appearance radiates reconciliation. For she does so only ephemerally. As a transitional figure she becomes an allegory of the artwork as a celestial apparition. "If *apparition* illuminates and touches," Adorno wrote in his *Aesthetic Theory*, "the image is the paradoxical effort to transfix the most evanescent instant. In artworks something momentary transcends; objectivation makes the artwork into an instant." And, revealing his source, he continued: "Pertinent here is Benjamin's formulation of a dialectic at a standstill, which he developed in the context of his conception of a dialectical image. If, as images, artworks are the persistence of the transient, they are concentrated in appearances as something momentary. To experience art means to become conscious of its immanent process as an instant at a standstill. This may perhaps have nourished the central concept of Lessing's aesthetics, that of the 'pregnant moment.'"[6] Adorno portrays Zerlina as such a dialectical image.

How can we make sense of this moment, Zerlina's standing in between, both historically and musically? To be sure, Adorno's Zerlina is not Mozart's Zerlina. Such plain and rigid historicism would contradict the premises of materialist historiography. Still, Adorno's critical insight grows out of a musical intuition that is grounded in the musical material and seeks to explicate its historical implications. Zerlina stands between epochs because she stands musically between classes. But she is not the typical *mezzo carattere*, who is decidedly part *seria* and part *buffa*. Unlike Donna Elvira, Zerlina is not torn apart by generic opposites but bridges the gap instead in her fleeting appearance. Naive at first, she learns quickly. Her social status is low, yet she rises in stature. Initially simplistic, her music attains an elegant simplicity. Whereas the relationship between Donna Elvira and Don Giovanni does not go anywhere (like that between Donna Anna and Don Ottavio), Zerlina's relationship with Masetto matures from the teasing submission of "batti, batti" to the loving control of "sentilo battere." Initially the object of Don Giovanni's game, she later directs her own play. In this context Adorno's most acute insight is also his most provocative: that Zerlina's light shines back on her seducer, that her "grace and loveliness" (put differently: her sexuality) has been awakened by Don Giovanni, that, therefore, she is "right to have liked him."

The music supports some of these claims. For Mozart molded Zerlina's two arias on one of opera's greatest hits: the ever charming "Là ci darem la mano." As Wye Allanbrook has shown, its two-part structure is nothing less than the blueprint for Zerlina's solo numbers (see example 13.1). "Batti, batti" (where the obbligato cello seems to resound Masetto's anger) and "Vedrai carino" (where he participates in Zerlina's gentle teasings) are seduction duets of sorts. Like the *Duettino*, "Batti, batti" switches from duple time to a compound meter whose lilting rhythm will be the point of departure for the triple time of "Vedrai carino." This metric mutation over the course of the opera becomes a measure of Zerlina's maturity. Amid the crumbling upper class relationships around her, she thus achieves reconciliation in "Vedrai carino" with an ease that no longer requires a change of meter but succeeds with a subtle change of "rhythmic gesture" (to use Allanbrook's term). The opening siciliano, whose "simple gravity" is "new to Zerlina," turns into an almost coquettish contredanse. The former line between the two stages of the seduction no longer needs the guiding hand of the Don to traverse it. In Zerlina's hands it has become but a faint fissure that functions as a mere foil for the rising refinement with which she tends Masetto's wounds. This way she helps him to become civilized.

	I	→	V	(X)	I	⌒	I	"X"	I
I,7 A major *Andante*	1-18 · 2/4 D.GIOV's song, ZER's dance	18-28 D.GIOV's fanfare, ZER's sigh's; no solid V cadence	29 · V^7	30-46 "stretto" version of 1-28	47-49 ascent to V^6_5 on "Andiam"		50-64 · 6/8 pastorale with musette	X contained in IV of French gigue	64-end French gigue
							└──────── PASTORALE ────────┘		
I,12 F major *Andante grazioso*	1-16 · 2/4 gavotte	17-24 move to V	25-34 drive to solid cadence; contredanse scansion	35-36 · V^7	37-52 gavotte with double	52-60 V-I oscillation as question	61-68 · 6/8 V-I oscillation as answer	69-78 IV phrase on "passar," delayed cadences	79-end cadences
							└──────── PASTORALE ────────┘		
II,5 C major *Grazioso*	1-16 · 3/8 siciliano (6/8 scansion)	17-24 move to V	25-32 V cadences	33 · V^7	34-48 mm 1-23, all on I	49-52 · V^7	53-63 · 3/8 contredanse	63-85 "beating" on V^7 and ii^6	85-end orchestra postlude summing up aria
	└───────────────── PASTORAL AFFECT ─────────────────┘								

EXAMPLE 13.1. The Key-Area Layouts of "Lá ci darem" (I, 7), "Batti, batti" (I, 12), and "Vedrai carino" (II, 5). Wye Jamison Allanbrook, *Rhythmic Gesture in Mozart* (Chicago: University of Chicago Press, 1983), p. 268; reprinted by permission of the author..

What Don Giovanni awakens in Zerlina, then, is the beginning of consciousness. That moment marks the boundary between natural and social states as imagined by modernity. Learning the art of love means for Zerlina becoming aware of the distinction between play and pretense—and there have been different schools of thought regarding where her awareness begins. Does she "follow" Don Giovanni in the *Duettino* "without any will in her answers" (Stefan Kunze) or does she play along willfully from the very beginning (Joseph Kerman)?[7] For Adorno it is crucial that Zerlina's newly acquired mastery of love is not manipulative (as it was with the Don) but based on mutuality. This is the mark of her humanity. What Don Giovanni cannot reach—social peace in the form of human love—Zerlina eventually attains. Paradoxically, however, he is necessary for her to break free from him.

This contradiction may help to address the pressing question whether Adorno's image of Zerlina—appearing like Goethe's portrait of Friederike in a sudden epiphany ("all at once")—is not also a product of male spectatorship (or patriarchal censorship), which positions the ideal female on the cusp between innocence and knowledge (or sainthood and sin). More urgent in this respect is the question to what extent this image seeks to vindicate the predatory man in the position of power, for Adorno himself was surely no saint—a question even recent biographies have addressed with candor but without sufficient critique. Indeed, this one moment between virginity and womanhood so prized by the male cultural imagination does not exist without its corollary: the fantasy of that "irresistible glance . . . cast at her." If Zerlina embodies utopia through rupture—the place that is not, the no-man's land—then looking at her is man's wish to be first, to penetrate the pristine, to reenter paradise (no *longer* man's land). Therefore, Zerlina's moment also belongs with other operatic moments that Adorno treasured for their embodiment of *natural* beauty, which Hegel had dismissed in favor of *artificial* beauty: Agathe under the starry sky in *Der Freischütz* and Leonore under the rainbow in *Fidelio*. What applies to Leonore calling out for the star of hope also applies to Zerlina: that she personifies a "connection of the ethical to natural beauty" and "that the solace and assuagement of a natural expression appears as a promise of goodness."[8]

Adorno's Zerlina thus stands for more than the idealized state halfway between girl and woman. She also functions as an allegory of momentous social and historical change: no longer a shepherdess, but not yet a *citoyenne*. In terms of musical genres she is no longer the *mezzo carattere pastorale* like Susanna; still she is not yet afflicted by the sentimental melancholy of Barbarina in *Le nozze di Figaro*. Moreover, in terms of social and political theory, she is no longer a class type, even if not yet an individual subject.[9] This putative position is both fragile and fleeting. The goodness that Zerlina promises is granted only as a brief repose between the old order and the new. Writing after Auschwitz, Adorno held that bourgeois barbarity was no better than feudal force. But neither of them, he fancied, could harm Zerlina. As the nonidentical surrounded by manifestations of identity gone awry, she hovers in between and thus suspends (and this "suspension" is the critical state of dialectics at a standstill) the historical dialectic Adorno perceived in the plot and heard in the music. Hence her reconciliation with Masetto takes place "in the name of freedom," while Da Ponte uses it at the same time to restore "the moral and social hierarchies." And hence "her breeze break[s] the spell of the ceremonial manner," while her music still remains in Adorno's words "surrounded by form" and "sheltered by a fading style." If that "manner" and that "style" are manifest in the generic strictures of the aria, the breeze that breaks them is the melodies sounding the simplicity of song. Zerlina's music stands between the unadorned tune that opens the *Duettino* with its "pluck-strum" accompaniment and the liberated *passagi* in the ensuing dance.[10] It is only because she was not traumatized by Don Giovanni upon their first encounter that Adorno could claim that she was "right to have"—initially—"liked him."

However, because of the Don's forced dance with Zerlina in the act I finale during the masked ball and the attempted rape that follows, one can hear his

"Viva la libertà" as a celebration of feudal freedom, which is really disguised as a harbinger of bourgeois license. Only in hindsight, to be sure, could Adorno claim that the emancipated subject of the postrevolutionary society became an exploitative one and the new "freedom for the subject" turned out to be "unfreedom for the other."[11] Only from the radically presentist perspective of his and Horkheimer's *Dialectics of Enlightenment* could so tortured an argument be advanced that Don Giovanni "was free from the lie that his despotism would be the freedom of others" and that he thus "honored what he took away." For honesty and honor are usually the last things associated with Don Juan. Yet, instead of justifying his tyrannical traits, Adorno (like Kierkegaard and many others) respected the tenacity with which Don Giovanni remains true to himself. As perfect lover, he is an allegory of the perfect work of art, who nevertheless knows that beauty and wholeness are an illusion, only served up to serve his own interests. In this sense the Don would indeed be free of the belief that is the premise of Hegel's philosophy, namely, that the true is the whole. Zerlina, by contrast, is true—but no longer whole.

In Mozart's opera, therefore, she becomes rupture of the total script—Leporello's catalogue with the score of women the Don seduced (and dishonored)—as an example of bad infinity. The Commendatore's revenge of his daughter's rape is also a grand gesture intended to rehabilitate all those women who have been wronged, but he can reinstall moral rectitude only at the cost of a failed redemption and Don Giovanni's death, which follows his refusal to repent. Hence Kunze suggested that the opera ends with a restoration, not reconciliation. The return to order after Don Giovanni has gone to hell is a restitution of a community that only seemingly restores the social equilibrium after the elimination of the extra male character and his excessive manhood. But, without such forgiveness, the final scene is a false celebration, a forged ritual, whose surface morality might have pleased the censors. Its balance appears as an illusion, an unconvincing convention that pastes over the damage done to two thirds of that restituted community. For the *scena ultima* is really only a penultimate one. The plot is finished, but not the story whose untied threads point to an uncertain future. The music's happy end jars with the sorry state of most of those who sing it. The rush of the generic stretto toward cadential closure clashes with a stark sense of incompletion: a woman abandoned by her lover, a couple traumatized by a rapist, and an employee left without a job by his boss. Behind the grim prospects of such restoration Adorno could sense the coming conditions of bourgeois society. Though free from the Don, the *lieto fine* is the sort of lie from which the Don was certainly free.

The opera's true "happy end" would then be the one that concludes "Vedrai carino." Because here the dialectic Adorno sensed in the opera—between purity and defilement, nature and artifice, love and power—comes to a standstill. And this is not only so because Zerlina takes over Don Giovanni's system of seduction, turning affect into genuine affection. Deeper still, if the Don's desire leaves a trace on her, it is not a stain but a mark—a musical mark. Kunze brilliantly saw Zerlina's "Vedrai carino" as the counterpiece to Don Giovanni's "Fin ch'han dal vino," with Mozart pitting her peace-giving gestures against his explosive dynamic. But as the antithesis to the champagne aria, Kunze's image of Zerlina in "Vedrai carino" is too pure. He retraces its "image of blissfulness" (*Bild der Glückseligkeit*) as painted by Ubilicheff, although he fails to notice it as an image of contrasts that are only momentarily resolved. The music leaves no doubt that Zerlina had been touched deeply by Don Giovanni: the hand that he took is the same that will lead Masetto's hand to her heart. Thus Daniel Heartz, equally brilliantly, draws attention to the fact that "Mozart saturated his score with expressive chromatic lines, especially descending ones such as had accompanied the death of the Commendatore," and that these chromatic lines "turn up unexpectedly in seemingly innocent and lighthearted pieces," for instance in the second part of the *Duettino* "as the violins, commenting on 'un innocente amor,' seem to say with their drooping chromatics, 'not innocent at all, but fatal'" (see example 13.2a). Or in "Fin ch'han dal vino," where "Mozart points up the chromatic descent in the vocal line by doubling it in the first violins and the flute [example 13.2b], which introduce at the same time the first sustained legato line in the piece."[12] If for Heartz these chromatic lines "spell death," they cast the shadow of lament over the joys of love.

EXAMPLE 13.2A. "Lá ci darem": first violin mm. 56–58.

EXAMPLE 13.2B. "Fin ch'han dal vino": vocal line mm. 21–25.

Significantly, however, in "Vedrai carino" the chromatic tinge of desire does not extend into a descending line (see example 13.3 mm. 76–77). Instead, its chroma colors (in the second section after the deceptive cadence) an exquisite moment of harmonic suspense—a true *Stillstand*. Here the music mimics the heartbeat with a two-measure oscillation between ii and vii^{o7}/ii^6, which is eventually reined in by the repeated cadences to the tonic. By telescoping that moment into the concluding ritornello, Mozart gently sutures the gap between the aria's dual structure. In the closing orchestral statement he combines material from the two sections into a single utterance and brings about an accord—literally—between *gravitas* and lightheartedness (see example 13.3 mm. 85-end). The image of Zerlina that Adorno saw in this moment of musical mimesis does not fall under the verdict of the *Bilderverbot* but is an instant where (to use another pertinent formulation by Adorno) *les extrêmes se touchent*. It thus offers the opera's only truly magic moment of reconciliation—both between Zerlina and Masetto and between the aesthetic and the historical, or, in Benjaminian terms, between the messianic and the materialistic.[13] If anything might vindicate Adorno's utopian imagination, it is that, for the sake of reconciliation, Don Giovanni can ultimately only look at Zerlina, while Masetto will have her. Seen that way, Adorno's Zerlina might forever look at us as a prime instance of Adorno's philosophy of the particular, his aesthetics of the *Augenblick*, and his hermeneutics of the moment. In that sense he was right to have fallen in love with her—and we, perhaps, in love with his ability to paint Mozart's portrait of her for us.

EXAMPLE 13.3. "Vedrai carino": mm. 76–end.

EXAMPLE 13.3. cont.

EXAMPLE 13.3. cont.

NOTES

My essay is dedicated to James Webster. Special thanks to Lydia Goehr and Nikolaus Bacht.

1. Theodor W. Adorno, "Huldigung an Zerlina," in *Moments musicaux, Gesammelte Schriften* (Frankfurt, 1982), 17:34–35; translation Berthold Hoeckner.

2. Adorno quotes here the third and fourth line of the second stanza of "Zephir nimm's auf deine Flügel," one of the famous "Sesenheimer Lieder" which the young Goethe wrote in Straßbourg. See Johann Wolfgang von Goethe, *Sämtliche Werke, Hamburger Ausgabe,* ed. Erich Trunz, 14 Bände (Munich, 1981), 1:26.

3. This is a quotation from Goethe's *Dichtung and Wahrheit,* ibid., 9:367. Translation with slightly modified from *The Autobiography of Goethe: Truth and Poetry, from My Own Life,* trans. John Oxenford (London, 1891), 1:375.

4. Theodor W. Adorno, *Notes to Literature,* ed. Rolf Tiedemann, trans. Shierry Weber Nicholsen (New York, 1991), 1:10 and 1:16.

5. Shoshana Felman, *The Literary Speech Act: Don Juan with J. L. Austin; or, Seduction in Two Languages* (Ithaca, 1983).

6. Theodor W. Adorno, *Aesthetic Theory,* ed. Gretel Adorno and Rolf Tiedemann, trans. Robert Hullot-Kentor (Minneapolis, 1997), 84, translation modified.

7. Stefan Kunze, *Mozarts Opern* (Stuttgart, 1984), 416. Joseph Kerman, "Reading Don Giovanni," in *Write All These Down: Essays on Music* (Berkeley, 1994), 307–321, at 309.

8. Theodor W. Adorno, *Beethoven: The Philosophy of Music*, trans. Edmund Jephcott (Stanford, 1998), 170. For a discussion of Leonore see my *Programming the Absolute: Nineteenth-Century German Music and the Hermeneutics of the Moment*, chapter 1, "Beethoven's Star" part 3 (Princeton, 2002).

9. Wye Jamison Allanbrook, *Rhythmic Gesture in Mozart* (Chicago, 1983), and Stefano Castelvecchi, "Sentimental and Anti-Sentimental in *Le nozze di Figaro*," *Journal of the American Musicological Society* 53 (2000): 1–24. See also Wye Jamison Allanbrook, Mary Hunter, and Gretchen A. Wheelock, "Staging Mozart's Women," in *Siren Songs: Representations of Gender and Sexuality in Opera,* ed. Mary Ann Smart (Princeton, 2000), 47–66.

10. Allanbrook, *Rhythmic Gesture in Mozart*, 262.

11. Adorno, *Aesthetic Theory*, 62.

12. Daniel Heartz, "An Iconography of the Dances in the Ballroom Scene of *Don Giovanni,* in Thomas Bauman, ed., *Mozart's Operas* (Berkeley, 1990), 181.

13. Theodor W. Adorno, "Zum Verhältnis von Malerei und Musik heute," in *Gesammelte Schriften*, ed. Rolf Tiedemann (Frankfurt, 1971–1986), 18:147.

Adorno and the Don

NIKOLAUS BACHT

Viva la libertà!
—Mozart and Da Ponte

In the false world all ἡδονή is false.
—Adorno

*I*f one were to count and name all versions of the Don Juan legend since its emergence in late-medieval Spain, one could easily
catalog well over 1,003 items. Even without the articles in the present volume,
there might be just as many interpretations of the legend's most influential
version, Mozart and Da Ponte's *Il Dissoluto Punito o sia Il Don Giovanni*. My
aim in adding yet another interpretation to the extant *mille e tre* is to analyze
the dialectics of pleasure and freedom that Adorno constructed in his continual engagement with *Don Giovanni* and especially with its main protagonist,
here referred to as "the Don."

Adorno's first documented engagements with *Don Giovanni* took place at
the opera houses in Berlin and Frankfurt am Main in 1926, 1928, and 1930
respectively. To judge by his reviews of these productions, published in the
Neue Musik-Zeitung and *Die Musik*, the one that he attended in February 1928
at the Kroll Opera Berlin was formative for him. In 1926 he had no qualms
about exaggerations of the opera's buffa elements or attempts to turn it into
a pseudo-Wagnerian music drama.[1] By 1930, then, he had grown acutely
sensitive to nineteenth-century manipulations of these kinds, still rampant in
the 1920s:[2] when Frankfurt am Main celebrated the fiftieth anniversary of its
opera house in that year with *Don Giovanni*, Adorno advised "urgent revision"

of the interpretive attitude toward the work.[3] He did not specify exactly what he meant by revision, but it is clear that he had the 1928 production at Berlin's controversial modernist opera house in mind. Of this production, he wrote, "the coquettish amoretti, which are so habitual in Mozart interpretation, have been toppled and the romantic expressive rendering of the melodies has lost its justification."[4] Under the baton of Otto Klemperer, who was the so-called *Kapellmeister* at the Kroll Opera at that time, Mozart and Da Ponte's tale of the *dissoluto punito* was no longer "opera buffa nor music drama" but *Ernstfall* ("a serious case").[5]

At long last, Adorno concluded, the main theme of *Don Giovanni* could be perceived as "the workings and reconciliation of fate."[6] To construe fate as the main theme of *Don Giovanni* is not unusual. *Don Giovanni* is obviously about the inevitability of the moral judgment passed by a society upon an individual that refuses to comply with its laws. This notion of fate has been at the center of much of the philosophically informed discourse on *Don Giovanni*. More often than not, it is linked with the dialectic of pleasure and freedom. The typical rendering of this dialectic is as follows: The Don, who treats his fellow beings as objects in his quest for pleasure and freedom, becomes an object himself, the object of fate (which in this opera means the inevitability of the negative moral judgment upon him). His violent action is ultimately resisted equally violently by the quasi-mythical power of society; fate consigns him to a place where there is neither pleasure nor freedom. Adorno both sharpens and modifies the dialectic. On the one hand, he capitalizes on the mythical-societal power that prevails over the Don; fate turns into Fate, as represented by the stone statue of the Commendatore, which, in his perception, "was never stonier"—that is, more mythical—"than in this production."[7] On the other hand, Adorno interprets the opera as ending not with the damnation of its title hero but, in Adorno's particular phrase, with a "reconciliation of fate" ("Versöhnung des Schicksals"). The counterintuitive nature of this position is increased by the fact that Adorno locates the reconciliation in the death scene and not in the apparently reconciliatory *scena ultima*—the final scene. Although Klemperer was one of the first to restore the final scene,[8] usually omitted in the nineteenth century, Adorno makes no mention of it. Instead, he places all his emphasis on the Don's encounter with the stone statue.

Neither were other contemporary reviewers any more effusive about the final scene; to the extent that they wrote about this scene at all, they indicated that one could well have done without it.[9] The second act's first finale, by contrast, must have been quite an experience. Ewald Dülberg, Klemperer's stage designer at the Kroll Opera, worked with stark contrasts of light and shade, directing the listener's gaze to the crosses at the center of the stage (see figure 14.1). The stone guest appeared from above through a door and then descended straight to hell, joined by the Don who, racing across the churchyard toward him, was turned on a last time by two female dancers.[10] The morbid eroticism of the second act's first finale was not commended by many reviewers; one found the appearance of the dancers superfluous,[11] and to another, Alfred Einstein, the Commendatore looked more like "an old aunt in a nightgown than a revered statue."[12] Adorno was one of the few who appreciated the scene. His notion of *Ernstfall* made good critical sense—not only for this scene, but for Klemperer's *Don Giovanni* as a whole: "Even in the catalog aria," as we are told by Arnold Schmitz, the musicological assistant who worked for Klemperer earlier in the 1920s, "laughter vanished."[13]

Seriousness, however, was only a concomitant feature of Klemperer's main intention, which was to bring out the demonic streak of Don Giovanni (the man and the opera). The gloomy set, the Don's readiness to surrender to fate, and the eroticized death scene were all part of this cause. Other major factors were Klemperer's attention to rhythm rather than to sound and the sheer speed with which he performed the scenes, even the recitatives.[14] Klemperer was held up only by the technical limitations of the Kroll Opera, which, as he recalled with regret some forty years later, did not have a revolving stage.[15] Still, his friend Georg Simmel, whom he invited to a performance of the opera, was "much struck by the unsuspected demonism that Klemperer

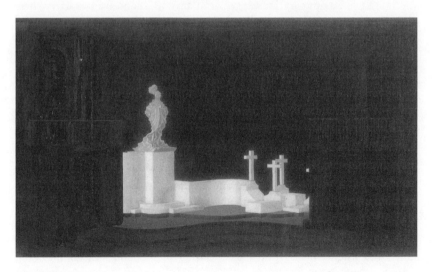

FIGURE 14.1. Ewald Dülberg's stage design for *Don Giovanni*, act 2, final scene (Kroll Opera, 1928). *Reproduced with the kind permission of the Theaterwissenschaftliche Sammlung, Cologne University.*

revealed in the score."[16] Interestingly, Klemperer's source of inspiration was philosophical: his view of the Don as a demonic character, according to Arnold Schmitz, was profoundly shaped by reading Søren Kierkegaard's writing about *Don Giovanni*.[17] This is important for the present argument because it reveals just how idiosyncratic Adorno's perception of the opera's ending was. For Kierkegaard the plot led inevitably to the damnation of the Don, and there is no reason to assume that Klemperer disagreed with him on that point. Although Adorno concurred with Klemperer about the necessity of a serious *Don Giovanni*, the interpretation of the second act's first finale put forward in the Klemperer review was a misunderstanding on Adorno's part.

With historical hindsight, Adorno's misunderstanding of Klemperer may seem arbitrary, but for him it was meaningful and compelling. What exactly made him think of the death scene in terms of reconciliation, however, is hard to tell from the Klemperer review because the concept of reconciliation is not qualified in this brief piece of journalistic criticism. To appreciate Adorno's misunderstanding, we need to take a look at other intellectual concerns of his around that time.

In the 1920s Adorno began to cultivate a deep metaphysical sympathy for all things transient. A metaphysics of death became especially prominent in his mind after Martin Heidegger's *Being and Time* (1927) came out. The key document was Adorno's essay entitled "Schubert" (1928), in which he attempted to rescue the concept of death from the ideological use to which he thought it was put by Heidegger. This text was conceived exactly when Adorno attended and reviewed Klemperer's *Don Giovanni*. The ideas elaborated here certainly colored and shaped his listening experience at the Kroll Opera,[18] a fact he conveyed to one of his closest allies, Ernst Bloch, who was in town at that time. Bloch himself suggested (likely after attending the same production) that "the *Don Giovanni* moment" contained "an element of depth . . . which in the end is not vanquished and undone even by the Commendatore's broad, moral, indeed cosmic *majestoso*."[19]

Ironically, Adorno substantiated his misunderstanding through an engagement with the very philosopher whom Klemperer read to get into the proper *Don Giovanni* mood: Kierkegaard. Kierkegaard had a fictitious aesthete, named "A," expound a theory about three immediate erotic stages, all of which were exemplified with reference to Mozart operas and characters therein. The model for existence in the third stage was the Don who, on A's account, never premeditates his future seductions, never reflects on his past ones and, most importantly, never bothers about questions of good and evil.[20] Kierkegaard made A indulge to the point of identification in the Don's pursuit of pleasure and freedom. Having thus established A's persona, Kierkegaard let him introduce the theory of the musical-erotic. In a bold deduction A was made to assert that the power of the immediate erotic "cannot be expressed in words; only music can give us a notion of it."[21] By music he means the music of Mozart, uniquely that of *Don Giovanni*. Such reasoning was not the only task that Kierkegaard set his authorial surrogate. He also made him carry a heavy theological charge: music, on account of its immediately erotic nature, is to be understood as the demonic Other of the Christian spirit. Music is that which theology posits as excluded from the moral domain. Its perfect embodiment is the Don.[22]

The Don, music, and aesthetics in general serve a strategy in *Either/Or* that combines Socratic diction and *épater le bourgeois*. Kierkegaard made this explicit in a text entitled "On My Effect as an Author" (1851). Temporarily removing the pseudonymic disguise, he explained with reference to Socrates that the intended effect of his writings on aesthetics had been to "*delude people into truth*."[23] For Kierkegaard truth was always religious and situated far beyond the reach of his bourgeois contemporaries, among whom he observed the spread of a new paganism. He did not attempt to win the bourgeois over with traditional means, such as sermons or edifying literature, but to awaken them from their lethargy with sensual shock effects and to seduce them out of their spiritual corruption and debauchery; hence his numerous hedonist pseudonyms and his deep interest in the Don. In Kierkegaard's later writings this strategy operated within a system of three distinct existential spheres: the aesthetic, the ethical, and the religious. In *Either/Or* the system of the spheres was still incomplete; the aesthetic sphere, i.e., the sphere of A and the Don, was contrasted with an ethical sphere only, represented by a pseudonymous "ethicist B" (also called "William the Judge"). B objects resolutely to A's hedonist activities, mapping out as an alternative—the "Or" of *Either/Or*—a path to freedom through an ethics of duty and marriage developed by Kant and Fichte.

Although we can safely assume sympathy on Adorno's part for any genuine attempt at *épater le bourgeois*, Adorno scathingly criticized Kierkegaard's construction of the aesthetic and, by extension, of the ethical. In his Kierkegaard book (written 1929–1930, published 1933), Adorno attempted in a series of rather problematic moves to defuse Kierkegaard's dialectic of pleasure and freedom in order to offer his own. In the process he focused on the dominant role of B in the construction of *Either/Or*, a role he tends to conflate with Kierkegaard's own position. To underpin his argument, Adorno claimed that Kierkegaard's authorial evasions are no more than flights into subjective inwardness, "the historical prison of primordial humanity."[24] Moreover, Adorno considered the conception of aesthetic *Schein* as mere delusion to be undialectical in itself and in relation to the ethical since "Kierkegaard's loneliness never reached" societal reality.[25] The project of a "delusion into truth" is therefore bound to fail. A's aesthetic hedonism and B's ethics of love remain locked within the boundaries of their respective spheres; pleasure and freedom are kept strictly apart. For Adorno this is the signature of bourgeois asceticism. Split between an aesthetics of the immediate erotic and an ethics of duty and marriage, Kierkegaard's Either/Or is thus repudiated by Adorno as "poor and deceptive class morality."[26]

Adorno's disagreements with Kierkegaard about the dialectics of pleasure and freedom are mirrored in a section devoted to the Don in the Kierkegaard book which, just like *Either/Or*, has *Don Giovanni* written all over it. The main point of contention between the two philosophers is whether or not the Don deserves to be damned for his refusal to submit to the bourgeois moral code, whether freedom ought ultimately to be taken from or given to him in an act of reconciliation of fate. As mentioned above, Kierkegaard advocated damnation. "No power on earth," he wrote in *Either/Or*, "is able to defeat Don Juan; only a spirit, an apparition from another world, can do that. . . . Don Juan can do everything, withstands everything, except the replication of life, precisely because he is immediate sensuous life, whose negation the spirit is."[27] Adorno cited this passage and identified the apparition from another world as the stone statue of the Commendatore who, exercising his mythical power against natural life, remained in Kierkegaard's reading "dedicated to its annihilation in spirit rather than to reconciliation."[28]

In Adorno's view, Kierkegaard reproduced the conventional configuration of the *Don Giovanni* dialectic and inadvertently exhibited its bourgeois substratum. This begs the question as to whether Adorno would have subjected Klemperer's *Don Giovanni* to the same critique had he known that it was influenced by Kierkegaard or whether, in the unlikely case that Adorno did know about Klemperer's philosophical leanings, he chose to protect the otherwise progressive Kroll Opera production through a misunderstanding of its first finale. Whether Adorno's misunderstanding was in fact deliberate or not, one can feel in his early *Don Giovanni* reading that he and the Don had an interesting development ahead of them.

We need to leave Adorno and the Don for a moment and trace the intellectual-historical effects of Adorno's ideas about pleasure and freedom. Adorno himself put the subject aside for a while, immersing himself instead in a monumental study on Husserl, but his colleagues in the Institut für Sozialforschung understood that the issues opened up by him were crucial for their specific brand of dialectical materialism. Shortly after Adorno's Kierkegaard book appeared in print in January 1933, Max Horkheimer, in an article entitled "Materialism und Morality," postulated that pleasure ought not to be sacrificed in the name of freedom.[29] In 1936 he reiterated this tenet of Adorno's in a more elaborate study, "Egoism and the Movement for Freedom."[30] Both texts were published in the institute's *Zeitschrift für Sozialforschung*. In the 1938 issue of that journal Herbert Marcuse adopted the dialectics of pleasure and freedom to support a political program. "Insofar as the materialistic protest of hedonism preserves an otherwise proscribed element of human liberation," he declared in his famous article "On Hedonism," "it is linked with the interest of Critical Theory."[31] The sense of reservation underlying this statement is important. In a detailed review from Epicurus to German Idealism and beyond, Marcuse demonstrated that the relationship of pleasure and freedom had always been volatile. He also asserted, following Hegel, that the pursuit of pleasure for its own sake amounts only to an abstract and not to a determinate negation of unfreedom.[32]

From such a perspective, Adorno's view of the Don can easily appear to be just that: a vindication of an abstract negation of unfreedom. Adorno must have been aware of this, but instead of revising his *Don Giovanni* interpretation, he embarked upon a sustained effort to reinforce and refine its theoretical foundations. The first step was a text that, according to a letter to Walter Benjamin dated February 29, 1940, "pursues further certain themes and directions of the Kierkegaard book."[33] This time Adorno did not refer to the ethics of love propounded by B in *Either/Or* but turned instead to religious sermons Kierkegaard published under his own name in a book entitled *Works of Love* (1847).[34] Again Adorno found much the same faults with Kierkegaard that he did with B, but used harsher critical language, probably because he was not dealing with an authorial surrogate but with the man himself. He wrote, in English, about a "lordly demonology of asceticism"[35] and defined the content of Kierkegaard's doctrine of love as "the oppression of the drive which is not to be fulfilled."[36] Adorno's only concession to Kierkegaard was that the latter, by virtue of the very misanthropy that allegedly conditions his doctrine of love, furnished an uncompromising analysis of the reified bourgeois character. Adorno held that such an analysis, properly decoded through social critique, could be valuable to the project of the Institut für Sozialforschung.[37]

Having ventured again into the frugal world of Kierkegaard and his alter ego B, Adorno also revisited the domain of A and the Don. In *Minima Moralia* (1944–1947) he demonstrated for the first time a concern with the Don's maltreatment of his fellow beings: "That Leporello has to complain of meager diet and shortage of money casts doubt on the existence of Don Juan."[38]

Adorno now also recognized, in response to Marcuse, that the Don achieves only an abstract negation with his ruthless acting out of desire. Commenting upon Goethe's portrayal of female characters, Adorno stated that the "absolute opposite" of Goethe's respectful distance to Adelheid, Klärchen, and Gretchen was "Don Juan." He continued: "When Kierkegaard says that in him [the Don], sensuality is comprehended as a principle, he touches on the secret of sensuality itself. In the fixity of its gaze, as long as it remains unawakened by self-reflection, lies the very anonymity, the unhappy generality, that is fatefully reproduced in its negative, the unfettered sovereignty of thought."[39] At this point Adorno could easily have abandoned the Don and joined the ensemble of those reveling in his damnation. However, he did not take this step; there is no indication here that Marcuse's insights made him change his mind about the reconciliation of fate that he perceived in the first finale of *Don Giovanni's* second act.

Actually Adorno did not fully agree with Marcuse on the dialectics of pleasure and freedom. In *Minima Moralia* he argued that moments of freedom could appear not only in the determinate negation of what is bad, but also, albeit to a lesser extent, in the abstract negation of what, in the bad world, is considered to be good.[40] This dialectical twist enabled Adorno later to "save" his *Don Giovanni* interpretation. It was prepared in his and Horkheimer's *Dialectic of Enlightenment* (1942–1944) through an examination of de Sade and Nietzsche's writings on morality. These "dark writers of the bourgeoisie,"[41] in Adorno and Horkheimer's view, exposed with unparalleled radicality the sacrifice of pleasure for freedom on which the bourgeois ideology of love is based. Not surprisingly, the authors of the *Dialectic* showed that this kind of critique, on account of its very radicality, reverts itself to ideology, conjuring up a reverse image of idealist morality. Adorno and Horkheimer, however, knew the importance of withstanding the calculated nauseating effects and the ubiquitous glorifications of violence with which antimoralistic pamphlets such as *Juliette* or *Beyond Good and Evil* abound. They also knew that it would be defeatist to abstractly negate de Sade's and Nietzsche's abstract negations. Adorno and Horkheimer thus concluded that de Sade and Nietzsche, in the final analysis, were "more merciful" with their unbridled hedonism than "the moralistic lackeys of the bourgeoisie."[42]

Having elaborated his dialectic of pleasure and freedom to a high degree of sophistication, Adorno entered into another major engagement with *Don Giovanni*: "Homage to Zerlina" (1952). This text, which pays just as much homage to the Don as it does to its title figure, begins with a brutal gesture toward the bourgeois listeners of *Don Giovanni*, undermining one of our most cherished moments in the opera: "Vedrai carino." Zerlina's *carino* was ridiculed by Adorno as "the one who lends his name to the blundering and the clumsy."[43] Zerlina only makes it up with her husband to be, laying his hand on her heart where she carries "un certo balsamo," because Da Ponte felt the need to make concessions to the opera buffa genre and to "restore the moral and social hierarchies" upset by the Don. Mozart's music enhances the effect: in his "orchestral postlude," Adorno wrote, "divided mankind seems to be reconciled." This use of the concept of reconciliation should not be conflated with the one discussed above. We are here dealing with an attempt by Adorno to locate reconciliatory moments not only in death but also in the opera's portrayal of love. Despite the slight revaluation of marriage in this passage, however, it is important to note that, for Adorno, divided mankind only *seems* to be reconciled in "Vedrai carino." The continuation of the passage that "such reconciliation takes place in the name of freedom" should also be handled with care for it was ultimately not "marital freedom" that Adorno was interested in.

Zerlina's reunion with Masetto served Adorno as a foil for an involved discussion of her erotic quandaries with the Don. She becomes a pivotal character between two men representing the different notions of pleasure and freedom that Adorno pits one against the other. Loving Masetto offers Zerlina lasting pleasure and freedom within the narrow constraints of Duty. Loving the Don, by contrast, affords her a merely momentary but qualitatively different experience of pleasure and freedom. It is not an experience, however, that can be lived in bourgeois society: Da Ponte, whom Adorno seemed to find every bit as bourgeois as all the others who throw themselves into the Don's way, prevents the ultimate consummation to which, as Adorno implied, the attraction between Zerlina and the Don would have led. Yet although the "promiscuous plottings" are thwarted by the librettist, Adorno found much reconciliatory potential in the attempted seduction of Zerlina. One important aspect for him was that the Don, valuing pleasure more highly than anything else, is quite ready to ignore social differences. His intended "exchange" with Zerlina is not modeled on the principles of bourgeois economy; it is not an "exchange of equal parts," as between Zerlina and Masetto. Although their banter is continually interrupted, the Don's message gets through to his "victim": "Zerlina," Adorno said, "was right to have liked him."

One might wonder why Adorno defends the Don, who, after all, is usually portrayed as a man with a considerably bad character (Bernard Williams) or as a "No-Man" (Wye Allanbrook).[44] However, Adorno did not give the Don carte blanche. He was quite aware that his protégé behaves as if he were beyond good and evil, as if freedom were a privilege of his, warranted by the unwritten statutes of *Herrenmoral*. He also recognized that the Don not only ignores social differences but also relies on them when he casts his "irresistible glance" at Zerlina, offering his hand to her "over the abyss of the classes." And, most important, Adorno drew attention to the fact that the Don, in honoring freedom through pursuit of pleasure, deprives Zerlina of honor. Why, then, did Adorno defend the Don? To answer this question, we need to return to the *Dialectic of Enlightenment*. The argument advanced there about radical critiques of the bourgeois ideology of love bears striking structural and substantive similarities to Adorno's defense of the Don: the latter's activities, like the ones described by de Sade and Nietzsche, are all abstract negations, that is, negations of unfreedom that reproduce what they negate. Adorno, it will be remembered, contended that such practice is still more humane than what is passed off as love by the bourgeoisie.

It is, however, not just dialectical sophistry that Adorno brought to bear in support of the Don. What Williams identified as the Don's "bad character" was explained by Adorno as a profound psychic deficiency. Adorno here reacted once more to Kierkegaard, who argued that the Don's erotic energy was "born in anxiety"[45]—the anxiety of the sinner, best expressed in music, the demonic Other of the Christian spirit. As such a diagnosis is only one step away from the Don's damnation, Adorno rejected Kierkegaard's notion that the Don suffers from anxiety; in fact, he called him "*der Angstlose*" in "Homage to Zerlina." On Adorno's account, the Don's condition cannot be explained theologically but only with reference to his sociohistorical experience. It is an experience of humiliation and ridicule: as a "half-powerless noble," his *Herrenmoral* is on the wane, and as a "messenger of desire" he is "already a little comical for the bourgeois." For Adorno the Don is, in short, a quixotic character who holds up, at the cost of losing his self, the standard of pleasure and freedom in a world where the former has become perverted and the latter prohibited.

Approximately one decade after paying homage to Zerlina and her promiscuous lover, Adorno engaged with *Don Giovanni* again. This engagement is the most complex and perhaps also the most important as it brings to the surface a theme that was latently present in the other engagements, namely, the definition and relation of aesthetics and ethics—pleasure and freedom—in Kant. The locus classicus of Adorno's late Kant critique is *Negative Dialectics* (1959–1966), where he wrote the following: "In the Italian title . . . the immoral hero is called *il dissoluto*, the disintegrated one." Da Ponte's descriptive epithet for the Don, *il dissoluto*, is thus attributed a double meaning: the Don is immoral and disintegrated at the same time. From this somewhat overdetermined linguistic perception, Adorno gained the possibility to explain the Don's psychic deficiencies as deviations from the Kantian norm of the integrated subject. Such deviations seem immoral, Adorno implied, if (and only if) one accepts Kant as the final authority on the whole gamut of subjectivity, aesthetics and ethics. According to Adorno, Da Ponte does exactly that. "Language," Adorno stated with a critical sidelong glance at Mozart's librettist in the continuation of the passage quoted above, "opts for morality as the unity of the person in accordance with the abstract rational law."[46]

Contrary to expectation, however, Adorno did not merely employ the double meaning of *il dissoluto* as "immoral" and "disintegrated" in an apologetic way. Rather, the Kantian context allowed him to revise, and thoroughly dialectize, his *Don Giovanni* reading. Technically, he achieved this by flanking the passage on the Don in *Negative Dialectics* with sentences marking the opposite poles that delimit possible readings of Kant's notions of pleasure and freedom. A few lines before the *dissoluto* is mentioned, Kant's constitution of morality on the grounds of the abstract unity of the person is criticized as hostility to the fulfillment of pleasure or, in Adorno's own words, as "diversion from the primary telos of desire."[47] We have already had ample opportunity to observe that this is the kind of morality from which the Don flees, roaming the world in a despairing and fatal pursuit of an idée fixe of freedom. A few lines after the reference to the Don, however, Adorno stated that Kant's notion of subjectivity, by virtue of its autonomy, also furthered the cause of freedom.[48]

Adorno here radicalized the third antinomy from the *Critique of Pure Reason*, the so-called antinomy of freedom, with an emphasis on the problem of pleasure. In constellation with this antinomy, Adorno's configuration of the *Don Giovanni* dialectic changed: certain ideas that were crucial for its earlier configurations are absent from the passage in *Negative Dialectics* under discussion. Adorno did not reiterate the Don's abstract negation of morality, probably because he realized that the reading of bourgeois antimoralism advanced in the *Dialectic of Enlightenment* and *Minima Moralia* could not be adopted without refinement in *Negative Dialectics*.[49] Moreover, there is no talk of a reconciliation in the second act's first finale any more, neither in *Negative Dialectics* nor in the passage in *Aesthetic Theory* that relates the antinomy of freedom to the *Critique of Judgment*.[50] Both passages also document a distinct loss of faith on Adorno's part in hedonism's potential for freedom. "In the false world," as Adorno said in the epigraph to the present essay, which appears at the climactic point of the passage on Kant in *Aesthetic Theory*, "all ἡδονή is false."

The Don's insistence that pleasure may be fulfilled and freedom gained in a lapse (out) of synthetic reason is therefore like riding against windmills—a futile attempt to assert the self against an antagonistic and insuperable reality. The sense of individual powerlessness in modern society that Adorno expressed through the radicalization of Kant's antinomy of freedom is also evident in his last engagement with the *dissoluto punito*, which took place in 1966, shortly after the publication of *Negative Dialectics*. This last engagement was, as the first, a review of Klemperer's *Don Giovanni*; this time, however, not of a stage production but of the famous EMI recording. Just as in *Negative Dialectics* and *Aesthetic Theory*, the theme of reconciliation is absent here, as is the problematic point about the possible good that abstract negations of morality might do in the bad world.

Nonetheless, many points that Adorno made in favor of the Don in the earlier texts recurred in the late Klemperer review. Da Ponte was reproached for blackening the Don's name already in the cast list "as extremely licentious."[51] The link between the Don and the characters of de Sade was for the first time made explicit.[52] So was the critique of Klemperer, whose decision to play the final scene was now described as a "forced naivety which retrospectively reduces the scene of the Commendatore . . . to silliness."[53] The Don's quixotic traits surfaced once more: "Don Juan among the bourgeois is not only a demon, but also, according to the rules of their game, a clown."[54] And finally, the Don's "outmoded libertinage" was said to "represent the potential of freedom against the morality that catches up with him."[55] All this suggests that Adorno, despite the caution in his late writings about the reconciliatory content of the opera, remained sympathetic to the Don's vision of a world where both can be had: pleasure *and* freedom.

NOTES

1. Theodor W. Adorno, "Frankfurter Opern- und Konzertkritiken: Juli 1926," *Gesammelte Schriften* (*GS*) 19:74–75, ed. Rolf Tiedemann, assisted by Gretel Adorno, Susan Buck-Morss, and Klaus Schultz (Frankfurt am Main, 1970–1986).
2. Adorno, "Berliner Memorial," *GS* 19:259–266, at 261.
3. Adorno, "Frankfurter Opern- und Konzertkritiken: Dezember 1930," *GS* 19:192.
4. Adorno, "Berliner Memorial," *GS* 19:261.
5. Ibid.
6. Ibid.
7. Ibid., 262.
8. Cf. the contemporary reviews reprinted in Hans Curjel, *Experiment Krolloper 1927–1931* (Munich, 1975), 226, 228, 229.
9. Klaus Pringsheim in his review in *Vorwärts* (January 11, 1928), reprinted in Curjel, *Experiment Krolloper*, 228–230, at 230.
10. Oscar Bie in his review in *Berliner Börsen-Courier* (January 12, 1928), reprinted in Curjel, *Experiment Krolloper*, 226–227, at 227.
11. Ibid.

12. Alfred Einstein in his review in *Berliner Tageblatt* (January 12, 1928), reprinted in Curjel, *Experiment Krolloper*, 225–226, at 226.

13. Peter Heyworth, *Otto Klemperer: His Life and Times,* vol. 1: *1885–1933* (Cambridge, 1983), 152.

14. Alfred Einstein in his review in *Berliner Tageblatt*, reprinted in Curjel, *Experiment Krolloper*, 226.

15. Peter Heyworth, ed., *Conversations with Klemperer*, rev. ed. (London, 1985), 71.

16. Heyworth, *Otto Klemperer*, 117.

17. Ibid., 152.

18. On the negotiation of Heidegger's concept of death in Adorno's Schubert text, cf. my "Temporalizing Strategies in Adorno's Schubert Interpretation" (unpublished MS). For a more comprehensive discussion of transience in Adorno cf. also my "Music and Time in Theodor W. Adorno," Ph.D. diss., King's College, 2002.

19. Ernst Bloch in *Blätter der Staatsoper* (January 1928), reprinted in Curjel, *Experiment Krolloper*, 340–342, at 342.

20. Søren Kierkegaard, *Either/Or,* part 1, trans. Howard V. Hong and Edna H. Hong (Princeton, 1987), 90, 98–99.

21. Ibid., 101.

22. Ibid., 64–65, 71–74.

23. Kierkegaard, "Om min Forfatter-Virksomhed," *Samlede Værker* 13 (Copenhagen, 1906), 487–509, at 495.

24. Theodor W. Adorno, *Kierkegaard: Konstruktion des Ästhetischen*, GS 2:89; *Kierkegaard: Construction of the Aesthetic*, trans. Robert Hullot-Kentor (Minneapolis, 1989), 60 (trans. modified).

25. Adorno, *Kierkegaard: Konstruktion des Ästhetischen*, 16; *Kierkegaard: Construction of the Aesthetic*, 8.

26. Ibid., 75; ibid., 50 (trans. modified).

27. Ibid., 155; ibid., 109. Hullot-Kentor's translation, here modified, is based on the translation of Kierkegaard's *Either/Or* used by Adorno.

    Walter Wiora, to whom we owe an excellent article on Mozart and Kierkegaard, seems to have overlooked this passage when forming his judgment, taken for granted by most musicologists writing in his wake, that Kierkegaard does not discuss the ending of *Don Giovanni*. Walter Wiora, "Zu Kierkegaard's Ideen über Mozart's 'Don Giovanni,'" *Beiträge zur Musikgeschichte Nordeuropas: Kurt Gudewill zum 65. Geburtstag,* ed. Uwe Haensel (Wolfenbüttel, 1978), 46.

28. Adorno, *Kierkegaard: Konstruktion des Ästhetischen*, 155; *Kierkegaard: Construction of the Aesthetic*, 109.

29. Max Horkheimer, "Materialismus und Moral," *Zeitschrift für Sozialforschung* 2 (1933): 162–197; "Materialism and Morality," *Between Philosophy and Social Science: Selected Early Writings*, trans. G. Frederick Hunter, Matthew S. Kramer, and John Torpey (Cambridge, 1993), 15–47.

30. Horkheimer, "Egoismus und Freiheitsbewegung," *Zeitschrift für Sozialforschung* 5 (1936): 161–234; "Egoism and Freedom Movements," in *Between Philosophy and Social Science,* 49–110.

31. Herbert Marcuse, "Zur Kritik des Hedonismus," *Zeitschrift für Sozialforschung* 7 (1938): 55–89, at 57; "On Hedonism," *Negations: Essays in Critical Theory,* trans. Jeremy J. Shapiro (London, 1988), 159–200, at 162.

32. On Horkheimer's and Marcuse's ideas about hedonism, cf. also Martin Jay, *The Dialectical Imagination: A History of the Frankfurt School and the Institute of Social Research, 1923–1950* (Berkeley, 1973), 57–60. On Horkheimer especially, cf. Herbert Schnädelbach, "Max Horkheimer und die Moralphilosophie des deutschen Idealismus," *Vernunft und Geschichte* (Frankfurt, 1987), 207–237.

33. Theodor W. Adorno and Walter Benjamin, *Briefwechsel 1928–1940*, ed. Henri Lonitz (Frankfurt, 1994), 419; *Adorno and Benjamin: The Complete Correspondence, 1928–1940*, trans. Nicholas Walker (Cambridge, 1999), 322 (trans. modified).

34. Kierkegaard, *Works of Love*, trans. Howard V. Hong and Edna H. Hong (Princeton, 1995).

35. Adorno, "Kierkegaard's Doctrine of Love," *Studies in Philosophy and Social Science* (= *Zeitschrift für Sozialforschung*) 8.3 (1939/1940): 413–429, at 418.

36. Ibid., 423.

37. Ibid.

38. Adorno, *Minima Moralia*, GS 4:217; *Minima Moralia*, trans. Edmund Jephcott (London, 1978), 191.

39. Ibid., 101; ibid., 90 (trans. modified).

40. Ibid., 106–107; ibid., 95.

41. Adorno and Horkheimer, *Dialektik der Aufklärung: Philosophische Fragmente*, GS 3:139; *Dialectic of Enlightenment: Philosophical Fragments*, trans. John Cumming (London, 1997), 117.

42. Ibid., 140; ibid., 119.

43. This and all subsequent citations in the present section from "Huldigung an Zerlina" follow the translation in this volume.

44. Bernard Williams, "Don Giovanni as an Idea," this volume; Wye Jamison Allanbrook, *Rhythmic Gesture in Mozart: Le nozze di Figaro and Don Giovanni* (Chicago, 1983), 207–208.

45. Kierkegaard, *Either/Or*, 129.

46. Adorno, *Negative Dialektik*, GS 6:237; *Negative Dialectics*, trans. E. B. Ashton (London, 1973), 238 (trans. modified).

47. Ibid., 237; ibid., 238 (trans. modified).

48. Ibid., 237; ibid., 239 (trans. modified).

49. Cf., especially on Adorno's late reading of Nietzsche, Gerhard Schweppenhäuser, *Ethik nach Auschwitz: Adornos negative Moralphilosophie* (Hamburg, 1993), 156–173.

50. Adorno, *Ästhetische Theorie*, 22–31; *Aesthetic Theory*, 9–15.

51. Adorno, "Klemperers 'Don Giovanni,'" GS 19:539–544, at 540.

52. Ibid.

53. Ibid., 544.

54. Ibid., 540.

55. Ibid.